EXPANDING THE HUMAN
IN HUMAN RIGHTS

EXPANDING THE HUMAN IN HUMAN RIGHTS

TOWARD A SOCIOLOGY OF HUMAN RIGHTS

Edited by

David L. Brunsma
Keri E. Iyall Smith
Brian K. Gran

Routledge
Taylor & Francis Group

LONDON AND NEW YORK

First published 2015 by Paradigm Publishers

Published 2016 by Routledge
2 Park Square, Milton Park, Abingdon, Oxon OX14 4RN
711 Third Avenue, New York, NY 10017, USA

Routledge is an imprint of the Taylor & Francis Group, an informa business

Library of Congress Cataloging-in-Publication Data is available from the Library of Congress.

Designed and Typeset by Straight Creek Bookmakers.

ISBN 13: 978-1-61205-776-7 (hbk)
ISBN 13: 978-1-61205-777-4 (pbk)
ISBN 978-1-61205-778-1 (library ebook)

CONTENTS

Introduction

David L. Brunsma, Keri E. Iyall Smith, and Brian K. Gran

Sociology of Human Rights and Human Rights Sociologies

According to the United Nations and human rights experts and activists, human rights are universal, interdependent, indivisible, inalienable, and promote equality regardless of context. The implementation of human rights principles of dignity and self-determination should work to support persons who are disadvantaged within the unequal structural realities of the contexts in which they live. Since the central subject of human rights is the person, the history of the global struggle for human rights has been, fundamentally, a struggle by oppressed peoples against the structures of their oppression. Some "people" throughout the history of the world have not been endowed with "personhood," and, as such, their experiences have been marginalized in the human rights discourse. Sociological work into the experiences of women, racial and ethnic minorities, children, elders, LGBTQ people, the mentally ill, and others helps us understand the promises and challenges of pursuing human rights. *Expanding the Human in Human Rights: Toward a Sociology of Human Rights* focuses on the fundamental insights gleaned from the scholarship on groups in society for the study of, understanding of, and, ultimately, realization of human rights. As the influence of sociologists and sociological insights has greater impact on human rights scholarship, so do key sociological concerns with groups, collective identity, social inequality, and collective action help us investigate the supposed universality, interdependence and indivisibility, equality, and inalienability of human rights.

This makes us excited about the potential of a sociology of human rights. A sociology of human rights can not only reveal successes and failures to achieve these objectives, it can also offer insights into different human rights experiences, as well as the various consequences and outcomes of meeting or failing to achieve these goals. By studying group identities and group experiences, sociologists can examine the degrees to which human rights truly are universal. Why are some groups (e.g., women, indigenous peoples, LGBTQ individuals) regularly excluded from human rights? Why do some groups, both historically and nowadays, seem to have reaped a disproportionate set of benefits from discourses and practices of human rights? Through such questions, sociologists investigate pressures that social groups endure when attempting to implement their human rights. They identify social forces that weaken human rights for some groups, as well as the various ways that human rights are implemented in practice. Sociologists and sociological research identify the consequences of selective enforcement of human rights. Sociologists use their methods to identify the ramifications of failing to achieve universal human rights and ask why inequality persists, and is sometimes endorsed, in the face of collective desires for and pursuits of human rights.

Over the past twenty years, sociology of human rights not only has started to make strong contributions to the scholarship on human rights, it is reshaping the discipline of sociology—a variety of human rights sociologies are emerging. Sociologists have long made invaluable contributions to human rights scholarship, including the works of Karl Marx, W. E. B. Du Bois, Vine Deloria Jr., Jane Addams, and other social scientists and sociologists, often stemming from research among, on, and centered within the perspective of oppressed groups. Contemporary work has also focused on the experiences of marginalized and oppressed groups in their struggles for dignity and self-determination. Yet, it is in the last decade that sociology of human rights scholarship has gained significant momentum. In the United States, a key component of the American Sociological Association is its Section on Human Rights. At the international level, the International Sociological Association's Thematic Group on Global Justice and Human Rights is relatively young, but its membership and impacts are growing. Other academic associations in the United States have expressed an interest in human rights. This is particularly true of the social sciences. For example, the American Political Science Association has a Human Rights Section. The American Anthropological Association has a Committee for Human Rights and a Declaration on Anthropology and Human Rights. The American Economic Association does not have sections, but members of this organization present conference papers on human rights. The American Psychological Association condemns torture and supports the UN Declaration and Convention Against Torture and Other Cruel, Inhuman, or Degrading Treatment or Punishment. It also recognizes that the discipline of psychology is relevant for securing and maintaining human rights and seeks to bring relevant UN documents to the attention of its boards, committees, and membership. The British Sociology Association has formed a Sociology of Rights Study Group. In South Korea, members of the Social Science Korea Human Rights Forum are studying diffusion of human rights with the eventual goal of using social science data to formulate human rights policies. These are all signs that human rights is becoming an important topic in the social sciences.

In recognition of the ever-present need to interrogate the "human" in human rights, *Expanding the Human in Human Rights: Toward a Sociology of Human Rights* concentrates on the intersection of the scholarship of human rights sociology and the study of group identities and group experiences. The authors of each chapter examine the relationship of sociology and human rights with sex and gender; aging and the life course; mental health; racial and ethnic minorities; Asia and Asian America; Latina/o sociology; children and youth; race, class, and gender; sexualities; animals and society; and disability and society. Along the way, the authors demonstrate crucial contributions the sociology of human rights can make to sister subdisciplines in sociology. These chapters also show that human rights scholarship can learn a great deal from sociology. Questions raised by these authors are imperative to the future of human rights scholarship, including the sociology of human rights. It is our hope that the questions raised within each chapter, as well as the resources provided at the end of each chapter, will encourage you to wrestle with the important question of who the "human" in "human rights" is as you understand what it means to build a sociology of human rights and human rights sociologies.

UNIVERSAL? INTERDEPENDENT? INDIVISIBLE? EQUAL? INALIENABLE?

A key feature of sociology is its ability to demonstrate how everyday tools and ideas are socially constructed, including human rights. Sociological studies have shown how different social groups work to construct human rights as well as the efforts that others engage in to deny such rights to others. The work of sociologists has demonstrated that the design of some human rights has intended to exclude some groups while empowering others. It is important to be clear that demonstrating social construction of human rights does not imply that human rights are not real. Rather, sociology of human rights has provided evidence of how social groups think about, fashion, employ, and struggle over human rights. Sociology of human rights also reveals how the construction of "human" and "rights" has real consequences in our daily lives.

Human rights are universal: they are available to all people. In studying disparities in human rights, sociologists tackle the concept of essentialism. Debates persist about how people and social groups are distinct from each other in essential ways. Some differences are used to exclude members of social groups. Such debates are sometimes even used to justify restricting human rights to some groups and not others. A crucial contribution sociologists have made to the broader debates consists of two parts: that nearly all differences are myths when it comes to participating in and sharing society, and that what differences do exist should not preclude availability and employment of human rights. Rather, all people possess human rights, no matter their differences. As a result, these differences should not and cannot serve as barriers to the universalism of human rights. Indeed, human rights are not only critical to eliminating the consequences of these differences; human rights are essential to changing, fundamentally, how people think about differences. Perceiving young people as rights holders requires changes in social structures, practices, and ways of thinking. Studying social interaction, including children's, may require similar awareness of competence and consent across all people.

Human rights are interdependent and indivisible. Human rights are interdependent: for a person to use one right effectively, such as free speech, a person must have the opportunity to enjoy, or have enjoyed, her right to an education. In order for a person to enjoy his right to an education, he must also have been supported to engage in the cultural life of his community. For a person to speak freely and enjoy the right to an education, she must have the right to experience these rights in her mother tongue. To be free to speak, he must be free to live, to move about public spaces, to possess dignity. We could create a web of rights connected to "free speech." Without one component, then speech is arguably less free. Thus, exercising the freedom of speech requires multiple other freedoms, and speech cannot be divorced from these components. The idea of interdependence is a profound one.

Human rights are indivisible: weakening one human right weakens an individual's overall set of human rights. For example, if a person's right to health care is violated, he may not be able to exercise his right to vote. Interdependent and indivisible human rights are interconnected rights. A person who experiences weakness in or absence of a human right may find their other human rights are compromised. Sociologists find patterns in deprivation of human rights across social groups. People experiencing mental health dilemmas often face deprivation of certain rights, such as maintaining health, which can hinder enjoyment of human rights to work and enjoy a socially acceptable standard of living.

Sociology of human rights highlights dimensions of intersectionality, a powerful idea of how intersections of power and oppression differentially empower members of some social groups while simultaneously weakening members of other social groups. Sociologists studying intersecting power dimensions can look to human rights to underscore and overcome these persistent differences. For some time, sociologists have examined how combinations of race, class, and gender not only perpetuate inequalities, they also exacerbate insidious differences and their harmful consequences. Human rights rejects such divisions and the resulting oppression and inequality.

Sociology of human rights contributes to analyses of diversity within groups. Sociological analyses of diversity across and within social groups can reveal significant inequalities, whether in terms of capital (e.g., social, cultural, and human), power, status, or other variables. The mere acknowledgment of diversity, rather than its erasure through the assumption of uniformity, is important to realizing dignity and human rights. Sociology can identify persistent differences in how societies separate individuals from other individuals, within and among groups. Because ideas of human rights include the concept of equality and reducing inequalities, sociologists can show differences within groups that human rights do not overcome.

Sociology often contends with ongoing discrimination. The sub-disciplines studied in this volume reveal pernicious discrimination—sometimes squarely facing us, sometimes carefully hidden behind social dynamics motivating key social institutions, including "law." Gender, race, class, sexuality, age, status, culture, and other factors that shape social life are often treated as individual characteristics, but these attributes are features of social structures that are external to an individual, yet shape what individuals experience and how they live. These attributes bring along particular statuses. They shape expectations of people and social groups. They may lead to consequences that shape social interaction. These attributes also affect the ways we live, including with other species and the environments in which we live. How do human rights change these social interactions? Can human rights challenge and even dismantle discrimination?

Sociology identifies aspects of social structures that shape individuals' experiences. Sociology of human rights demonstrates how social institutions affect every aspect of human rights. Sociology of human rights demonstrates what factors obstruct justice and what factors promote justice. It shines a light on dynamics behind decisions made by actors and institutions to enforce human rights. Why do judges use the courts over which they preside to implement or disavow human rights? Are some socioeconomic systems prone to hindering human rights? Can human rights overcome segregation in its various guises? To what degree is violence an enemy to human rights? Sociology can present evidence of whether boundaries are built around human rights for some social groups.

Human rights are inalienable. Sociologists of human rights can show that, despite the inability to sell, transfer, or give away a human right, members of some social groups face pressures when attempting to use their human rights. Sociologists study transactions by which an individual concedes a human right to obtain a scarce resource. Some institutions are set up on the basis of an individual conceding her liberty to obtain a medical service, such as an individual who is forced to live in an institution to receive health care, shelter, and food. Across the globe, young people are bought and sold into slavery. The traffickers treat these young people as commodities: humans without rights. Sociologists have demonstrated that some people forego their human rights in the face of domestic violence.

Sociologists have also shown that human rights appear meaningless in some parts of society. The private sector, a space with fuzzy borders and meanings, is a location where human rights are ineffective for some social groups. The family home is, for instance, often a place of unequal power. In the family home, many young people do not possess rights to making decisions about their religious beliefs. In the workplace, employees often do not possess rights to free speech or privacy.

Many governments have limited impacts on enforcing human rights of some social groups and in some social spaces. Indeed, in many countries, by law, government cannot intervene in private domains to reduce inequalities or challenge violent power structures. Some social groups strive to weaken human rights in private domains. The inability of human rights to change social relationships in private domains suggests that some social groups rely on government to implement their human rights.

TOWARD A SOCIOLOGY OF HUMAN RIGHTS THROUGH EXPANDING THE "HUMAN" IN HUMAN RIGHTS

In *Expanding the Human in Human Rights: Toward a Sociology of Human Rights* we have invited leading and emergent scholars to engage revolutionary questions, resituate their substantive concerns within new terrains, and begin mapping the intellectual and practical contours of a human rights sociology. Each chapter contributor responded to two primary questions: (1) How does a human rights perspective change the questions that sociologists ask, the theoretical perspectives that sociologists utilize, the methods that sociologists use, and the implications of sociological inquiry? And (2) How can the sociological enterprise (its epistemologies, theories, methodologies, and results) inform and push forward human rights theory, discourse, and implementation toward a better world for all humanity?

Sociologists walk a delicate line, identifying patterns and creating useful generalizations to understand how society distributes resources and harms. At the same time we must recognize that individuals are the ones who experience the benefits or harms based upon their membership in these groups. In this book you will find groups of people and individuals who live within those groups. You will see how some struggle more for their group membership, while others benefit. You will see how access to human rights—which by definition belong to all humans—is frequently limited by group membership. But you will also see how paths to human rights are emerging in the darkest corners, how human rights give language and a basis for group and individual demands, and how human rights entitle all people to claim their humanity.

The contributions to this volume demonstrate the potential of sociology for human rights scholarship and practices. Sociology presents evidence of the extent to which human rights are universal. Sociologists give a voice to groups whose human rights interests and concerns are ignored. Sociologists offer insights into the everyday practices of human rights. Sociologists can show patterns of human rights enforcement across social groups. Sociologists provide evidence of the consequences of failures in human rights, including how denials of specific human rights affect other human rights. Sociologists have shown that some groups face severe burdens when trying to enforce their human rights. Some members of these groups face the dangerous dilemma of giving up their rights to obtain resources that many consider necessities. Sociology of human rights identifies complexities of current human rights practices. Sociologists are shining a bright light on the future of human rights.

≈≋

CHAPTER ONE

SEX AND GENDER

Barbara Gurr and Nancy A. Naples

The intellectual history and topics of interest in the sociology of sex and gender are tied intimately to human rights scholarship and activism. The field was generated through the advocacy of activists inside and outside the discipline inspired by the women's movement of the late 1960s and early 1970s (Fox 1995). Recognizing that women's knowledge and experience had been either erased or diminished in importance by a discipline dominated by men and fueled by patriarchal assumptions of what counts as knowledge and who should be the primary conveyers of sociological insights, women sociologists challenged the gendered assumptions of the field (Smith 1987). In 1969, Alice Rossi, who would become one of the first women presidents of the American Sociological Association (ASA) in 1983, presented data at a business meeting demonstrating the underrepresentation of women and the discrimination they faced in the discipline. As a consequence, in 1971, feminist sociologists formed their own association, Sociologists for Women in Society (SWS), and produced a separate journal, *Gender & Society*, which is now one of the leading journals in interdisciplinary gender studies. SWS dedicated itself to establishing the importance of sex and gender research for sociology; ensuring that women's contributions to knowledge and other aspects of social, economic, political, and cultural life were acknowledged in academic literature; challenging sexist language in sociology journals; and increasing women's visibility in the ASA (Fox 1995). The ASA's Sex and Gender Section was formed in 1973 and is now one of the largest sections of the ASA. SWS members hold prominent leadership positions in the ASA, including the presidency. Since the Sex and Gender Section's founding, three new ASA sections have been added that developed directly from the feminist scholarship on sex and gender.

The topics that are prominent in the field of sex and gender are also at the heart of human rights scholarship. They include processes of discrimination and economic inequalities, the roles of social activism and law in challenging gender inequality, the sources of violence against women, and the role of culture in shaping gendered understandings and practices. Sociologists of sex and gender also address the gendered processes of economic development and migration as well as militarization and global capitalism, among other social structural and historical processes (Fukumura and Matsuoka 2002; Mendez 2005; Salzinger 2005). In this regard, sociologists of sex and gender argue that a gender lens offers a powerful tool for uncovering the social dynamics shaping all major institutions (Brush 2003; Coltraine and Adams 2008; Lorber 2002). To capture the diversity of these experiences, sociologists of sex and gender frequently approach their work from an intersectional perspective (Baca Zinn and Dill 1996; Collins 1990; Naples 2009), paying attention to the intersections of gender, race, class, sexuality, age, culture, and other factors that differentially shape social life rather than concentrating on a single dimension.

THE SOCIOLOGY OF SEX AND GENDER

EXAMINING PROCESSES OF DISCRIMINATION AND ECONOMIC INEQUALITIES

Sociologists of sex and gender focus attention on how sex and gender shape structures of inequality and power. Their research addresses structural factors that derive from gender inequality, including the wage gaps between men and women and other forms of discrimination in the labor force (Britton 2003; England 2005); the gender gap in electoral politics (Rossi 1983); and sexist and heteronormative assumptions embedded in law and social policy (Bernstein and Reimann 2001; Naples 1991).

Another dimension of this scholarship relates to understanding the contribution of global economic restructuring for gender dynamics and economic inequalities. Sociologists of sex and gender highlight the fact that globalization is a result of particular actions taken by identifiable actors and that globalization lands in particular places (Sassen 2006, 2007). Rather than view globalization as a process that occurs at a distance from the everyday lives and activities of particular actors, they demonstrate that global economic and political change is manifest in the daily lives and struggles of women and other members of communities in different parts of the world in ways that are often hidden from view in analyses of globalization that start from the perspective of multinational corporations, transnational organizations, and international political institutions (Naples and Desai 2002, vii).

UNDERSTANDING THE ROLE OF SOCIAL ACTIVISM AND LAW FOR CHALLENGING GENDER INEQUALITY

Until sociologists of sex and gender focused attention on women's political activism, especially the important roles they play in their communities, the extent and variety of women's political participation were ignored or unexamined (Naples 1998). Women's community work and activism, when noticed at all by academics, were understood primarily as a natural extension of their caretaking roles and as part of a maternalist politics in which women's engagement in the public sphere was justified through their identities as mothers (Koven and Michel 1993). In contrast to these assessments, women as community activists contribute countless hours of unpaid labor to campaigns to enhance the physical and environmental quality of their communities while tending to the emotional and social needs of other community members. Their approach to community development and leadership often involves collective and empowering strategies that encourage other women and other residents frequently left out of decision-making roles in formal voluntary associations and political parties to increase their political participation (Naples 2011). This scholarship also explores the role of transnational women's, LGBT, and social justice movements that challenge gender oppression, sexual violence, and other human rights violations (Adam, Duyvendak, and Krouwel 1999; Naples and Desai 2002; Tripp and Ferree 2006).

ANALYZING THE SOURCES OF VIOLENCE AGAINST WOMEN IN PUBLIC AND PRIVATE SPHERES

One of the most important issues addressed by sociologists of sex and gender involves analyzing the many ways that women, minority men, and sexually nonconforming men become targets of violence. Studies of domestic violence were noticeably missing in early sociological literature on the family. With the recognition of the ways power inequalities in marital relations contribute to women's risk of violence in the family, as well as how women become targets of sexual harassment at work and in public spaces, sociologists of sex and gender revealed the daily costs associated with gender and sexual inequalities (Baker 2007).

In considering factors that contribute to violence against women, sociologists and other feminist scholars of sex and gender also brought attention to the roles of militarization and global capitalism in increasing risks of violence against women—for example, through the development of coercive sexual labor in military zones and gendered constructions of violence in armed conflict (Enloe 1990, 2000, 2007; Fukumura and Matsuoka 2002); the use of rape as a tool of war (Allen 1996); and the international crisis of sex trafficking and forced marriage, both of which have been centralized by international human rights groups (Gill and Sundari 2011; Zheng 2010).

ASSESSING THE ROLE OF CULTURE AND DIFFERENCE IN SHAPING GENDERED UNDERSTANDINGS AND PRACTICES

A main topic in the sociology of gender focuses on examining how cultural understandings of gender shape the norms of how a feminine or a masculine body should look and act (Connell 2002; Hughs and Witz 1997; Messner 1992; Witz 2000). This contributes to the attention that feminist sociologists have paid to standards of femininity and masculinity as they apply to evaluations of appropriate body size and shape for women and men, stigma attached to those who do not adhere to these standards, and the ways in which early childhood socialization and media serve to enforce these norms (Hesse-Biber and Nagy 2006). Sociologists of sex and gender also use an intersectional approach to explore the power dynamics between women of different racial and ethnic backgrounds (Becker 1994; Kang 2003) and with different abilities (Shakespeare 2006; Zitzelsberger 2005). Feminist scholars also analyze the role of the medical profession, pharmaceutical companies, and new technologies for providing the means by which women and men can reshape their bodies to fit into narrow definitions of appropriate gender and sexuality (Haiken 1999; Loe 2006).

Feminist sociologists of science are especially interested in new reproductive technologies and their ability to challenge the notion of the "natural" mother and father as older, infertile, or same-sex couples access alternative forms of reproduction (Mamo 2007). They point out the inequities in who can access new technologies and the expansion of "reproductive tourism," where wealthy couples travel to poorer countries to purchase reproductive services, including surrogacy arrangements (Purdy 1989). The new field of transgender studies further complicates analysis of the social construction and production of gender as well as the myriad of ways that gender shapes social policy—for example, by challenging hegemonic understandings of gender as a binary system that maps onto bodies that are understood as "male" or "female" (Currah, Juang, and Miner 2007; Valentine 2007).

Sociologists of sex and gender draw insights from postcolonial and third world feminist analysts who emphasize the ways that cultural diversity and other differences, including class, race, ethnicity, country of origin, age, ability, and sexuality, contour the lives of women and men, thus contributing to their different gendered expectations and experiences (Grewal and Caplan 1994, 2000; Alexander and Mohanty 1997; Mohanty, Russo, and Torres 1991). These complexities are particularly salient, for example, when we examine the lives of poor women, who are disproportionately women of color and disproportionately shoulder the burden of the economic and social dislocation resulting from gendered, racialized, and internationalized processes (Buvinic 1998; Sanford 2003; Women's Refugee Commission 2011). This insight relates to an approach that is at the heart of contemporary feminist sociological analyses, namely, intersectionality.

The call for intersectional analyses was first heard from feminists of color who critiqued approaches that constructed women's concerns without attention to the ways that race, class, and sexuality shaped the experiences of women (Baca Zinn and Dill 1996; Collins 1990). The most powerful approaches to intersectionality also include attention to the ways in which these interactions produce contradictions and tensions across these different levels of analysis and dimensions of difference (McCall 2001, 2005; Maynard 1994).

RESEARCH METHODS FOR THE STUDY OF SEX AND GENDER

Prior to the intervention of feminist sociologists, when included at all, sex was merely considered as a variable in sociological studies. Feminists first argued for a distinction between the biological category of sex and the social construction of gender, then recognized that the biological category is also socially constructed (Lorber and Moore 2007). Beginning in the 1970s, researchers informed by a feminist call to describe women's experiences and perspectives in their own words began to make women's lives central in ethnographic and other qualitative accounts (Smith 1987). A gendered lens on men's lives and the development of men's studies was inspired by a growing sensitivity to the ways in which femininities and masculinities are coconstituted (Connell 1987, 2005; Kimmel 2005; Pascoe 2007). Since the 1980s, feminist sociologists who are influenced by postmodern analyses of power and knowledge have become particularly concerned with the role of discourse and the myriad of ways power shapes women's lives (Ferguson 1991). Differences in feminist epistemologies of knowledge influence what counts as data and how data should be analyzed; therefore, a postmodern feminist researcher would approach the collection and analysis of interviews differently from a scholar who draws on positivist or symbolic interactionist perspectives (Naples 2003).

Feminist sociologists have been particularly effective in identifying the processes by which power and "relations of ruling" are inherent in disciplinary practices (Smith 1990). Feminist sociologists have raised questions about the ethics of social research, especially as relates to power imbalances in fieldwork and interviewing (Stacey 1991; Wolf 1996). As one strategy, sociologists of sex and gender recommend addressing these inequalities through reflexive practice designed to interrogate how personal and situational factors contribute to power imbalances. For example, Nancy Naples explains that this form of reflexive practice "encourages feminist scholars to examine how gendered and racialized assumptions influence which voices and experiences are privileged in ethnographic encounters" (2003, 22). She also argues that a reflexive "approach also implies the development of more egalitarian and participatory field methods than traditionally utilized in social scientific investigations" (201).

Sociologists of sex and gender employ a number of research methods to better understand the complexities of sex and gender. Small-scale, locally focused studies such as those conducted by Patricia Richards (2005) in Chile and Vincanne Adams (1998) in Tibet often incorporate various interview methods, including in-depth interviews and focus groups, as well as observations of and, occasionally, participation in local communities, nongovernmental organizations, and state-sponsored organizations. Sociologists interested in larger demographic trends such as poverty levels, refugee status, education attainment, and maternal mortality and morbidity frequently employ statistical methods through censuses and surveys (Hafner-Burton 2005; Hafner-Burton and Tsutsui 2005; Spirer 1990). Other quantitative approaches are used to capture aggregate patterns such as wage inequality and gender division of labor in employment across different regions (McCall 2001). Sociologists of sex and gender have also turned to policy and document analysis to better understand the bureaucratic and discursive development of instruments intended to identify and meet women's human rights needs (Merry 2006; Naples 2003; Wotipka and Tsutsui 2008).

HUMAN RIGHTS AND THE SOCIOLOGY OF SEX AND GENDER

SEX AND GENDER IN HUMAN RIGHTS DOCUMENTS

The Universal Declaration of Human Rights (UDHR) affirms the "dignity and rights" of all humankind. However, the near invisibility of sex and gender as specific categories for protection in the UDHR renders addressing the rights of women problematic, particularly in a global or transnational context (Bunch 1990; Freeman 1999; Gaer 1998; Binion 1995). Largely as a result of feminist scholarship and activism, particularly since the mid-1980s, human rights abuses based on or related to sex and gender have become increasingly noted; yet there is still no clear consensus as to how to understand these categories or appropriately address violations of women's and sexual minorities' human rights in an international human rights context. This lack of clarity continues to circumscribe the ability of activists and scholars to adequately frame gender-specific abuses as human rights violations in an international legal framework and also presents challenges to those seeking redress. However, progress has been made toward delineating women's and sexual minorities' human rights and demanding that they be formally recognized and protected. Sociologists of sex and gender contribute to this work through increasingly intersectional analyses of the interactions between gender and the state, citizenship, governance structures, and local and global political economies, among other factors.

HISTORICAL PERSPECTIVE ON SEX AND GENDER IN HUMAN RIGHTS DISCOURSE

Attention to sex and gender in human rights discourse and documents can be traced to the late nineteenth century (Lockwood et. al. 1998) and is more evident in the UDHR, which was adopted in 1948. The elaboration of concern for women's rights in particular was further evident in the efforts that resulted from the United Nations Decade for Women (1976–1985), during which women from many different geographical, ethnic, racial, religious, cultural, and class backgrounds took up the task of improving the status of women transnationally. The United Nations sponsored three international women's conferences during this time: in Mexico City in 1975, Copenhagen in 1980, and Nairobi in 1985. Several important human rights documents developed out of these conferences and the efforts of feminist activists and scholars.

The 1976 International Covenant on Civil and Political Rights recognized the equal right of men and women to the enjoyment of all civil and political rights set forth in the covenant (Article 3). This right was further codified in 1979 when the UN General Assembly adopted the Convention on the Elimination of All Forms of Discrimination against Women. Some scholars note that its references to sex include sexual freedom, thereby offering protection to sexual minorities (Mittelstaedt 2008).

In 1990, following decades of concerted effort from feminist activists, organizations, and scholars, Dr. Charlotte Bunch published a foundational call for women's rights as human rights, criticizing the reluctance of states and international structures to address the needs of women and homosexuals from the legal framework of human rights. Three years later, the participants in the World Conference on Human Rights produced the Vienna Declaration and Program of Action, which specified a platform on women's human rights as inalienable from the individual and indivisible from universal human rights, noting that the eradication of sex discrimination is a priority for the international community.

The 1994 International Conference on Population and Development in Cairo featured discussions on sex, sexuality, and sexual health but linked these rights to heterosexual reproduction with no mention of freedom of sexual expression or sexual orientation. At the Fourth World Conference on Women in Beijing in 1995, sponsored by the United Nations, feminist activists finally saw the global emergence of the idea of "women's rights as human rights" (Bunch 1990). Developed by conference participants, the Beijing Platform for Action focused on removing obstacles to women's active participation in all spheres of public and private life through a full and equal share in economic, social, cultural and political decision-making. However, this platform failed to include support for the rights of lesbians and rejected the term "sexual orientation" (Bunch and Fried 1996; see also Baden and Goetz 1997).

KEY AREAS OF CONCERN FOR WOMEN'S HUMAN RIGHTS

Sociologists have identified numerous areas of concern for the development and protection of women's human rights, and they generally understand these areas as linked globally (Naples and Desai 200; Reilly 2009). We offer here three brief illustrations: economic security, gendered violence, and reproductive health.

ECONOMIC SECURITY

The United Nations asserts that women's economic security is at far greater risk than men's globally, and this is particularly true in rural areas that rely heavily on agricultural production (UNFAO 2010). Differential access to employment opportunities continues to reflect and reproduce gendered conceptualizations of women's domestic roles and to inhibit their ability to engage fully in civic life. Further, approximately 75 percent of the world's women are not entitled to property ownership and cannot receive bank loans due to underemployment, unemployment, and insecure employment (Moser 2007). These restrictions impact not only women but families and communities as well (Cagatay 2001).

GENDERED VIOLENCE

Anthropologist Sally Merry points out that "the idea that everyday violence against women is a human rights violation has not been easy to establish" (2006, 2). Part of the difficulty lies in the tensions between global and transnational institutions and local structures. The translation of human rights laws and ideologies between multiple locations is complicated by cultural differences, questions of sovereignty, and access to resources, among other potential impediments (Bunch 1990). In this context, the role of intermediary institutions such as nongovernmental organizations is pivotal. Further complicating the ability of scholars and activists to address gendered violence as a human rights violation is the continuing construction of a public-private dichotomy in which violence against women is framed as a family issue in which state actors are reluctant to intervene (Clapham 2007; Tomasevski 1995). However, there has been some progress toward understanding gendered violence as an issue that transcends public/private dichotomies, particularly when this violence occurs in the context of war. In 2008 the UN Security Council passed Resolution 1820, which formally recognized the particular vulnerabilities of women and girl children to sexual violence during armed conflict and reaffirmed states' obligations to address sexual violence against civilians.

REPRODUCTIVE HEALTH

Maternal and child health continue to be a priority for women's human rights activists in the twenty-first century. Growing attention and increased resources from local, global, and transnational institutions over the last several decades—particularly since the 1994 International Conference on Population and Development explicitly linked the reproductive health and human rights of women to global efforts to reduce poverty—have resulted in important improvements in women's access to adequate health care (WHO 2010). However, globally women experience unequal access to health care. For example, according to the World Health Organization (2000), global maternal mortality and morbidity rates are highest in developing nations.

Guang-zhen Wang and Vijayan Pillai (2001) explain that sociologists have applied two general analytical frames to reproductive health: (1) identifying social-structural factors shaping reproductive health, and (2) examining a rights-based paradigm to elucidate states' obligations to provide reproductive health care. Utilizing these frames has enabled sociologists to offer critical analyses of the interactions between health and social environments that elucidate foundational causes for the disparities in health between sexes, genders, geographic locations, socioeconomic locations, and racial-ethnic identities, among other key factors (Doyal 1995, 2001; Warner-Smith, Bryson, and Byles 2004).

KEY SOCIOLOGICAL QUESTIONS AND INSIGHTS IN THE STUDY OF WOMEN'S HUMAN RIGHTS

A primary question emerging from the feminist sociological study of human rights is, What obstacles challenge universal recognition of women's human rights and prevent a comprehensive consideration of gender within the prevailing human rights frameworks? Findings in response to this question vary but often include the influence of religious groups, social and political constructions of a public-private gendered dichotomy, masculinized notions of citizenship, and the fact that the concept of "universal" human rights tends to mask the multiple dimensions of difference emerging from racial-ethnic, class, and cultural locations, as well as sex and gender differences, and to impose a Western conceptualization of individual rights.

ASSESSING THE INFLUENCE OF RELIGIOUS GROUPS IN CIRCUMSCRIBING WOMEN'S HUMAN RIGHTS

The lack of women's voices in the development of religious institutions and the concurrent influence of religious doctrine on state practices impose multiple and, at times, severe restrictions on women's freedoms (European Women's Lobby 2006; Winter 2006). For example, at the time of the Beijing Conference for Women, Roman Catholic authorities rejected what they considered the ambiguity of the term "gender" and noted that they understood "gender" to be "grounded in biological sexual identity" (UN Report 1995, 165), thus reinscribing an essentialist role for women that curtails women's opportunities (European Women's Lobby 2006). The role of religious doctrine in determining women's rights is complicated by these essentialist ideas about gender as they intersect with issues of cultural relativism and fundamental human rights (Sunder 2003; Winter 2006). These complications have led many scholars, such as Madhavi Sunder, to assert that "human rights law has a problem with religion" (2003, 1401; see also Reilly 2009).

EXAMINING THE PERSISTENCE OF THE PUBLIC-PRIVATE DICHOTOMY IN HUMAN RIGHTS DISCOURSE

Sociologists of sex and gender interrogate the social construction of a public-private dichotomy in which some aspects of human lives are conceptualized as occurring or belonging in a public sphere and others are deemed private and thus, in some measure, protected from surveillance or state control (Collins 1994; Okin 1989). Many violations of women's human rights, such as domestic violence, forms of sexual slavery, and child-preference practices that disadvantage girl children, are often considered "private" matters in which global and local states are reluctant to intervene (Bunch 1990; Freeman 1999; MacKinnon 1993). The occurrence of these and similarly gendered phenomena in what is constructed as the "privacy" of family and home constructs boundaries around how these issues are addressed and inhibits the abilities of international systems to intervene in such rights violations.

GENDERING HUMAN RIGHTS DISCOURSE AND PRACTICE

Sociologists of sex and gender point out that the dominant image of the political actor is male (Haney 2000; Bunch 1990; Yuval-Davis 1997), and most human rights institutions are male dominated (Freeman 1999). Therefore, women are largely invisible as human rights institutions deal with human rights violations on a large, public scale (for example, through the institution of democracies, fair housing, and economic security); "it is assumed that women benefit" (Freeman 1999, 515) as members of the larger populace. Failure to specify the needs of women as women presents an obstacle to recognizing the many ways their human rights can be and are violated through an imposed public-private dichotomy (Bunch 1990; MacKinnon 1993). Within this dichotomy, notions of citizenship become conflated with the presumably male political actor (Yuval-Davis 1997), and the human rights of women are subsumed or delegitimized under this rubric of masculinized citizenship.

UNIVERSALIZING NOTIONS OF HUMAN RIGHTS AND OF WOMEN

Citizenship for women is further complicated by political and cultural location, as the women's-rights-as-human-rights frame potentially implies a universalizing notion of women and of rights derived from Western conceptions of citizenship and the state. Sociological perspectives point out the ways in which this runs the risk of further masking local structures and institutions such as diverse family forms, law-enforcement practices, and religious beliefs (Bonnin 1995; Chow 1996; Howard and Allen 1996; Ray and Korteweg 1999). When theoretical space is allotted for the recognition of women outside a Western paradigm, it is often limited in scope. For example, as Chandra Talpade Mohanty argues, "Assumptions of privilege and ethnocentric universality (can) lead to the construction of a ... reductive and homogeneous notion of '... Third World difference'" (2006, 19), wherein third world and postcolonial women and U.S. women of color are produced as a "composite, singular 'Third World Woman'" (Narayan 1997). Women's human rights, therefore, potentially work from a binary framework of "West/not West" as well as "male/not male."

REDEFINING THE HUMAN RIGHTS PARADIGM FROM A FEMINIST PERSPECTIVE

Gender requires a revisioning of human rights as a universal concept as well as a reconstruction of the systems used to create and ensure the sanctity of women's human rights (Staudt 1997; Binion 1995). This includes a blurring of imposed boundaries around "public" and "private" and recognition of the inherently political nature of the "private" lives of women, including domestic lives, religious beliefs and practices, and sexualities. Sociologists recognize that political borders are blurred in the transnational context of global economy, migration, and armed conflict (Freeman 1999; Naples and Desai 2002). Therefore, a feminist and intersectional sociological study of relevant social structures includes, but is not limited to, family and community; local, regional, and global political economies; culture, religion, law, and education; and national and transnational governance, including nongovernmental organizations.

Just as political boundaries are not permanently fixed, a human rights framework is not a static paradigm, as our local and global conceptualizations of what counts as human rights issues and what they require continue to evolve. Feminist sociologists' particular perspective on the intersections of social institutions and structures, such as the family, state, economy, and religion, and individual experiences of power and inequality renders visible the links between the lives of women and sexual minorities, violations of their human rights, and opportunities for protection and redress.

Sociological inquiry into gender and gendered structures and institutions has helped to reveal the ways in which definitions of citizenship; local, national, and transnational institutions and structures; and even the law itself are frequently informed by gendered notions of masculinity that exclude women and their experiences. Sociological analyses of gender thereby offer theoretical tools with which to understand, highlight, and advance an agenda of women's rights as human rights. Emerging emphases in feminist sociological work on the intersections of gender with race, class, sexuality, and other social and political locations (Collins 1994; Richards 2005) provide still greater space for consideration of women's diverse lived experiences under the rubric of human rights, allowing human rights scholars and activists greater opportunity to avoid essentializing women and imposing inadequate Western concepts of "rights."

WHERE DO WE GO FROM HERE?

Recognizing the diversity of women's and men's lives, yet striving to understand "women" and "men" as universal categories, produces a theoretical tension for sociology and for human rights praxis. Women constitute a "group" that exists everywhere; yet they are often differentiated by political, cultural, racial, economic, ethnic, religious, and other considerations. The specific needs of women and non-gender-conforming men for recognition and protection of their human rights share some similarities but vary in many ways. Sensitivity to the differences among women requires nuanced, locally grounded analyses of women's and men's diverse lived experiences; yet, as Gayle Binion asserts, "The facts and conditions of cultural diversity among societies cannot, from a feminist perspective, justify a failure to rectify the conditions in which women live worldwide" (1995, 522), conditions that include gendered violence, economic insecurity, and reproductive health concerns. The international instruments of human rights retain an uncomfortable relationship with culture and gender that requires ongoing reflexive practice and attention to local structures and cultural diversity as well as global economic and political processes that shape everyday life in different parts of the world.

CHAPTER TWO

AGING AND THE LIFE COURSE

Robin Shura and Rachel Bryant

For sociologists, age—like gender, race and ethnicity, social class, and other characteristics typically construed strictly as attributes of individuals—is a feature of social structure that is both external to and coercive of individual experience (Riley, Johnson, and Foner 1972; Kohli 1986). Age carries particular statuses, expectations, and consequences in highly age-conscious societies that influence interaction, regardless of the individual (Chudacoff 1989). Age can also carry with it expectations for human rights. However, the acceptance of human rights instruments (e.g., UDHR, UNCRC) has not had explicitly noticeable effects on scholarship within the sociology of age and the life course (hereafter, SALC), particularly in the United States (Townsend 2006). Indeed, with some exceptions (see Townsend 2006), scholarship in SALC does not include significant explicit conceptual or methodological attention to human rights. This is not due to a lack of considerable sociological scholarship that draws attention to laws and policies and how they relate to age and aging (e.g., Binstock 2007; Rowe et al. 2010; Binstock and Post 1991), including issues of age discrimination (Quadagno and Street 1995), and scholarship on the political economy of age and aging (e.g., Estes et al. 2006). It may reflect the propensity to overlook realities of age segregation and ageism as robust features of social reality that bear on human rights, while being all too aware of the salience of kindred concepts within sociology regarding discriminatory structural segregation and cultural beliefs based on gender, race and ethnicity, or social class. However, attention within SALC to age segregation (Hagestad and Uhlenberg 2005, 2006) and ageism (e.g., Butler 2002 [1972]; Dannefer and Shura 2009) is significant and synergistic with human rights concerns, and debates about generational equity (including rationing health care to "seniors") within SALC are highly relevant (e.g., Binstock and Post 1991; Callahan 1987). These substantive areas speak to the ideological and structural manifestations of prejudices and systematic discriminatory treatment based on age. Yet even this scholarship has generally fallen short of making explicit, formalized scholarly connections to human rights.

This lack of explicit focus on human rights within SALC cannot be understood as due to a failure to make major empirical and theoretical gains or an absence of vigorous scholarship in SALC. "Human rights" largely has not been clarified within SALC scholarship in terms of its conceptual, theoretical, or methodological relevance because this relevance has not, or not yet, been made widely known, articulated, and accessible across sociology. Further, we speculate that the lack of explicit focus on human rights within SALC may be explained by one issue that a diversity of approaches within SALC have in common: a reluctance to make strong and direct claims that social problems exist relevant to their subject matter, in favor of emphasizing descriptive and highly sophisticated analytical approaches using increasingly robust empirical data sources (e.g., see Kohli 2007 or Mayer 2009), or in favor of making refined theoretical contributions to the subfield that allege claims of problems within sociological scholarship itself (Dannefer 2011; Baars et al. 2006; Bengtson et al. 2009a, 2009b). Omission of explicit attention to human rights may be less specific to SALC and more broadly descriptive of perennial disagreements within the field about our roles as sociologists and the proper focus and locus of our work writ large.

The diversity of perspectives and issues within SALC speaks to a deeper, paradigmatic divide within SALC, as both conventional approaches to research and more critical approaches exist within SALC. Dale Dannefer (2011) alleges that the former are more represented than the latter. The dominance of conventional research within SALC in some ways makes understandable the lack of explicit attention to human rights, whereas the significant minority of critical perspectives within SALC unavoidably raises issues that have synergy with human rights concerns—for example, power, ideology, and conflict. And these paradigmatic divides do not touch on debates over whether there is a place for advocacy in sociological scholarship or human rights sociology.

THE SOCIOLOGY OF AGE, AGING, AND THE LIFE COURSE: KEY CONCERNS AND QUESTIONS

The sociology of age and the life course consists of very heterogeneous orientations to research, including subject matter, methodology, and theory. Even inconsistency in the language used to describe its subject matter—older adults versus elders versus the elderly; later life versus later adulthood versus old age; life course versus lifespan—suggests extreme heterogeneity of approaches, including disagreement within the field (Dannefer and Uhlenberg 1999; Thomas 2004; Settersten 2005). Interestingly, SALC includes gerontological approaches (research focused on late life) and research on the life course, which is broadly inclusive of midlife and later life as well as early life events and childhood. However, in part a legacy of section development within the American Sociological Association, and in part reinforced by divisions of major federal funding agencies (e.g., NIA versus NICHD), SALC typically does not subsume scholarship devoted to childhood. SALC research has in the past been accused of being rich in data but lacking in theory (Birren 1959). Perhaps in response to this criticism, several developments have ignited renewed theorizing and attention to theory within SALC.

The life-course perspective within sociology is deceivingly singular, as a plurality of frameworks comprise life-course sociology. In brief, these include seeking to understand how early life experiences or events influence the courses of lives over time (e.g., Elder 1999; Elder et al. 2009; Crosnoe and Elder 2004); how life-course transitions (e.g., transitions from childhood to adulthood, from adulthood to later life/"old age" or retirement) relate to individual and cultural circumstances (e.g., Settersten and Hagestad 1996a, 1996b); how macro-level social structures produce regularity (homogeneity or heterogeneity) in these life-course patterns en masse (e.g., Kohli 1986; Brückner and Mayer 2005); and how these patterns vary over time and place. Through the mid-twentieth century, as cohorts navigated social structures highly regulated and organized by age as a key criterion for role entry and exit, people within these cohorts tended to experience key life transitions (e.g., entry into the workforce, family formation, retirement) at increasingly similar ages. This has created such strong age-linked patterns in human lives that the life course is described as "institutionalized" (Kohli 1986; Kohli and Meyer 1986; Mayer and Müller 1986). Yet shifts in these macro-level structures, as well as new data, raise the question of whether deinstitutionalization of the life course is occurring (Brückner and Mayer 2005; Dannefer and Shura 2007). Some SALC scholars emphasize aging as a process; others criticize a focus on "aging" as reification of the presumption that aging is a "natural" process and prefer to identify age as an influential social construct (Dannefer 1984).

A few substantive areas within SALC include population aging; aging policy and welfare state scholarship; health, ability, and aging (including health changes across the life course, health disparities, caregiving, long-term care, structure and organization of health-care services and aging, chronic illness, end-of-life issues); work and retirement (pensions, retirement policy, later-life employment patterns); intergenerational relationships; later-life migration; cumulating dis/advantage and aging; ageism; quality of life (including ethical issues about medical care and quality of life at the end of life); and gender, race, and social class and their relationships to age. For more robust overviews of substantive, methodological, and theoretical work in SALC, see recent handbooks by Robert H. Binstock and Linda K. George (2006, 2011), Richard A. Settersten Jr. and J. L. Angel (2011), Peter Uhlenberg (2009b), and Dale Dannefer and Chris Phillipson (2010). Additional key SALC areas and findings are elaborated in the following sections.

SUMMARY OF KEY METHODS

There is high value within SALC on quantitative data and sophisticated quantitative analytical techniques, specifically advanced forms of multivariate longitudinal and/ or hierarchical modeling that are used to tease out such social patterns as trajectories of age-related trends and changes over time within populations in terms of health, wealth, well-being, and so forth, as well as to tease out cohort and period effects (e.g., Alwin, Hofer, and McCammon 2006). Other methods are also utilized in SALC, with qualitative research generally less represented than quantitative work (for a hallmark exception, see Gubrium 1997), and with participatory and community-building methodologies much less prominent within SALC (for exceptions, see Blair and Minkler 2009; Shura, Siders, and Dannefer 2010). Yet a mainstay of SALC is sophisticated and rich analysis of population-representative data sets. More robust population-representative data sets are becoming available to study processes and patterns related to age and aging, particularly longitudinal data sets (Alwin, Hofer, and McCammon 2006; Kohli 2007). Within SALC, significant portions of strongly data-driven research can be considered social-psychological in orientation, with emphases on individual-level outcomes such as individual health and well-being (Hagestad and Dannefer 2001).

WHAT CAN HUMAN RIGHTS LEARN FROM SOCIOLOGY OF AGE AND THE LIFE COURSE?

Connections between human rights sociology and scholarship within SALC that has salience to human rights remain underdeveloped. Three SALC areas that are promising for integration are explored here: age segregation, ageism, and the extent to which age is an axis of differentiation and discrimination for human rights among groups and individuals across the life course. In relation to these three major areas, population aging, globalization, and debates within SALC about age-linked vulnerability are briefly considered. We present our ideas here not as an exhaustive treatise but as targeted and thought-provoking discussions that we hope may spur further consideration.

For human rights scholarship, inequality is a major concern. A pervasive feature of modernity is the reliance on age as a major basis of social organization across education, work, and other social settings. SALC scholars have examined the social phenomena of age segregation (Hagestad and Uhlenberg 2005, 2006) and ageism (Butler 2002 [1972]; Dannefer and Shura 2009; Hagestad and Uhlenberg 2005); yet there is room for clearer articulation of how these areas of research may intersect with human rights. Age segregation, or the physical and social separation of groups within society based on age, is a systematic and structural feature of "developed" societies. In these societies, norms and expectations linked to age provide an often taken-for-granted guide to "age-appropriate" behavior and social practice, which is not the case in other societies (Rogoff 2003). Based on the rapid rise in age consciousness and the social salience of age as a key meaning-laden status of individuals in the early twentieth century (Achenbaum 1978, 2009; Chudacoff 1989; Rogoff 2003), age segregation is currently a widespread form of social segregation within most major social institutions. This pattern is reinforced by pervasive cultural beliefs that place high social value on some age categories, yet denigrate others. Age during later life is a major and concentrated target of devaluation. Cultural ageism, then, refers to the differential social value and meaning attributed to individuals and groups based on age and has particular salience to the nexus of SALC scholarship and human rights. Ageism and age segregation share a mutually reinforcing relationship in society (Dannefer and Shura 2009;

Hagestad and Uhlenberg 2005). This work in SALC has laid the groundwork for potential integration with human rights scholarship: inasmuch as other forms of social segregation and culturally patterned inequalities and prejudices (e.g., racial or ethnic segregation and racism, gender segregation and sexism) are concerns of human rights, there is an opportunity to integrate these important substantive areas within SALC more explicitly with human rights.

Age segregation creates various forms of social vulnerability for many in later life (Hagestad and Uhlenberg 2006; Riley and Riley 1994). Evidence of age segregation within social networks is robust, indicating a large degree of homogeneity of age within people's networks of closest ties (e.g., Uhlenberg and Gierveld 2004), particularly in nonfamily networks (Hagestad and Uhlenberg 2005). Ironically, age segregation endures within a historical period in which the effects of other forms of systematic social segregation (e.g., racial segregation) have been deemed harmful and unjust (Fry 2007), despite assertions that structural opportunities for older people are increasingly mismatched with their capacities (Riley, Kahn, and Foner 1994) and evidence of benefits of age integration for young and old (Hagestad and Uhlenberg 2007; Uhlenberg 2009a; Uhlenberg and Cheuk 2010). Age segregation has placed some elders in particularly vulnerable social positions, especially since many older adults face concentrated loss due to death within their age-homogenous social networks (Dannefer and Shura 2009). This amplifies the probability of social isolation in late life. Issues raised by age segregation and ageism take on special significance as older people are becoming an increasingly large proportion of many countries' populations (e.g., Uhlenberg 2009a). Human rights scholars have an opportunity to build from these SALC findings in ways that frame increased social vulnerability and isolation in later life not as natural problems related to physiological aging processes but rather as socially constructed barriers to full human rights, barriers that limit or obstruct social participation and are reified through ageist social discourse, including ageist discourse within SALC.

An irony of ageism is that, except those who die relatively young, we will all inherit the relatively denigrated status that accompanies older age unless there is a cultural shift. This statement ought to evoke concern and a sense of the importance of tying ageism to broader sociological literatures about human rights that target other "isms" and concomitant forms of social segregation (Hagestad and Uhlenberg 2005). For example, praising others for how "young" they are, or for trying to "stay young" in order to avoid social devaluation, reifies and reproduces ageism: it does not question or undermine the differential value attributed to human beings, human experience, and social reality based on age. It is heuristically informative to develop sociological parallels that make visible the cultural and structural realities of ageism. For instance, is the imperative to "stay young," which is largely celebrated in today's culture, similar to asking a woman to "be manly" or an African American to be "whiter"? Age hegemony, marked by the relative devaluation of oldness and valorization of some aspects of youth, becomes visible through such exercises. Sociologists who link human rights scholarship to age may benefit from considering the ways in which ageism is similar to, or different from, racism and sexism. The connections between dynamics of hegemony and dominance, as well as inferiority and prejudice, as they relate to age and human rights need to be further studied and elucidated.

Human rights scholarship may benefit from a deeper examination of the extent to which age is an axis of differentiation and discrimination for groups and individuals across the life course. Analyses of shared or similar age-linked social vulnerabilities in early and late life, often indicated by "dependency," are needed within human rights scholarship. This includes the need for attention focused on the rights and responsibilities allocated to individuals or groups based on age and the implications for how this changes as individuals grow older. Some basic, starting questions to explore potential linkages between SALC and human rights include the following: Which age groups have which rights? Do any social groups have "special," age-specific rights? Who is responsible for protecting these rights? Which stakeholders (social groups or social institutions) rally against age-specific constructions of rights (e.g., for the old, for institutionalized elders, for adults, for the young) and why? Do some rights turn on or off at specific ages? If so, why? Such questions reframe basic considerations of human rights with a specific emphasis on how age as a social construct may explicitly relate to how human rights are socially constructed. These questions also remind us of the importance of examining power differences according to age: there is a need to consider how social vulnerabilities are shared by both the young and the old in society (e.g., Hagestad 2008; Uhlenberg 2009a).

The concept of the life course can inform human rights scholarship. Rights may change, formally or informally, based on age: a person's rights may look different from different points in his or her life course (Janoski and Gran 2002). SALC may offer conceptual insight and methodological tools to research age-based variations in rights (e.g., voting) by forcing questions of the extent to which age is used to confer and constrain various rights across the life course and why.

Finally, SALC offers strength in terms of its methodological and analytical rigor, as well as some critical theoretical advances. In these areas, SALC might challenge scholars using human rights as a perspective or conceptual framework to hone methods and measures in analyses, identify robust data sources, refine measurement, and employ diverse theoretical perspectives rather than proclaim or reify an ideological line. It is not yet clear within SALC, or not clearly communicated to or by SALC scholars, what human rights sociology entails, what explicit or implicit theoretical premises it employs, what methods it considers primary, upon what forms of data it most heavily relies, and what prominent disagreements or debates may currently exist among scholars who identify as human rights sociologists. Communicating about the tools of human rights sociology, therefore, is a surmountable challenge, as human rights orientations may be seen as too activist and not as mainstream scholarship within SALC without clear theoretical and empirical justification. SALC can challenge human rights perspectives regarding making universal claims and exporting them without nuanced understandings of social-historical contexts that shape experiences and understandings of age.

What Can Sociology of Age and the Life Course Learn from Human Rights?

Unlike with some other socially charged and consequential social statuses (e.g., race, gender), unless one dies relatively early, one will experience all ages, replete with more or less social value and potentially with more or fewer rights, different rights, more or less protection of rights, more or fewer responsibilities for protecting others' rights, and even special rights relevant to specific stages of the life course (Bryant and Shura 2009; Foner 1974). Because few SALC scholars are actively engaged in such a perspective, human rights sociologists may make key contributions that will inform this area. Furthermore, age is often presumed to be helpful in determining an individual's competency, a presumption that some SALC scholars heavily critique and that has relevance to human rights. It may be socially acceptable to restrict full participation in specific rights based on presumptions about age-related deficits, even if formally and legally the specific rights in question are conferred irrespective of increased age. There may be a "rising sun" in the life course of human rights, in which various legal rights are not realized until "adulthood" (usually at the arbitrary age of eighteen), and some rights may become informally restricted with greater age (Bryant and Shura 2009). For example, both minor children and adults in late life may experience formal and informal limitations placed on their participation in medical decision-making. Are there counterexamples in which the young and the old possess comparatively stronger rights, or specialized rights, when compared to other age groups? An assessment of the United States suggests that young people benefit more from social rights, such as the right to education, compared to working-age adults, who typically possess weak entitlements to public health insurance unless they can demonstrate financial hardship or enter older age (e.g., Medicare, Medicaid). The contingency and transition, then, of human rights throughout the life course are areas ripe for SALC scholarship, and this research could potentially be bolstered with tools used by human rights sociologists. Further, how potential age-related contingencies that shape the use of human rights intersect with hierarchies of race, class, gender, and health could be fruitful areas to integrate with other sociological research devoted to human rights.

SALC scholars face the challenge of not reproducing ageist assumptions in their work and not taking age segregation or its purported social value for granted in their scholarship. One distinct challenge we pose to SALC scholars is to consider seriously in their scholarship the view of elders as active individuals with continuing capacities to play valued roles within myriad social institutions and in their communities (see, e.g., Shura, Siders, and Dannefer 2010), particularly at a time in history when rapid population aging has led some to recognize that older people may be the world's only expanding natural resource (Freedman 2007). We consider it an important heuristic exercise, and one with relevance to human rights, to pit the ageist assumption as a hypothesis against the hypothesis of "elder as capable," if only to shed light on the extent to which scholars often internalize status quo ageism and age segregation as inevitable, or even desirable, social realities. Prominent messages within mainstream media often perpetuate ageist perceptions, including references to population aging that are almost always negative or even ominous and references to later-life policies that emphasize the social burdens and costs of an aging population rather than potential social benefits. In an increasingly globalized world, one with many rapidly aging populations, SALC and human rights scholars ought to consider the extent to which cultural ageism and the concomitant positive and largely unquestioned value placed on age segregation are being exported globally from the Economic North to the Economic South. Human rights sociology may offer useful insights and tools for meeting these SALC challenges.

The Universal Declaration of Human Rights (UDHR), adopted in 1948 by the United Nations, emphasizes the dignity and rights of all people, which includes people of all ages. SALC scholars give little explicit attention to age as an axis of social differentiation that has real implications for rights. The extent to which beliefs about aging and elders, the lack of prominent and socially valued roles for elders, and other practices and institutions relevant to later life uphold human dignity and rights is another possible perspective through which SALC scholars may benefit from increased attention to human rights. Whenever claims about "rights" and "best interests" are made on behalf of one group by another group, and the target social group does not have a direct, leading role in identifying its own best interests (and it is not clarified how the social division between such groups is justified in the first place), there is fertile ground for analysis from both sociological and human rights perspectives. Upon sociological examination, hegemony and disenfranchisement are likely to be found. Additionally, various substantive areas in SALC are ripe for further consideration of how age explicitly relates to human rights, including end-of-life issues regarding legal and medical decision-making, rights within institutionalized care settings, age-based inequality in social opportunities, debates about later-life policy (e.g., pensions and US Social Security), and specific rights-relevant contexts of midlife experience (e.g., incarceration and disabling conditions), to name just a few avenues of investigation. The sociology of age may be well served by not reifying intergenerational equity debates (e.g., Do children's rights threaten adults' rights? Do elders' rights threaten the idea of rights belonging to adults at midlife and young people?). It is the task of sociology to adopt such questions and social phenomena as subject matter for sociological analysis and to apply appropriate tools of theory, measurement, and analytic rigor in the quest for answers. Combining strengths in SALC with strengths in the sociology of human rights could produce gains in these important areas.

CONCLUSION

The UDHR goal of upholding human dignity and rights, irrespective of age, provides one potential starting point for integration of SALC and human rights scholarship. Approaches to integrated research might begin from analysis of age-segregated and age-pluralistic communities and the value attributed to age therein and, from there, explore how all constituents could be afforded greater opportunities for social participation and positive social value. Rather than raise a flag to rally for "older adults" to become the next social group on behalf of which human rights campaigns are framed, we call sociologists' attention to the need to clarify methods and theories that might allow myriad fruitful substantive areas within SALC to be better integrated with human rights considerations and with pursuits of upholding human dignity across the life course.

Age—a powerful social force and social fact that is coercive of individual experience and organizes social life—may often not be explicitly framed as relevant to human rights by SALC scholars, and it may be overlooked by human rights scholars as a key axis of social differentiation and discrimination. SALC offers rich methodological and theoretical orientations, substantive contributions, and scientific rigor, all of which may be useful tools for research on human rights as they relate to age. SALC may illuminate how people experience human rights over their life courses and how other age-related structures or experiences interface with rights. Finally, SALC is a hugely diverse subdiscipline and can make vast contributions to human rights in regard to policy analysis, population aging, and intergenerational relationships, to name a few. Further communication about, and clearer elaboration of, the tools of human rights research within SALC circles—from clear conceptual definitions of human rights, to elaboration of theories that organize research of human rights, to methods and data in sociology of human rights, to clarification of the respective roles of conventional research, critical research, and advocacy-based sociology within human rights sociology—will most effectively promote increased integration of perspectives. This chapter is intended to suggest thought-provoking, yet limited, substantive ways to further such integration.

CHAPTER THREE

MENTAL HEALTH AND HUMAN RIGHTS

Giedrė Baltrušaitytė

Nearly 54 million people around the world have severe mental disorders such as schizophrenia and bipolar affective disorder (manic-depressive illness). In addition, 154 million people suffer from depression. Mental disorders are increasingly prevalent in developing countries, the consequence of persistent poverty, the demographic transition, military conflicts, and natural disasters (World Health Organization 2007).

Recognition of the effects of social, economic, political, and cultural conditions on mental health and well-being is a current feature of social-policy agendas, with debate increasingly framed in human rights terms. The most significant international effort to protect the rights of those with mental health disorders is UN General Assembly Resolution 46/119 on the Protection of Persons with Mental Illness and the Improvement of Mental Health Care, adopted in 1991. This resolution, while not formally binding, serves as an influential aid in developing human rights–oriented mental-health-care systems and policies. In addition, the World Health Organization (WHO) continues to draw attention to the impacts of human rights violations and refers to social isolation, poor quality of life, stigma, and discrimination as central issues for those with mental disabilities (Lewis 2009a).

Despite the increasing policy attention, sociological attention to the intersection of mental health and human rights remains marginal. While there is a long tradition of sociological research on the phenomenon of mental illness (Goffman 1961; Scheff 1999; Busfield 1996), sociologists have rarely framed their research questions explicitly within the framework of human rights. Analysis of human rights issues and their implications for the situation of people with mental illness, however, is clearly within the sociological terrain.

This chapter provides a summary of key topics and issues in the sociology of mental health and explores the ways in which the sociology of mental health could frame some of its central questions in relation to the paradigm of human rights. I start with the presentation of major sociological ideas about mental illness, psychiatry, and psychiatric care and then provide a summary of the key findings within the field. The subsequent sections cover a discussion of how the sociology of mental health could enrich human rights research as well as redirect its constituent questions toward the human rights paradigm. The chapter concludes with a discussion of the possibilities for a human rights approach to the sociology of mental health.

THE SOCIOLOGY OF MENTAL HEALTH

The sociology of mental health is concerned with several key issues. Scholars in this area of inquiry are interested in a variety of questions in their research, including (1) the linkages between social factors and mental disorders, (2) the ways in which professional discourses and practices shape the phenomenon of mental illness, (3) societal reactions to individuals with mental illness, (4) the effects on the individual of the stigma associated with mental illness, (5) the effects that changes in mental health policy have on mental health care, and (6) the experiences of using mental health services.

SOCIAL FACTORS IN MENTAL ILLNESS

Much of the sociological contribution to our understanding of the onset of mental illnesses is grounded in social epidemiology. Sociologists account for variations in the prevalence of mental illness among various social groups by examining differences in levels of adversity, stressful events, and individual management of stress (Turner, Wheaton, and Lloyd 1995; Pearlin and Schooler 1978; Kessler and McLeod 1984). Pilgrim and Rogers (1999) provide a solid summary of some key assumptions of the sociological research that investigates the links between social factors and mental illness.

According to the scholarship, the probability of mental health problems, particularly severe mental illnesses like schizophrenia, increases as socioeconomic status decreases, with the lowest social classes being clearly disadvantaged. There remains considerable debate about whether poverty increases vulnerability to mental illness or whether individuals, particularly those who are already socially disadvantaged, drift further into poverty because their illness makes them socially incompetent and vulnerable (Kohn 1981; Link, Dohrenwend, and Skodol 1986; Eaton 1980; Miech et al. 1999).

Women are diagnosed as suffering from mental illness more often than men, though most of this difference is accounted for by diagnoses of depression. Men are more likely to have diagnostic labels that refer to and incorporate behavioral threats (e.g., alcoholism, pedophilia). There is still no clear sociological account of these differences, particularly concerning why women are overrepresented in psychiatric populations. Some studies show that gender differences in common mental disorders virtually disappear in the lowest income group (Busfield 1996; Rosenfield 1999; Ridge, Emslie, and White 2011).

The prevalence of mental health problems seems to vary among different ethnic groups, seemingly becoming more common in African-descended rather than European-descended populations. This difference, however, needs to be explained with caution, as there may be methodological problems inherent in such studies. The overrepresentation of minority ethnic groups in psychiatric statistics may reflect continuing disadvantages rooted in slavery, enforced migration, colonialism, and racial discrimination rather than real differences in psychiatric morbidity (Omi and Winant 1986; Brown et al. 1999; Mossakowski 2008; Williams et al. 1997).

Other sociological work has been focused on wider social structures and the capitalist social order as implicated in mental illness. Warner (1994), for instance, attempted to demonstrate that in industrialized societies, recovery rates for schizophrenia are closely linked to fluctuations in state economies and the requirements of the labor market. He concludes that changes in the outcome of schizophrenia reflect changes in the perceived utility for the labor market of those with mental health disorders. Despite the critiques and various methodological problems, the strength of research that investigates the linkages between social factors and mental illness is its focus on the inequalities in mental health among various social groups as related to the social circumstances in which they live.

PROFESSIONAL DISCOURSES AND PRACTICES

Contemporary Western psychiatry is not an internally consistent body of professional knowledge and practice. Despite the variety of conceptual approaches, mental illness in psychiatric discourse is conceptualized as a pathology that, in more severe cases, may affect the ability of the individual to apprehend reality and retain critical insight into his or her health problem (Baltrušaitytė 2010).

By defining those with mental illness as incapable of self-mastery, the psychiatric discourse sustains the need for continuous professional supervision of the patient and legitimates paternalism in psychiatric care. The presumed lack of insight on the part of the affected individual often serves as a ground for the involuntary treatment of people with mental disabilities. Playle and Keeley (1998) have analyzed the notion of treatment nonadherence in psychiatric discourse. They note that nonadherence to treatment is regarded as a symptom of illness. If the patient fails to comply, the presumed lack of critical insight may provide the justification for the professional to diminish the autonomy of the individual by paternalistically imposing compulsory treatment. The close association developed in psychiatric discourse on mental pathology between the notions of mental illness and perceptions of "dangerousness" provides further basis for compulsory psychiatric examination or hospitalization (Dallaire et al. 2000).

Other studies point out that paternalistic health care may, in various ways, inhibit patients' abilities to participate actively in or critically evaluate the medical encounter (Edwards, Staniszweska, and Crichton 2004; Goodyear-Smith and Buetow 2001; Williams 1994). Mead and Copeland (2001) maintain that long-term psychiatric patients may eventually get used to the identities and roles constructed by the psychiatric discourse and imputed to them. These roles and identities often, in turn, alter the relationship of mental patient and caregiver into one of dependence and deference.

Much sociological work has focused on examining the psychiatric conceptualizations of mental illness, noting that categories of mental disorder are socially and culturally relative (Busfield 1996; Warner 1994). An emphasis is often made that mental health and illness are negotiated social concepts and, as such, cannot be understood simply in terms of bodily phenomena. The strength of this sociological work is that it questions the assumed impartiality of psychiatric diagnosis and highlights the socially contingent nature of mental illness. For instance, in D. L. Rosenhan's 1991 study, eight researchers with no history of mental illness or obvious psychiatric problems gained admission to different psychiatric hospitals in the United States by complaining that they heard voices. This study showed how readily psychiatric hospitalization can be achieved, particularly if the patient voluntarily agrees to hospital admission. Rosenhan concluded that it is not possible to distinguish the sane from the insane and that psychiatric diagnoses are not reliable.

The overarching tendency of psychiatry to medicalize social problems is another prominent theme within the sociology of mental health. Sociologists note that the medicalization of life takes away individuals' right to self-determination and creates a dependence on the medical profession. According to Sarbin and Keen (1998), medicalization of mental distress may have even more significant consequences for the affected individual than typically assumed. By relegating mental distress to the realm of neurotransmitters, brain damage, or even psychological processes, the medical model in psychiatry challenges the validity of individual action and agency. All of these ideas, together with other work on professionalization, professional power, and professional practice (Foucault 1995 [1961]; Castel 1988; Scull 1984), have shaped the sociological understanding of psychiatry as an institution of social control that aims at regulating deviant behavior.

STIGMA AND MENTAL ILLNESS

Mental illness is the disability with which the general public seems to feel the least comfortable (Cook and Wright 1995). Public perceptions toward the mentally ill vary by country. The Eurobarometer survey on the self-perceived mental health of European citizens, conducted in 2010, found that, on average, two-thirds (67 percent) of European Union citizens believe they would feel comfortable talking to a person with a significant mental health problem. Notably, the highest prevalence of respondents feeling they would find it difficult to talk to a person with a mental health problem was found among countries that had recently joined the European Union (e.g., Lithuania, Latvia, Bulgaria, Estonia, Poland, Slovakia)—countries sharing long histories of institutionalization of the mentally ill (Eurobarometer 2010). Sociologists continue to investigate the effects of stigma and shame related to mental illness on persons with severe mental disorders and their strategies to cope with perceived devaluation and discrimination (Onken and Slaten 2000; Link et al. 1997; Link and Phelan 2001). According to Onken and Slaten (2000, 101), the ideology of "ableism" that prevails in many societies systematically promotes negative differential and unequal treatment of people because of their apparent or assumed physical, mental, or behavioral differences. Mental health service users know that in the public imagination, they are believed to be unpredictable and dangerous, and this contributes to their own feelings of being rejected and feared (Link and Phelan 2001). This, more often than not, results in their devaluing themselves.

Most persons acquire generalized beliefs that people with mental illness are devalued and discriminated against, but these beliefs do not become personally applicable unless an individual is officially labeled mentally ill. Once such a label is applied, the likelihood increases that a person will devalue him- or herself, fear rejection by others, have a lower income, and become unemployed. Studies show that stigmatization has a dramatic bearing on the distribution of life chances in such areas as earnings, housing, criminal involvement, health, and life itself (Link and Phelan 2001). Employers consistently rank persons with mental disorders last as potential employees, and people suffering from severe mental illness report the difficulties of reentering or staying in the labor market (Schulze and Angermeyer 2003).

CHANGES IN MENTAL HEALTH POLICY AND THE EXPERIENCES OF MENTAL HEALTH SERVICE USERS

In the early 1960s, social researchers noticed that persons who spent long periods in psychiatric hospitals tended to develop "excessive dependence on the institution," which hindered their reintegration into society after they left the hospital (Lamb 1998, 665). Psychiatric hospitals and other custodial institutions where individuals resided for long periods (often involuntarily) became seen as depriving them of their civil rights and reinforcing their stigmatization. Consequently, a policy of deinstitutionalization was introduced in the United States and other Western countries that led to the shift away from large-scale mental hospitals to community-based mental health care, which may include supported housing with full or partial supervision, psychiatric wards of general hospitals, day centers or clubhouses, community mental health centers, and self-help groups for mental health. These services may be provided by government organizations, mental health professionals, or private or charitable organizations.

Today a majority of individuals with mental illness receive community-based mental health services. However, as Fakhoury and Priebe (2002) note, the quality of the community mental care systems varies substantially across countries worldwide. The World Health Organization (2007) notes that in many developing countries, the closing of mental hospitals is not accompanied by the development of community services, leaving a service vacuum. As a result people with mental illness do not receive adequate help. Countries with advanced deinstitutionalization attempt to tackle such issues as confinement of those with dangerous behaviors and successful integration into the community of those with mental illness and their concomitant access to employment and housing. Countries with recent histories of institutionalization, where the development of community mental health care is at its beginnings, face challenges related to the allocation of financial resources, social acceptance of deinstitutionalization, and degrading approaches toward those with mental illness. As a result of these differences, the experience of being a mental health service user may vary significantly across countries and among various social groups.

An early study by Hollingshead and Redlich (1958) examined the links between social class, pathways to treatment, and type of treatment received; it suggested that the lower classes are clearly disadvantaged when it comes to imposing involuntary and restraining treatment. Compared to other social classes, the lowest social class experienced more mental illness, particularly psychosis, and was more likely to enter treatment via courts and official agencies, as well as to receive somatic rather than psychological therapies. Some studies continue to report that members of racial and ethnic minorities receive limited or inadequate mental health services and hold more negative beliefs about the mental health profession. Racial and ethnic minorities are more likely than whites to experience discriminatory treatment and to be restrained (physically or chemically) and secluded, escorted by police, and admitted involuntarily (Cook and Wright 1995).

Furthermore, despite the increasing emphasis in contemporary legal frameworks and professional codes of ethics on patients' autonomy and informed decision-making, some studies show that withholding illness- or treatment-related information from the patient may be common both in inpatient and outpatient settings (Shergill, Barker, and Greenberg 1998). Patients with schizophrenia are less likely to be informed of their diagnosis, and psychiatrists are also more reticent regarding the diagnosis of personality disorders.

THE KEY METHODS UTILIZED IN THE FIELD

Sociologists studying the phenomenon of mental illness utilize a variety of methods. Scholars interested in psychiatric concepts, classifications, and mental-health-related media messages use textual and/or content analysis; sociologists studying professionalization, development of psychiatric care, and mental health policies draw upon archival data. Survey methods are applied in studying users' expectations, needs, and satisfaction with mental health services. Mental health service utilization is assessed by studying patient statistics. Some sociologists have used path models to understand how psychiatric consumers/survivors fare in community settings (Hall and Nelson 1996).

Qualitative research methods are also increasingly used in the field, both by sociologists and by other researchers. Schulze and Angermeyer (2003), for instance, have applied the focus-group method to explore stigma from the subjective perspective of people with schizophrenia. Bradshaw, Roseborough, and Armour (2006) carried out semistructured interviews in their hermeneutic phenomenological study on the lived experience of persons recovering from serious and persistent mental illness.

WHAT THE HUMAN RIGHTS PARADIGM CAN LEARN FROM THE SOCIOLOGICAL WORK ON MENTAL ILLNESS

Human rights scholars can learn from sociological work in the field of mental illness in several ways. First, mental health and illness, as well as treatment options, are unequally distributed among various social groups, with the lowest income groups as well as racial and ethnic minorities being at a clear disadvantage. Experience of social exclusion, discrimination, and poverty (i.e., being denied basic human rights) correlates with vulnerability to mental distress. In turn, socially disadvantaged groups are more likely to experience restrictive and discriminatory psychiatric treatments, resulting in their further stigmatization and social exclusion. Second, health and illness are negotiated social concepts and, as such, cannot be understood simply in terms of bodily phenomena; psychiatric labels are socially contingent. Third, some psychiatric conceptualizations of mental illness (for instance, those emphasizing genetic predisposition to mental pathology) may challenge the individual's right to self-determination and serve as a basis for imposing paternalistic professional practices or compulsory treatment. Finally, paternalism, if structured into mental health care, as well as the stigma of mental illness, may impede individuals' abilities to take a more active and critical stance and prevent realization of their basic rights or questioning of the denial of those rights.

A RESITUATION OF THE SOCIOLOGY OF MENTAL HEALTH WITHIN A HUMAN RIGHTS PARADIGM

Sociologists focus on the various manifestations of discrimination and mistreatment of people with mental disabilities. The resituation of the sociology of mental health within a human rights paradigm encourages us to readdress these issues by exploring more specifically the underlying and sustaining mechanisms of human rights violations in mental illness, as well as the conditions that help people to flourish and enjoy their rights, freedoms, and good mental health.

One potential area for this kind of sociological study is the implementation of mental health policy and law both locally and internationally. There is a long tradition of sociological research on deinstitutionalization policies (Prior 1996; Barham 1992; Scull 1984) and an interest in psychiatric legislation (Dallaire et al. 2000; Carpenter 2000), but this kind of research has not engaged directly with the issue of universal human rights for those with mental illness. Sociologists could start by asking how mental health laws, policies, and programs enhance or limit the rights of people with mental illness. What triggers the implementation of human rights for those with mental illness locally and globally? Who are the key players and interest groups in this process? In his analysis of mental health policy under welfare capitalism, Carpenter (2000) has noted that in some countries, mental health service user movements and the focus on civil liberties have had a significant impact on the development of mental health policies and rights for individuals with mental illness. In other countries, professional groups have been more prominent in debates about procedures and rights in mental health care, leading to more restrictive mental health policy regimes. The peculiarity of the cultural, economic, and political contexts as implicated in mental health policies, initiatives and programs directed toward preserving the mental health of the population, involuntary commitment laws, and their comparative historical analysis might become the starting points for those who wish to get engaged with the human rights issues within mental health.

Sociologists have been actively engaged in exposing the degrading effects of institutional care. The analysis of the nature of psychiatric care in both institutions and community mental-health-care settings remains highly pertinent to the rights-related sociology of mental health. However, if we center the human rights paradigm in our studies, we are prompted to ask not only how psychiatry interferes with the individual's right to self-determination but also how it may enhance the individual's ability to lead an independent and full life. Sociologists have typically rejected the possibility of a genuine concern on the part of psychiatry for the welfare of the mental patient. Are we ready to rethink our position? How should we approach the coercive psychiatric care that seems to be necessary at times?

Furthermore, how do we reconcile the dominant sociological ideas about mental illness with those inherent to the human rights paradigm? Sociologists tend to reject mental illness as a natural, universal phenomenon and prefer to see it as socially constructed. This kind of reasoning has provided a background for much sociological critique of psychiatric care and the unjust social situation of those labeled as "mentally ill," although at the same time it has led to a neglect of the reality of human suffering due to mental illness (Gerhardt 1989). The human rights paradigm, on the contrary, approaches mental illness as a natural phenomenon. One way to solve this apparent problem would be to accept the ontological reality of mental illness but to see it as culturally and socially mediated (Busfield 1996). Then, for instance, the reinforcement or denial of human rights becomes crucial for mental health. Still, these and similar questions remain to be answered.

Finally, if we center the human rights paradigm in our research, we are impelled to focus on the mental health user's life. How do these people fare in the community? How does the experience of mental illness, treatment, or the status of the mental health user itself interact with the opportunity to enjoy other human rights (e.g., an adequate standard of living, the right to work)? How do the answers to these and other pertinent questions change if we introduce socioeconomic status, gender, and ethnicity/race into analysis?

What Is the Future?

As human beings we possess rights simply because of our humanity. Thus, mental illness by itself provides no justifiable ground for unjust treatment or denial of an individual's autonomy. This approach is advocated by both the sociology of mental health and the human rights paradigm. The sociology of mental health continues to offer a conceptual and theoretical foundation that helps to challenge the negative beliefs and practices related to the phenomenon of mental illness. Human rights scholars assert that people with mental illness need not prove that they deserve certain rights or that they are able to exercise them. Both sociology and the human rights paradigm are interested in social justice and empowerment of socially disadvantaged populations. Thus, a sociology of mental health and human rights could become a powerful tool in fostering positive changes in the situation of people with mental disabilities.

Sociologists have distinctive theoretical tools and a long tradition of empirical research into the phenomenon of mental illness. Sociology goes beyond medical conceptualizations and locates what is often understood as a natural category or a personal tragedy within the broader social context and analysis of social and power relations. By further examining the link between institutional arrangements, societal reactions, professional power, and social control, we can continue to explore and challenge the limitation of rights that may be imposed on those with mental illness.

What about the professional prerogative—which, although restricted, is still preserved—to decide when such limitations are needed? Do there exist ways to challenge this still overly medicalized approach to the rights of people with mental illness? And how about mental health laws and policies shaped by the social construction of violence and mental illness at a sociopolitical level and by the dominant societal perceptions of the mentally ill? Viewing those with mental illness as violent and unpredictable, for instance, may prevent us from acknowledging discriminatory behaviors and practices toward them. As Beresford and Wilson (2002) note, increased claims in favor of restricting the civil and human rights of individuals with mental illness constitute an emerging international development that has also tended to be racialized in its public presentation. The authors argue that these claims are fueled by increasing emphasis in both the media and government policy on the danger, threat, and "otherness" of mental health service users. Such public fears are reinforced by genetic approaches to severe mental illness and mental distress that are gaining increasing power and official legitimacy. These and similar issues should be a focus of a sociology of mental health and human rights.

For a long time, sociologists have devoted relatively little attention to the subjective experience of living with mental illness. Thorne et al. (2002) have analyzed qualitative studies published between 1980 and 1996 that dealt with some aspect of what it is like to live with a chronic illness from the perspective of the individual involved. They noted that studies typically focused on individuals with rheumatic, cardiovascular, or endocrine disorders, and "rarely were persons with chronic psychological or psychiatric disorders related to the physical illness included in these kinds of studies" (Thorne et al. 2002, 443). Cook and Wright (1995, 106) have noted several reasons why a focus on the mentally ill individual has not been very prominent in sociological research. According to them, interaction with people suffering from mental illness is often difficult, as they experience mood swings, tend to withdraw from social contact, or cannot tolerate long survey interviews. Patients in long-term care settings may be inaccessible. Besides, in order to study mental illness, sociologists probably need to be familiar with and understand basic psychiatry. By exploring subjective experience of stigma and discrimination, sociologists might provide useful insights into how people with mental illness themselves define their rights and what impediments they see to realizing them. This would enrich the human rights paradigm from the "bottom-up point of view" (Lewis 2009b).

Finally, what about involving people with mental illness as active participants in our research projects? Participatory action or collaborative research methods have become increasingly used by disability researchers. This kind of research strengthens sociological commitment to social justice and social activism. Indeed, a sociology of mental health and human rights provides a strong reason to redefine our relationship to those we study. By reconstructing people with mental disabilities as credible agents whose views we must respect and take into account when designing legal instruments, implementing mental health policies, and protecting human rights, we could contribute to the empowerment of these people. This is also a way to challenge and reverse negative and stereotypical societal perceptions of mental illness and the mentally ill.

In sum, a sociology of mental health and human rights could contribute to societal and political awareness of the importance of human rights promotion and protection for the mentally ill. The wealth of data produced by our research may in turn serve as a basis for developing legal instruments that would be grounded in sound empirical evidence.

Chapter Four

Racial and Ethnic Minorities

James M. Thomas and David L. Brunsma

As we slowly make our way through the twenty-first century, the sociological enterprise is rapidly expanding. With more than forty-five sections in the American Sociological Association, an increasing number of doctoral degrees being earned, and more outlets for publishing scholarly works than ever before, the rapid growth of the sociological enterprise has made room for the potential to begin to answer the most pressing social and cultural questions of our time. Problems of the past are not going away; nor are they simply being recycled. They are fundamentally transforming as our social worlds collide with one another, producing new problems (and solutions) in an increasingly transnational world.

The sociological study of racial and ethnic minorities, then, is no different. As the former strengths of national borders begin to give way to corporate power and collective identity movements in various parts of the globe (Sassen 1999), how we think about the relationship between identities and power is shifting—from questions of the local to questions of the global. In this transition, we must not lose sight of one historical and contemporary fact: the study of racial and ethnic minorities must be the study of oppression and resistance. That is, the very definition of the term "minority" refers specifically to a location absent of social power. Starting from here, sociological analysis requires a question that asks how this absence of power has been produced, what mechanisms allow for it to sustain itself, and how this force can be stopped or reversed. Thus, we repeat for effect: the study of racial and ethnic minorities must be the study of oppression and resistance.

In this chapter, we think about one way that the study of racial and ethnic minorities can be reframed, not simply as a struggle for civil rights and social recognition but fundamentally as a struggle for human rights. As we move forward in an era witness to increasing transnational flows of capital, information, and even people, as sociologists we must incorporate a rights-based paradigm to understand the evolution of racial and ethnic minorities, in terms of both their oppressions and their resistances. This is no easy task, however. A rights-based paradigm requires sociologists of racial and ethnic minorities to fundamentally take a moral position through their research agenda. Such a claim to moral authority is not without its problems, and the debate about whether it is our place as social scientists to claim such authority has been a long and complex one. We wish to table this debate until the conclusion for the purposes of reviewing the field of racial and ethnic minority studies. At the end of the chapter, however, we take up this question with great respect and articulate a position in which moral authority becomes a question of sociological analysis and, more importantly, one that deserves a definitive answer.

REVIEW OF THE FIELD

Any review of a field of study requires some sort of organization from which the researcher and the reader can make sense of an otherwise vast and confusing body of knowledge. In a pursuit of such organization, depth is often sacrificed for breadth— ours is no different. By and large, there are currently three general categories into which the majority of sociological scholarship on racial and ethnic minorities can be organized: stratification studies, identity studies, and movement studies. We propose a fourth wave that could center itself in human rights. Within the first three categories, there exists a weak presence of an analytic of rights in general, not to mention human rights specifically. Such discussions are often relegated to secondary analyses or a strongly worded conclusion.

Though there are studies that do not fit these categories, the typology we present here is useful for thinking through the varieties of research in the sociology of racial and ethnic minorities. Such categories are not necessarily separate but often imbricate one another, and scholars often find their work falling within more than one of these categories. For instance, if we take the works of W. E. B. Du. Bois, much of his early work documented social ills facing black America during the post-Reconstruction period in the United States. However, if we single out his groundbreaking *The Souls of Black Folks* (1903), then we see an entirely different Du. Bois, one devoted to understanding and articulating the mechanisms through which black American identity is structured through the metaphor of the "veil." With this in mind, we wish to proceed by first unpacking what these categories entail and how a rights-based paradigm both contributes to their current scholarship and can also improve upon them.

STRATIFICATION STUDIES

Stratification studies of racial and ethnic minorities stem in large part from the empirically oriented works of the Chicago School, as well as some of the classic sociological theorists. Contemporary works often follow the foundations set forth by many of the giants in this field: Oliver Cox (*Caste, Class, and Race*, 1948), W. E. B. Du. Bois (*The Philadelphia Negro*, 2010 [1899]), and Robert E. Park (1914, 1928a, 1928b), who, along with Cox, was influential in developing the Chicago School approach to the study of race and ethnic relations. In these bodies of scholarship, the various ills of racial and ethnic minorities, primarily in the Western context, are exposed through a variety of methodologies, though they are predominantly positivist in their epistemological orientations and lean heavily on the idea that particular methods must be employed in order to document societal ills.

Over time, as sociology has had to respond to the theoretical and methodological critiques of positivism, particularly after the 1950s, stratification studies have become much more diverse in their epistemological and methodological orientations. What has not changed, however, is their primary focus on the documentation and explanation of how particular racial and ethnic minority groups have come to be arranged in relation to the dominant majority. Contemporary works that highlight this particular category of research are Omi and Winant's (1994) influential work on racial formation in the United States and the subsequent revisions to racial formation theory, both in the US context and internationally, that have followed (e.g., Thomas 2010; Bonilla-Silva 2003); Charles Mills's (1997) philosophical treatise on how contemporary race relations were constructed through a racialized social contract during the period of European Enlightenment; and Joe Feagin's research agenda of documenting and problematizing systemic racism in both the US and global contexts (Feagin 2006, 2010). In all instances, these scholars attempt to answer two fundamental questions: how race and ethnicity themselves, as well as the resultant racial social structure, came to be, and what the social, political, and cultural consequences of these hierarchical arrangements are.

The most obvious contribution of stratification studies is the empirical breadth and depth they offer for documenting societal ills and concerns. This is of utmost importance in the current political global climate, where questions of race and ethnicity are often viewed by those in power as a relic of the past. In the Western context, the prevalence of color-blind racism (Bonilla-Silva 2003; Forman and Lewis 2006; Hill 2008) has been well documented and theorized as the overarching contemporary logic behind ethnic and racial stratification. Studies that highlight multiple levels of inequality among racial and ethnic minorities continue to abound, from research on overt discrimination in the European Union (Wrench 2011), to comparisons of rates of success for political incorporation of new immigrants into the US and western European political systems (Mollenkopf and Hoschschild 2010), to documentation of disparate home appreciation between whites and minority groups in the United States (Flippen 2004). Without a doubt, stratification studies continue to serve as a strength of the sociological enterprise in addressing the lack of actualized human rights among racial and ethnic minorities the world over. However, this brings us to questions that still remain for this particular area.

Though stratification studies have their place within the sociological enterprise, particularly concerning the sociological analysis of racial and ethnic minorities, there exists a tendency within these studies to focus strictly on the noticeable presence or absence of inequality, with little or no intellectual debate over remedies for these processes and outcomes. Of course, this is no easy task for sociologists, and there exists within the discipline of sociology an ongoing debate as to whether it is even our job, as academics, to make the case for or against a global human rights agenda as a form of social policy (Sjoberg, Gill, and Williams 2001). This is not to suggest that all stratification studies ignore the merits of advocating for a human rights agenda within the discipline. Such contemporaries as Zuberi and

Bonilla-Silva (2008) and Feagin and Vera (2008) in fact take an explicit stance on the role of human rights in addressing the many inequalities and injustices faced by racial and ethnic minorities around the world. However, simply looking through the recent abstracts of *American Sociological Review, Social Forces,* or *American Journal of Sociology* demonstrates that scholars who study racial and ethnic stratification through a human rights perspective are in the minority.

IDENTITY STUDIES

In addition to the central tendency of sociology to focus on stratification, another realm of inquiry might be called identity studies. Identity studies in the social sciences, particularly those on ethnic and racial identities, derive a large portion of their theoretical strength and empirical foundations from the work of two scholars who shared a similar time period but little else: pragmatist George Herbert Mead and the critical race theorist W. E. B. Du. Bois.

Generally speaking, Mead's cornerstone collection of writings, *Mind, Self, and Society* (1967), provides the building blocks for understanding how social scientists talk about the concept of the self and how that concept shares a relationality with social forces external to it. In particular, Mead's (1967) use of the I, the Me, and the Other provides a social explanation of how individuals who belong to particular groups come to recognize their own sense of self and community through an opposition to a generalized other. Over time, various revisions to and iterations of this theory of the self have emerged. In particular, the theoretical strain of symbolic interactionism and its derivatives, especially dramaturgy, were of particular importance in shaping our current understandings of how identities come to be made and reproduced over time (Goffman 1959; Garfinkel 1967).

Currently, identity studies in race and ethnicity that follow this particular theoretical strain are often categorized under the label "performative studies" or "dramaturgical studies" and attempt to respond to questions centered on how identities come to be produced and maintained within particular contexts and in response to certain cultural forces and constraints. For instance, Johnson (2003) explores the contradictory ways in which blackness is put together in American culture. She argues that when blackness as an identity is appropriated to the exclusion of others, it becomes political. More importantly, Johnson's (2003) work questions the notion of an "authentic black self" by problematizing the hypothetical other that would have to exist as its counterpart. Authenticity as an identity configuration for black Americans or any other racialized group of people, according to Johnson, is simply "another trope manipulated for cultural capital" (2003, 3).

Another example of the dramaturgical approach to ethnic and racial studies in sociology would be Picca and Feagin's (2007) work on the Janus-faced nature of whites' attitudes toward race. Here, Picca and Feagin investigate not just how whites code their racial attitudes among peers and coworkers in public spaces (e.g., Bonilla-Silva 2003), but also the various ways in which whites display their attitudes toward race and difference among family, friends, and other whites, or what Goffman (1959) would refer to as the back stage.

The second strain of identity studies within the social sciences concerning race and ethnicity stems from W. E. B. Du. Bois and his oft-quoted passage from *The Souls of Black Folks* concerning the metaphor of the veil. Though Du. Bois and Mead were contemporaries, they were hardly interlocutors. However, Du. Bois's use of the metaphor of the veil to explicate how blacks come to see themselves through both their own eyes and the eyes of others—double consciousness—is dramatically similar to Mead's theorizing of how a generalized other comes to be the referent for the development of the I in social life. In many ways, these two theorists were explaining two sides of the same coin: Mead, how whiteness comes to reproduce itself over time through a constant reference to that which it is not; Du. Bois, how the racial and ethnic other comes to recognize that it is not a part of a community through a recognition of its own lack.

Du. Bois's illumination of the experience of racialized others in the American context provided much-needed ground for later critical race theorists to stand upon. Further, as Du. Bois himself became more global in his travels and writings, his ideas on Pan-Africanism and racism as a global force, rather than an American one, became building blocks for future generations of critical race theorists (Du. Bois 1983). Of special importance were the works of the early postcolonial writers, such as Aimé Césaire (2001), Frantz Fanon (2005, 2008), Edward Said (1979), and Stuart Hall (1986). These postcolonial theorists in particular began to advance a theory of race and ethnicity that examined the formation of these othered identities without losing sight of the fact that these identities were born out of a dialectic of struggle and resistance. This particular branch of identity studies has been much more open to interdisciplinary ideas and research, as evidenced by the multiple perspectives that touch, and have been touched by, postcolonialism—from film and narrative studies (Minh-ha 1997), to literature (Kincaid 2000), to cultural theory (Bhabha 2004).

Whether deriving their theoretical and empirical strength from the Meadian tradition or that of Du. Bois, identity studies by and large share some common strengths in the study of race and ethnicity, as well as some common weaknesses. First, let us speak to the strengths of this area.

As a whole, these studies provide great insight into the particular mechanisms and technologies through which particular identities come to be expressed. The Meadian emphasis on language, specifically talk (Garfinkel 1967), allows us to understand how race and ethnicity come to be conceptually made and repackaged over time through the production and deployment of language (McIntyre 1997). For example, Ruth Frankenburg's (1993) study on how white women come to make sense of racism and sexism through their lived experiences illustrates how whiteness as a concept is both socially constructed and meaningful in the same ways that otheredness is meaningful to those who experience social life from that perspective (Tatum 2003).

Meanwhile, the emphasis on language, specifically discourse, that arises in part from the tradition of postcolonialism and poststructuralism's influence over the body of literature in the sociological study of racial and ethnic minorities that we call identity studies demonstrates the dialectical nature of identity and the interplay between social forces and social agents, between resistance and oppression. David

Goldberg's (1990) edited volume stands as an exemplar of this model in identity studies, offering essays from such scholars as Kwame Anthony Appiah, Frantz Fanon,
Roland Barthes, Paul Gilroy, and Homi Bhabha, among others, to demonstrate the
multiple forms and methods through which racism is generated and maintained in
philosophy, literature, and social institutions such as politics and law. The connective
tissue of these essays, and in most identity studies that begin through a poststructuralist and postcolonial theoretical examination, is that the illumination of these
discursive forms of power that create ethnic and racial hierarchies is meant both to
reveal and to subvert its multiple manifestations. In this way, the Du. Bois tradition
of identity studies takes us, as sociologists, to a platform of advocation, critical questioning, and hope—something that the symbolic interactionist tradition does not
necessarily provide with its meticulous attention to explicit forms of language such as
conversation, narrative, and conceptual construction (Holstein and Gubrium 1999).

Identity studies, whether in the tradition of Mead or Du. Bois, are not without
their flaws. Having already spent some time identifying the limits of Meadian analysis, particularly as it concerns a lack of agenda setting for policy-making or critical
engagement with social structures and forces, we wish to discuss some concerns
we have with the tradition of identity studies stemming from the work of Du. Bois
and other more critical scholars of race and ethnicity.

Lawrence Grossberg's (1992) examination of popular culture and the formation of conservativism makes the compelling argument that the notion of identity
politics is a dead end for a progressive political agenda, in part because the tradition
from which identity politics has arisen argues for an essentialized political identity
of the other. In a separate but equally important criticism, Grossberg writes that
traditional theories of otherness "assume that difference is itself an historically
produced economy, imposed in modern structures of power" (1992, 94), rather
than seeing difference as fundamentally constitutive. Criticizing Said (1979) specifically, Grossberg argues that Said's form of Orientalism assumes that people who
participated in Orientalism traveled to places and cultures that already existed,
rather than understanding the Orientalist and Orientalism as a particular logic
of difference that, through description of the Oriental other, constituted the very
thing it was seeking to describe.

This, then, has been the problem with much of the Du. Bois tradition of the
racial and ethnic other, as well as contemporary postcolonial theories and writings on the matter. These contemporary studies seek to essentialize the other into
a political category, where political agency comes to be defined haphazardly as a
politics of resentment. Grossberg's claim, and our critique, is that this limits the
possibilities for what subjectivity, agency, and a progressive politics can mean in a
world where there is no essential self and where agency is more and more coming
to be understood by activity rather than simply by presence.

MOVEMENT STUDIES

The above concern brings us to the third category of scholarship on racial and ethnic minorities: movement studies. The tradition of movement studies, in general,

draws its strength from the early works of Karl Marx, in particular his argument that social movements are, for the most part, the end result of historically determined conditions. Movements for social change arise from the collective action of social actors when, in Marx's analysis, they become aware of their social class as a contradiction to the antagonists of those conditions that produced their social class in the first place (Bottomore 1963; Tarrow 1998). Later developments in Marxism reconfigured social-movement theories around the conceptual framework of "resource mobilization" spurred by those in positions of power (Lenin 2007) and later as centered on the need to build consensus through the development of a collective identity (Gramsci 1971).

By the 1960s, however, and influenced heavily by the French student movements, the modern-day civil rights movement in the United States, second-wave feminism, and Black Power, sociology underwent a paradigm shift that emphasized a politically connected view of social movements (Tarrow 1998). Resource mobilization began to take on an entirely different perspective, one spurred forward by political scientists and economists who wanted to understand the rise and success of movements in terms of incentives, sectors, and industries (McCarthy and Zald 1977).

Such an account of social movements did not resonate with many in the discipline of sociology, and by the 1980s an alternative model was being put forward that emphasized culture as a counterparadigm to resource-mobilization theories (Tarrow 1998). This shift in how we understand social movements resulted in a strong emphasis being placed on what was termed "identity politics" and subsequently deemphasized structural approaches to the understanding of social movements and change. The newly placed emphasis on identity formation as part of the social-movement process allowed for culture to play the role of metanarrator in the trajectory of movements and also in how identities come to form a collective around such interactive processes as framing (Goffman 1986), ideological and emotional packaging of grievances (Gamson 1988), and the multiple processes by which social concerns and conditions become social problems (Best 2007).

As relates to the study of racial and ethnic minorities, movement studies scholarship has largely focused on the identity politics paradigm, where the formation of collective politics is emphasized, most typically through the essentializing of racial and ethnic others under a generic political condition they are all assumed to share. For instance, Vermeersch's (2003) study of the active construction of Romani identity within the contemporary Czech and Slovak republics provides a rich analysis of how Romani identity is framed by politically active members and how this framing is tied to explicit political strategies. However, left out of this analysis, and others similar to it (Kuroiwa and Verkuyten 2008; Leibovitz 2007; Nordberg 2006), is the plurality, hybridity, and relationality that is most typical of any ethnic or racial group and how these characteristics constrain and enable any given collective movement.

Also typical of most movement-studies scholarship is the emphasis on social movements among ethnic and racial minorities as they relate to political, cultural, or economic recognition. For instance, much scholarship has been produced on the Black Power movement within contemporary America (Bush 2000; Rojas 2007).

In most of this work, analysis focuses on the movement's goals as they relate to political and economic rights—the right to vote, the right to equal housing and schooling, the right to work, and so forth. Little scholarship, however, focuses on the emphasis of these movements toward recognizing blacks in America as humans worthy of dignity, justice, and other human rights as defined in the Universal Declaration of Human Rights. In fact, there is almost no mention of the influence of such historically significant and, during the 1960s, well-circulated documents on the formation and sustainment of movements that, if we look at the rhetoric of the political leaders of Black Power, was obvious in their speeches, demonstrations, and political platforms. It is from this final point that we can begin to build an agenda for the sociological study of racial and ethnic minorities that incorporates the human rights perspective currently trending within political science, legal studies, and international studies scholarship.

REDEFINING THE FIELD FROM A HUMAN RIGHTS PERSPECTIVE

To return to our opening assertion: the study of ethnic and racial minorities is, and should remain, the study of oppression and resistance. With this statement, we do not declare that sociologists abandon the categorization of scholarship that we presented in the above review. Rather, we demand as scholars and advocates of social justice that sociologists attend to the substantive questions of concern in this twenty-first century—questions of how human rights can be attained for racial and ethnic minorities. Stratification studies must of course continue to document the many instances where groups of ethnic and racial minorities are hierarchically arranged, but must begin to emphasize the effects of such arrangements on the affording and limiting of human rights as acknowledged by international law in the Universal Declaration of Human Rights; the International Covenant on Economic, Social, and Cultural Rights; the International Covenant on Civil and Political Rights; and other human rights instruments ratified by the vast majority of nations the world over since 1948.

Stratification studies, for instance, must begin to examine the effects of the aforementioned human rights instruments on the increasing and decreasing rates of disparity between ethnic and racial minorities and those in power, not just in specific regions but also on a more global scale. And, stratification studies must, from the empirical evidence they find, begin to generate real claims grounded in social-scientific methodology. Sjoberg, Gill, and Williams (2001) contend, as do we, that sociology *necessarily has to* investigate the moral dimension of social life. Citing the works of the philosophers Hilary Putman and John Dewey, Sjoberg, Gill, and Williams (2001) argue that the moral order is neither God-given nor biopsychological in nature. Therefore, it must be sociological at its core. If morality is a product of social and cultural activities, then it deserves sociological attention at the empirical level. Taking it one step further, if morality is accepted as a key component of sociological inquiry, then it follows that we are required as social scientists to explore the nature of moral commitments within our own discipline.

This means, for the purposes of stratification studies, that sociologists begin to not only document social inequalities, but also exert particular moral claims upon those hierarchical arrangements (Brunsma and Overfelt 2007). To maintain an empirical quality, however, these claims must be made at the level of human rights, as these rights are universally recognized among various governing bodies around the world, and are therefore better able to stand the moral position of relativism popular among sociologists of culture and radical constructionism.

For identity studies, a human rights paradigm opens up the possibilities of fostering a politics of community not predicated upon essentialized categories of racial and ethnic difference, but rather a politics of community predicated upon shared experiences and commitments to a shared vision among racial and ethnic minorities. The former is essentially a slippery slope, as a politics of community built upon essentialized categories of difference can only be, in the end, a politics of resentment and a reactionary political platform. What we advocate, however, is a shift toward thinking about ethnic and racial difference as historically grounded in shared experiences, but also oriented toward a progressive future in which commitments among members of oppressed groups are aimed toward achieving a shared vision of hope (Brunsma 2010). The dilemma of intersectional analyses in the social sciences is that, due to the nature of moral relativism that has taken a hold of sociology since the cultural turn in the late 1970s to early 1980s, intersectional analysis has become an "add and stir" form of sociological investigation. Axes of difference have been articulated as being more *problematic* for developing a sense of community and shared visions for a progressive politics because common ground can never truly be found among those who share a racial category but not one of gender, or who have similar class backgrounds but differing sexualities.

We take intersectionality seriously, but through a human rights paradigm in which the rights of all are acknowledged simply because they share the commonality of being human, identity studies can potentially develop a praxis of hope through the investigation of shared commitments toward this hope from those who come from different identity configurations. Rather than an "add and stir" analysis, then, identity studies in the twenty-first century can redirect their focus toward how human rights organizations, instruments, and movements allow those from different ethnic and racial backgrounds to achieve those same rights across the board. Further, identity studies can begin to focus on how human rights themselves are mechanisms for articulating particular identities, including racial and ethnic categories, and what these human rights tools are able to accomplish in the articulation of these identity locations (Brunsma and Delgado 2008).

Last, movement studies in ethnic and racial minority scholarship perhaps have the easiest task of the three categories. A human rights paradigm simply requires a shift in analytical attention—from movements for civil or economic rights to one that centers on movements for human rights. We have already mentioned how a historical sociology could investigate the rhetoric of the Black Power movement, for example, and see it for its articulation of human rights for the black diaspora rather than for political and economic rights for black Americans. Similar measures could be taken in the examination of activist rhetoric among those involved in the movements for indigenous rights among First Nations people in Canada, Aborigines in Australia, the Maori of New Zealand, and American Indians within the United States, both contemporarily and in a historical context. Much of the claims making among these groups has been documented by social scientists as oriented toward achieving political and economic rights, such as reparations (Thomas and Brunsma 2008). However, it would be a relatively simple task for sociologists to examine the ways in which rhetoric that advocated for these various groups' rights was actually a product of a larger human rights paradigm shift in international political movements and legal actions.

CONCLUSION

The human rights paradigm within sociology is both a serious shift in epistemology among sociologists and an evolving field of inquiry. In addition to the growing membership of the Section on Human Rights of the American Sociological Association, an increasing number of publication outlets focus explicitly on illuminating cutting-edge research in the field of human rights and moral inquiry. Further, various organizations around the world with a mission to advance the pursuit and purpose of human rights are seeing a growing number of sociologists enter into their folds, including Sociologists Without Borders (of which we ourselves are members), Human Rights Watch, Amnesty International, and the International Society for Human Rights, to name just a few. The turn toward human rights, then, is not a fad or a passing trend; instead, it should be seen as both a social and a scientific revolution, in the Kuhnian sense (Kuhn 1996). That sociologists are just now beginning to enter into its enterprise in large numbers simply indicates to us that this revolution has been in the making for over sixty years, as indicated by the advancements already made in legal studies and political science, and that our presence as sociologists is necessary for the human rights enterprise to become truly central to both the scientific investigation of social and cultural life and the advancement of a moral inquiry focused on the development, deployment, and achievement of human rights in practice the world over.

CHAPTER FIVE

ASIA AND ASIAN AMERICA

Mary Yu Danico and Phi Hong Su

The Universal Declaration of Human Rights in 1948 argued for the dignity of all human beings and their rights to freedom, justice, and peace. While such sentiments appear straightforward, the constructed meaning of human rights has been heavily swayed by Western thought and ideals about what constitutes dignity and justice. For Asia and Asian America, the human rights paradigm is often contested and questioned for its applicability to people of Asian descent. Does the human rights doctrine assume universality in the reality of the individual lives in particular spaces?

This chapter begins with a discussion of traditional human rights research and paradigms and questions the applicability of a universal human rights paradigm to a world of sovereign states, problematizes whether human rights exist for the stateless or those without a nation or citizenship, and examines the role of "Asian values," including Confucianism, in the evolution of human rights in the diaspora. We then discuss key human rights issues in Asia and Asian America from the past and present and the human rights violations that continue across the globe. We end with a discussion of the limitations of the human rights discourse in its application to Asia and Asian America and frame a critical discussion of what the human rights paradigm can learn from scholarship in Asia, Asian America, and the interstices of states, in order to better enrich human rights research and the reality of human rights for all. We suggest new questions and new possibilities for the study of and advocacy for Asia and Asian America.

HUMAN RIGHTS PARADIGM AND ASIA/ASIAN AMERICA

Are human rights, premised on universal personhood, ultimately universal in their application? It is abundantly clear in the literature on human rights in Asia that this is a persistent concern, posing the following challenges: Do human rights exist outside the West? Can a universalistic paradigm of human rights work in a world of sovereign states? A universal framework is often criticized for Western bias, for cultural blindness to Eastern ways or Asian values, and for being restrictive and assimilative (Kausikan 1995; Zakaria and Lee 1994). While the concept of universality is enticing, does it come at the cost of denying the reality facing individuals and the societies in which they live (Evans 2001b)?

Such problems stem from the fact that the constructed meaning of human rights is not universally shared. Fulfillment of basic survival needs for food and shelter is a human right that may be more pressing for developing Asian countries than broader political and economic concerns. These considerations are embodied by an "Asian values" perspective characterized by collectivism, a strong emphasis on the family and discipline, and denial of the universality of human rights (Hoang 2009; Sen 1999a). From this perspective derive communiqués such as the 1993 Bangkok Declaration, which criticizes human rights universalism. Defense of cultural relativism, however, has in turn been criticized "as a defense against human atrocities, including the suppression of women" (Amirthalingam 2005; Goonesekere 2000).

Human rights is a universal obligation, with allies from around the world subscribing to its tenets. Confucian values, widespread in parts of Asia, for example, have human rights ideals embedded in their philosophy. The key principles of Confucianism promote humanistic philosophy, free conscience, personal dignity, equality before the law, fair punishment, freedom of ideology and speech, patriotism, and a harmonious relationship with the world. Yet, the standard of the West as defender of human rights and the non-West as violator of them persists. Ownership over human rights has conceptually been ascribed to and claimed by the West. While some contend that Western parentage of the notion of human rights is a historical fact (Donnelly 1982), others propose an overhaul of the notion of ownership (Penna and Campbell 1998).

Beyond a state framework, owning human rights is glaringly problematic for those without states, or stateless persons. More than 1 million people are ignored in human rights discourse—these are the noncitizens of the world (Weissbrodt and Collins 2006). The Universal Declaration of Human Rights dictates that everyone has the right to leave and return to his or her homeland. In reality, the concerns of those who escape from ethnic/religious conflict, war, and genocide are not addressed because these individuals often are stateless. People who have been separated by war (e.g., South and North Korea) are denied the right to return to their homes or have only recently been able to do so (as in the case of diasporic Vietnamese); those who are "undocumented," typically as well as their children, are denied human rights because of their stateless status.

CHALLENGING TRADITIONAL HUMAN RIGHTS DISCOURSE

The case of China further evidences the paradoxical boundedness of human rights constructs. Sovereignty is an invaluable virtue in this era of interdependent states, one that exists with as much reverence as, and in contradiction to, a discourse of borderless human rights (Soysal 1994). In problematizing human rights as universal, scholars and activists have addressed the questions of for whom human rights are important and who is responsible for human rights. Consequently, opposition to the perceived imperialist project of universal human rights has manifested in a form of cultural relativism. In Asia's case, this relativism takes the stance of "Asia's different standard" (Cerna 1995). This perspective complicates universalist discourse by noting that rights are conceived differentially across cultures, that the rhetoric of universalism is not useful in implementation, and that universalism confronts and conflicts with the principle of national sovereignty (Kausikan 1995). Engaging this rhetoric of a different standard, Ali Alatas, former Indonesian foreign minister, noted that "in the developing countries we are still struggling to overcome the blights imposed by past colonialism and new exploitation, and by the pervasive effects of an inequitable international order, and consequently, must spend more time on basic needs" (cited by Cerna 1995, 153). Alatas defends the need for developing countries to first secure material conditions for living over and above—perhaps at the expense of—what the West considers pressing human rights concerns. In prioritizing policies that delay the implementation of human rights, these political leaders demonstrate how state sovereignty may present difficulties for a universal pursuit of human rights.

Yet, like its dialectical opposite, relativism is also riddled with problematic implications. The case of *sati*, or Indian ceremonial widow burning based in religious tradition (Stein 1998), drives at the heart of the cultural relativist/universalist debate. How does a relativist approach resolve the problems of practicing human rights? Simply put, perhaps it cannot. That is, cultural relativism is not a panacea for challenges afflicting human rights advocacy. Relativism can foster a dilemma that dictates inaction against atrocities to avoid the charge of cultural chauvinism (Hershock 2000; Turner 2006). From this perspective, relativism invites human tragedy under the guise of difference. In human rights discourse, the debate continues: How do we disentangle this universalist/relativist divide?

While theory, central to sociological work, is borderless, policy and implementation of rights are not. With this in mind, the following section addresses violations of and struggles for human rights in a way that is inclusive of the experiences of individuals and communities. It provides an abridged, and therefore incomplete, portrait of human rights violations in Asia and draws attention to recurring forms of social and political violence.

PORTRAIT OF HUMAN RIGHTS IN ASIA

By the turn of the millennium, media and academic outlets reporting on conditions in Asia decried bleak realities. Tibetans faced forced intermarriages with or sterilization by Chinese to induce cultural genocide (Adams 1998); blogging, protesting, and other forms of political protest continued to be suppressed in Singapore (Rodan 2006). In mainland Southeast Asia, the lack of response toward the spread of HIV/AIDS in Cambodia and Myanmar was noted (Beyrer 1998); the latter state was then also under international scrutiny for the jailing of Nobel laureate Aung San Suu Kyi and for continuing violence against ethnic minorities by the military junta (Hlaing 2005; James 2006). Religious conflict between Buddhists and Muslims and assassinations of police, soldiers, teachers, religious leaders, and other civilians in

Thailand led newspapers to condemn the "Crisis of the South" (Albritton 2005). Less-targeted acts of violence, in the form of public bombings, highway ambushes, and general political unrest and religious persecution, plagued Laos (Thayer 2004).

Examples of human rights violations in Asia span a broad range, from the individual level of a twenty-five-year-old Australian hanged in Singapore for heroin possession (Rodan 2006) to the macro threat of extermination by China confronting Tibetans. Journalists and watchdog groups often bring these issues, posed as violence inflicted against individuals, groups, or societies, to international attention. Notably, violations of rights based on personhood can be intended for collectivities, as demonstrated by the case of Tibet, where the struggle for survival is as much cultural as it is physical (Adams 1998).

Gendered violations of human rights have rightfully received tremendous attention, with much research addressing human trafficking, sex work, bride burnings, and a host of forms of violence against women (Amirthalingam 2005). Asia is particularly susceptible to human trafficking due to endemic poverty coupled with rapid development and a highly stratified social structure. Efforts to address interrelated issues of trafficking, HIV/AIDS, and violence against sex workers often look to conditions in South Asia, where these axes of injustice together result in the trafficking of hundreds of thousands of women, children, and men every year and an atrocious rate of HIV/AIDS second only to South Africa. In Southeast Asia, youth orphaned by the 2005 tsunami were kidnapped and sold into slavery. Innumerable instances of such devastating realities can be recalled; yet even within this discourse, there is division over whether to regard those trafficked as actors with agency or as "victims" (Huda 2006). We cannot hope to expediently resolve issues that are inextricably bound to the structural denigration of women, poverty, exploitation, and abuse without contextualizing these actors' experiences, without being aware, for example, that the resettlement houses for sex workers may be judged as even less hospitable than brothels (Jayasree 2004).

In recognizing the complex causes and implications of human tragedy, we implore scholars to take a more grounded and contextualized approach to studying and advocating for human rights. A holistic approach necessitates looking at flagrant abuses of rights in their institutional and historical contexts. The flouting of habeas corpus and detention of suspected communist sympathizers in Indonesia (van der Kroef 1976), then as now, evidences systemic constraints on political expression within a border. Contextualizing human rights concerns in consideration of political and social structures and historical implications, and in the spirit of solidarity with those who confront violations of their rights, is critical to ushering human rights research beyond its current impasse. Far from proffering a solution, we simply suggest demonstrating more effort in understanding the human condition, beyond the universalist/relativist theoretical divide.

PORTRAIT OF HUMAN RIGHTS IN ASIAN AMERICA

Research and work on human rights in Asian America often adopt the form of civil rights and social justice. However, a human rights framework should and must be applied to the lives of Asian Americans. Since the United States professes a human rights agenda, political and social human rights are taken for granted for Asian Americans in this millennium. This was not always the case. Legal policies have historically hindered rights for Asian Americans. Executive Order 9066, in particular, forced Japanese Americans into concentration camps, stripping them of their basic human rights. Detailed accounts of governmental wrongdoings after the Pearl Harbor attack led to the wrongful internment of Americans of Japanese descent. Michi Weglyn's *Years of Infamy: The Untold Story of America's Concentration Camps*, along with the case of Fred Korematsu, in which Korematsu challenged his internment (323 U.S. 214), highlight the overt and subversive tactics used by the government to disregard basic human rights. Various challenges to these human rights violations led to repatriation.

While glaring institutional violations are not as prevalent today, there are still numerous case studies and reports of discriminatory practices against Asian Americans in areas of hiring, salary, and promotion in private industries, health fields, civil services, and even academic institutions (Jo 1984). Social discrimination also continues to haunt Asian Americans. Anti-immigrant sentiments and racism are realities confronted daily by many Asian Americans (Ancheta 1998). Thus, Asian Americans continue to fight for social justice to gain rights that are due to them.

While citizens of the United States have an easier time finding legal routes to rights, those who are undocumented or trafficked into the US underground economy (e.g., sex workers, sweatshop workers, domestic workers) are exploited and deprived of their basic human rights. Feminist human rights activists have challenged the contradictions of human rights. They push to ensure that the rights of women and girls are seen as an inalienable and integral aspect of human rights (Binion 1995). Along with gender, sexuality is still a shared human rights issue for those living in the United States. With only a limited number of states having legalized civil unions or marriages, continued hate crimes toward lesbian, gay, bisexual, and transgender (LGBT) individuals and enduring legal and social violations highlight the hardship for LGBT communities. There has been a cultural and political shift with the repeal of Don't Ask, Don't Tell in 2010 and the Obama administration's announcement that it would no longer defend the Defense of Marriage Act because it was unconstitutional. Yet, there is still cause to argue that the human rights framing does not address LGBT issues in the United States (Mertus 2007). Asian Americans, women, LGBTs, and those whose identities intersect in dimensions of inequality in race, class, gender, and sexuality continue to face a bigger challenge in gaining justice and rights.

One form through which intersectional issues impacting structural opportunities for Asian Americans are obscured is the myth of the model minority. While the model minority stereotype in itself appears positive and innocuous, the fuel of hostility toward foreigners who are "making it" is evident. During the 1982 US recession, for example, at the peak of anti-Japanese sentiment, Vincent Chin was murdered by two laid-off Detroit autoworkers who saw him as a foreigner responsible for taking jobs from Americans (Kurashige 2002). After 9/11, Sikhs and other South Asians mistaken for Muslims were targeted, and in some cases killed, by those who blamed them for the attacks (Maira 2004). As Tuan (1999) argues, Asian

Americans are perceived as "honorary whites and forever foreigners." Under the human rights framework, every individual should be free to live without fear of violence or death; yet the racialized climate in the United States fosters hostility.

For those without a state or country, the problems are even more glaring, as some individuals face discrimination, assaults, detention without due process, and, in extreme cases, deportation to other countries (Ashar 2003; Paust 2004). The stateless in the United States are most vulnerable and are not offered the human rights protections bestowed upon citizens. Undocumented or stateless people are often homogenized as a single group of criminals. In reality, those who seek refuge in the United States find it is not the safe haven they envisioned.

The climate of intense xenophobia is not new. From the 1940s to the civil rights movement and the 1980s, cities and states across the nation confronted pressure to assimilate at all costs. San Gabriel Valley, California, a suburban community nestled near Los Angeles, faced an influx of affluent Asian immigrants in 1985. As Asian languages popped up in California cities such as Monterey Park, Alhambra, and Arcadia, business owners lobbied their city councils for an "English-only initiative" (Saito 1998). While the United States does not have an official language, various cities, counties, and states have attempted to make English the official language (Arington 1991). These attempts have failed, yet anti-immigrant sentiments continue to haunt various states and cities across the United States.

Much like Asians in Asia, Asian Americans confront structural and social obstacles in obtaining and maintaining basic human rights. Hence, there is a need to rethink and reconstruct a human rights framework that can better adapt to sovereign Asian nations and address issues confronting those in the United States who are perceived to be from another nation.

LESSONS FOR HUMAN RIGHTS FROM THE SOCIOLOGY OF ASIA AND ASIAN AMERICA

The Sociology of Asia and Asian America spans numerous subareas, including ethnic/racial studies, international migration, religious studies, political sociology, and gender and sexuality. Sociological work in and about Asia and Asian America transcends centuries of political and social activism that challenge oppressive governments, organizations, and communities. It is important to recognize that the birth of the human rights framework began in the West; hence, there are cultural barriers that hinder understanding what human rights encompass. When Chinese president Hu Jintao met with President Barack Obama in 2011, he received stern warnings from the US administration about China's human rights policies. President Hu Jintao articulated his commitment to working on human rights in China, but there were concerns that his idea of human rights did not include the political, gender, and religious rights of China's peoples. The work in Asia demonstrates a need for Western activists to learn how best to work in collaboration with governments, communities, and organizations seeking to find ways to avoid human rights violations. Further, the case of China draws attention to just one example of contested territories, including Tibet and Taiwan. In this regard, persisting conflict in Asia also raises questions about how human rights are conceptualized and how violations are avoided.

A human rights paradigm can also learn from the lessons of a century and a half of Asian Americans working toward social justice. Intersecting these efforts with human rights allows for addressing concerns such as the right of ethnic studies to exist as a discipline, realities confronting migrants (Fujiwara 2005), and rights without citizenship (Turner 1993). As Asian American studies programs (and ethnic studies generally) around the nation face potential dismantling, and consequently silencing, by universities, the need for Asian Americans to continue to fight for democracy and to confront oppression is glaring.

Currently, the literature interrogates the conditions under which human rights can be sustainable and whether human rights are universal (Franck 2001; Hoang 2009); there is a continuing discussion of how human rights are applied to Asia (Bell 2000). Less frequently problematized is the question of who violates human rights. Violations of human decency in countries of the West are framed as infringements of civil rights, which somehow appear less insidious. For example, the right to be with family should be inherent to humans, yet border policing in the West results in familial separation. Habitually, it is the developing countries, such as those in Asia, which are riddled with social, economic, and political quandaries, that are condemned as perpetrators of human rights abuses. Efforts undertaken by nongovernmental organizations such as the World Trade Organization have also been decried for degrading human rights and living conditions in the interests of capital (Cohn 2001).

Existing research has suggested ways to rethink and address issues of human rights (Donnelly 2003), including by interjecting a Buddhist framework (Hershock 2000). Yet limited research has accounted for conditions that circumvent or complicate the implementation of human rights, such as those to clean water and fulfillment of basic material needs (Beyrer 1998). This disregard raises an epistemological issue: How do we know what we know? It harkens back to our earlier assertion that allegations of human rights violations are disproportionately levied against developing, not developed, countries.

Studies and contemporary human rights efforts have often taken the form of shaming governments, with few calling the effectiveness of this approach into question (Franklin 2008). Bourgois (1990) also remarks on the constraints of doing human rights work in the academy, noting the need to be mindful of the practical implications of scholarship for the lives of populations being studied. These and other considerations for studying and implementing human rights remain. Short of offering a universal answer to these very pertinent concerns, we celebrate the call to prioritize, as a broader moral imperative of researchers, the ways in which their work incorporates and impacts communities.

CHAPTER SIX

LATINA/O SOCIOLOGY

Rogelio Sáenz, Karen Manges Douglas, and Maria Cristina Morales

Latina/os represent the fastest-growing racial and ethnic group in the United States. Indeed, over the period from 1980 to 2009, the Latina/o population more than tripled—from 14.6 million in 1980 to 48.4 million in 2009—while the overall US population increased by only 36 percent (Sáenz 2010a). Currently, Latina/os account for one of every two persons added to the US population. The rapid growth of the Latina/o population has been fueled by the group's youthfulness, reflected in a median age of twenty-seven compared to forty-one among the white population in 2009.

The variation in the age structures of these two groups will result in an expansion of the Latina/o representation in the United States alongside a declining presence of whites in the coming decades. It is projected that the Latina/o share of the US population is likely to increase from 16 percent in 2010 to 30 percent in 2050, while that of the white population is expected to decline from 65 percent in 2010 to 46 percent in 2050 (US Census Bureau 2008). This divergent demographic future has led to the rise of policy initiatives to halt Latina/o immigration and to apprehend and deport undocumented Latina/os.

The increasingly hostile environment against Latina/os has threatened their basic human rights for US citizens and noncitizens alike. Despite their long presence in the United States, especially in the case of Mexicans and Puerto Ricans, Latina/os continue to be viewed as an invading threat that does not belong in the United States (Chavez 2008). The antagonism against Latina/os is driven by racism and a fear that they are encroaching on the safe and comfortable space where whites have thrived and benefitted from their racial status.

Despite major encroachments on the basic human rights of Latina/os in the United States, human rights concerns continue to be a sidebar in research on Latina/os. Only in the last decade have we seen an increase in research on Latina/os directly addressing matters of human rights. For example, a search of *Sociological Abstracts* using the keywords "Hispanic," "Latino," or "Latina" and "human rights" reveals only twelve entries, all published since 1999, with two-thirds of these published since 2005. The absence of work on human rights related to Latina/os reflects the US practice of granting rights on the basis of citizenship rather than one's being a human being (Turner 2006). Nonetheless, attention to human rights issues affecting Latina/os has increased in the post-9/11 period with the heightened criminalization of immigrants and militarization of the border (Golash-Boza 2009; Sáenz and Murga 2011).

This chapter has several goals. First, we provide an overview of the theoretical perspectives and sociological tool kits that Latina/o scholars have employed in the study of Latina/os. Second, we provide the historical context in which whiteness became an asset for US citizenship along with the racialization of Latina/os. Third, we summarize the contemporary context in which Latina/os live. Finally, we conclude with a discussion of the sociology of Latina/os and its potential linkage to a human rights perspective.

SOCIOLOGICAL TOOL KITS IN THE STUDY OF LATINA/OS

Sociologists who study the Latina/o population use a variety of methodological tools to conduct their research (Rodríguez, Sáenz, and Menjívar 2008; Rodríguez 2008). As scholars try to gain a deep understanding of sociological phenomenon on Latina/os, they tend to rely on qualitative methods including ethnographies, in-depth interviews, and observations (Dunn 2009). In addition, scholars who are interested in historical and legal studies of the Latina/o population tend to make use of historical and legal archives in their research. Court cases, including Supreme Court decisions and dissenting opinions, for instance, are quite revealing of the assumptions undergirding them (López 2006). Moreover, sociologists who are interested in media studies tend to analyze textual, visual, and digital sources. Content analysis of programming content and advertisements, along with newspaper column-width coverage, are all common methodological tools used for studying the media. Furthermore, persons who examine structural forces impacting the behavior of Latina/os tend to rely on quantitative data including census information and large-scale surveys. Additionally, sociologists who examine the transnational aspects of the lives of Latina/os use a variety of methodological approaches, including ethnographies, in-depth interviews, and surveys, in the communities of origin and destination across international borders. Finally, sociologists who study the Latina/o population use a variety of theoretical approaches that capture the inequalities that continue to mark the lives of Latina/os. These approaches include the structural racism (Feagin 2006) and critical race (and LatCrit) (Trucios-Haynes 2001) perspectives.

A HISTORICAL OVERVIEW OF THE RACIALIZATION OF LATINA/OS

Ngai's (2004) concept of Latina/os as alien citizens (or Heyman's [2002] reference to "anticitizens") provides an appropriate point of departure from which to discuss human rights and the US Latina/o population. Alien citizenship ensued from the

US legal racialization of people based upon their national origins. Accordingly, the use of racial categories for inclusion and exclusion from the United States dates to the nation's first immigration and naturalization laws of 1790, which limited eligibility for naturalization to free, white aliens (Ngai 2004).

Following the Civil War, naturalization laws were amended to confer citizenship on persons of African descent (former slaves) while continuing the eligibility criterion of white, thereby establishing a black-white color line for the granting of US citizenship (Daniels 2004). The 1924 National Origins Act established a racial hierarchy of the world's inhabitants (Ngai 1999, 2004) in which northern and western Europeans received large quotas, southern and eastern Europeans got small quotas, and Asians were barred from immigrating to the United States.

Western Hemisphere residents (Latin Americans and Canadians) were excluded from the act's quota restrictions, reflecting the political clout of southwestern agricultural interests desiring cheap Mexican labor. Instead the bill established visa requirements for entry into the United States, which resulted in a new category of persons in the racial taxonomy: the "illegal alien" (Bustamante 1972). Although people without proper documentation included all nationalities worldwide, over time the term became synonymous with "Mexican" (Ngai 2004).

The requirement that US citizenship be limited to those defined as either white or black meant that the courts were called upon to make racial determinations. Between 1887 and 1923, the federal courts made more than twenty-five racial determinations (López 2006; Ngai 2004). For the nation's Latina/o population, who per the US black-white citizenship requirements were legally designated white, there are numerous examples of ways the dominant white group defined Latina/os as nonwhite. In the case of *In Re: Rodriguez* (1897), Ricardo Rodriguez, a Mexican-born resident of San Antonio, Texas, was denied naturalization on the grounds that he was not white (De Genova 2005; Sáenz and Murga 2011). However, a district court judge ruled that although Rodriguez was not white, he was nevertheless eligible to become a naturalized citizen because the Texas state constitution recognized Mexicans as citizens of Texas, all citizens of Texas were granted US citizenship when Texas became a US state, and the Treaty of Guadalupe Hidalgo signed in 1848 granted US citizenship to Mexicans living on these lands (De Genova 2005; Sáenz and Murga 2011).

The discomfort of the white population over the Latina/os' default white designation is further reflected in the creation of a "Mexican" racial category for the 1930 census. Due in part to the lobbying efforts of Mexican American leaders who argued that Mexican Americans were white (Snipp 2003, 69), the issue of how to classify the Latina/o population of the United States remained a work in progress. Ironically, whites were quick to view Latina/os as white when *Brown v. Board of Education* pressured the South to desegregate. Accordingly, Texas officials sought to achieve school desegregation by placing Latina/o and black students in the same schools (San Miguel 2005).

The alien citizenship of Latina/os stems from the conquest of the two largest Latina/o groups—Mexicans and Puerto Ricans—characterized by warfare, power, and resource asymmetry between the United States and Latin America (see Bonilla-Silva 2008). US employer demand for cheap Latin American labor (particularly Mexican), supported by legislative initiatives such as the Bracero Program and more recently NAFTA, continue to pull Latina/os into the United States despite highly racialized immigration and naturalization legislation intent on limiting "undesirables." Policy initiatives in several states (notably Arizona and Alabama) are aimed squarely at the Latina/o undocumented. While individual pieces of legislation have been legally challenged, the racial nature of the efforts, the conflation of legal and illegal, citizen and noncitizen, and the Supreme Court's sanction of racial profiling of "Mexican-looking" people send an unwelcoming message. Further, these types of policy initiatives have intensified over the last few decades as the Latina/o population has grown.

THE CONTEMPORARY CONTEXT

The expanding Latina/o population and its spread to states that have historically not had a significant presence of Latina/os challenge the racial hierarchy and the power monopoly that whites have enjoyed (see Moore 2008). To stem Latina/o encroachment on the existing racial structure, US states have employed a variety of tactics, including highly restrictive immigration laws such as Arizona's Senate Bill (SB) 1070, mobilization of local militias such as the Minutemen to patrol the border, state-mandated abolition of ethnic studies courses (e.g., Arizona's House Bill 2281), passage of English-only legislation and repealing of bilingual education in several states, and local ordinances criminalizing property rental to undocumented immigrants. These efforts have served to set Latina/os once again as a class apart.

At the federal level, revamped immigration laws such as the Illegal Immigrant Reform and Immigrant Responsibility Act of 1996 enhanced border-enforcement activities and loosened deportation criteria. Additionally, the law established a mechanism for partnerships between local law enforcement and federal immigration enforcement via the 287(g) provision. In 2006, the United States passed the Secure Fence Act of 2006 authorizing construction of a US border wall. Further, the Fourteenth Amendment to the US Constitution, which grants citizenship to all persons born in the United States, is at the epicenter of nativists' efforts to overturn the principle as a mechanism to slow the growth of the rapidly expanding US Latina/o population (Wood 1999).

As López (2006) notes, these targeted actions are far from color-blind and share the same highly racial imprimatur of earlier policies that oversaw the internment of Japanese American citizens during World War II and the deportation of Mexican Americans during Operation Wetback in the 1950s. This hostile environment against Latina/os has contributed to citizenship and human rights violations—acceptable collateral damage to maintain white supremacy.

SOCIOLOGY OF LATINA/OS

The sociological study of Latina/os is relatively new, with major developments beginning in the 1970s. However, over the past several decades, the field of the sociology of Latina/os has expanded dramatically. Major substantive areas of study include demography, crime, education, family, gender, health, immigration, inequality, and labor. While much of the research in the area has focused on Latina/os in the United States, research has also addressed the larger transnational context in which Latina/os exist.

Transnationalism describes the processes whereby immigrants maintain ties to the native/sending communities and participate in varying ways in the activities of their communities of origin and destination. In part due to the proximity to Latin American countries, Latina/o immigrants to the United States, particularly more recent arrivals, continue to be linked to their originating communities (Fink 2003; Smith 2005).

Transnationalism impacts both individuals and entire families. Transnational families are created when one or both parents emigrate from the household of origin (Menjívar and Abrego 2009; Parreñas 1998). In the context of the aftermath of 9/11, the "war on drugs," and the global economic recession, crossing borders and maintaining transnational ties has become difficult and dangerous for Latin American migrants. Human rights concerns have escalated along the US-Mexico border due to border-control measures—that is, the erection of a physical and virtual wall, increases in border agents, and the militarization of the border (use of surveillance technology and military personnel) (Dunn 2001). Consequently, what was once a circulatory migrant flow has become increasingly a one-way journey. Sending-community involvement in this migration is constricted, transnational family reunification is hindered, and undocumented immigrants are often "entrapped" along the southern border (Núñez and Heyman 2007).

Particularly alarming is the increase in migrant deaths resulting from the more dangerous and treacherous terrain migrants are forced to travel from Mexico into the United States due to enhanced urban-border enforcement (Eschbach et al. 1999; Massey, Durand, and Malone 2002). Unfortunately, these and other human rights abuses have largely been ignored in the United States. Further, because nation-states maintain power in implementing international human rights, there appears to be little legal recourse for these human rights abuses as the United States refused to sign the International Convention on the Protection of the Rights of All Migrant Workers and Their Families adopted by the UN General Assembly in 1990. This is problematic for Latina/os because many lack citizenship rights afforded by nation-states (see Turner 2006).

Border-control initiatives also create human rights abuses for US-born Latina/os. Heightened border enforcement disrupts the stability of life for all inhabiting this militarized zone. Under the pretext of the "war on drugs," the military is used for domestic policing along the US-Mexico border (Dunn 2001). The militarization that Latina/os are subjected to in the border region parallels other state-sanctioned forms of social control. Border-control operations racially profile all "brown" people regardless of citizenship status (Morales and Bejarano 2009). The Border Network for Human Rights (2003) has documented the extensive use of race as a basis for immigration-related questioning leading to constitutional violations against US citizens and documented immigrants, such as wrongful detentions, searches, confiscation of property, and physical and psychological abuse.

As Latina/os have settled in new destinations (Sáenz, Cready, and Morales 2007), border-control enforcement tactics have followed (Coleman 2007). Turner (2006) notes the increasing need for human rights enforcement in situations where everyone is vulnerable. In this case, all US residents are vulnerable as the militarized state and border-control tactics expand across the country.

No doubt, the historical and contemporary story of the US Latina/o population is far from straightforward. Latina/os encompass a heterogeneous population with differing histories and modes of incorporation into the United States. This heterogeneity makes human rights issues more complex and not neatly encompassed in a single narrative or tradition. Although there are variations, one constant has been the inferior status of Latina/os relative to whites.

WHAT CAN THE HUMAN RIGHTS PARADIGM LEARN FROM THE SOCIOLOGY OF LATINA/OS?

The sociology of Latina/os can expand the human rights paradigm given Latina/os' status as the largest US minority group, their diversity, and their transnational lives, which create a gray area between the human and citizenship rights paradigms. To begin, despite being the nation's largest minority group, Latina/os remain marginally integrated into mainstream institutions. The sociology of Latina/os has been inspired by several societal conditions that Latina/os face, such as precarious employment situations, poverty, educational inequality, injustice in the criminal justice system, a system of rights that does not protect its immigrant community, and other human rights abuses that reflect the group's lack of integration. The human rights abuses that Latina/os confront are not merely associated with the newcomer status of a segment of the population. Indeed, despite their long historical presence in the United States, Mexican Americans continue to occupy the lowest economic positions (Sáenz, Morales, and Ayala 2004) and are largely regarded as "foreigners" (Douglas and Sáenz 2010).

The human rights implications of the extensive social control of Latina/os are reflected in public policies. For instance, SB 1070 made residing in Arizona without legal authorization a crime and conflates the policing of immigration with racial profiling (Heyman 2010; Sáenz and Murga 2011). Arguably, this state-level policy is a response to the threatening Latina/o growth (see Sáenz 2010b) and targets all Latina/os, regardless of citizenship status, who are perceived to be "foreigners" (Heyman 2010). Human rights concerns arise from the exercise of state power to disproportionately target Latina/os, leading to their subjection to extensive social controls, deportation and separation from families, harassment, and criminalization.

The sociology of Latina/os has highlighted Latina/o heterogeneity, which has important implications for the human rights paradigm. Latina/os are stratified by racial identification, skin color, citizenship status, and class (Morales 2009), which increases the complexity of applying the human rights paradigm. The diversity of the Latina/o population, particularly in terms of citizenship status, illustrates a challenge in utilizing the human rights paradigm for the equality, safety, and prosperity of the entire group. The difficult theoretical work of how to grapple with the human rights of Latina/o immigrants—many of whom are outside the umbrella of citizenship rights and simultaneously deprived of human rights given the focus of nation-states—has yet to be done.

Yet, the citizenship diversity among Latino immigrant families has a myriad of human rights implications. There are many "mixed-status families," which consist of members with a variety of statuses, including citizens, visa holders, naturalized citizens, and undocumented individuals. Indeed, Fix and Zimmermann (2001) found that one-tenth of families have mixed status, where one or both parents are noncitizens and the children are citizens. In a study of mixed-status families in the detention/deportation system, Brabeck and Xu (2010) found that parents with higher levels of legal vulnerability experienced greater problems associated with emotional well-being, ability to provide financially, and relationships with their children. In this context, children's emotional stability and academic perfor-mance are jeopardized (Brabeck and Xu 2010). Moreover, in the legal system, the onerous requirements to override deportation proceedings create a hurdle few can overcome and one that is nearly insurmountable for undocumented parents of US citizen children (Sutter 2006). Human rights perspectives must consider the ces-sation of individual deportations in order to maintain "intact" families, a notion that several nations recognize as important (Sutter 2006). Thus, this adds another layer of complexity to the application of human rights when considering whether the locus of protection should be the individual or the family.

INCORPORATING THE HUMAN RIGHTS PARADIGM INTO THE SOCIOLOGY OF LATINA/O RESEARCH

A review of the human rights literature concerning the Latina/o population reveals significant attention to human rights based in Latin America but not in the United States before the 9/11 period. With the rise of human rights abuses in the post-9/11 period, research addressing human rights among Latina/os has shifted toward the United States since 2000. Of the sixteen entries in *Sociological Abstracts* published since 2000, eleven were based in the United States. The research on Latina/os in the United States that has incorporated human rights dimensions includes themes such as the ambiguity of the US-Mexico border (Ortiz 2001), the militarization of the border (Dunn 2001), the US minority rights revolution associated with the civil rights era (Skrentny 2002), abuses against immigrants (Dunn, Aragones, and Shivers 2005; Krieger et al. 2006; Redwood 2008; Vinck et al. 2009), the growth of the prison population (Modic 2008), youth activism and the struggle for human rights associated with the immigrant rights marches of 2006 (Velez et al. 2008), and antigay family policies (Cahill 2009).

Still, the relative dearth of material within the established human rights tradi-tion represents the difficulty the perspective faces in addressing the multiple and continuing human rights violations confronting the US Latina/o population. There are several reasons for this. First, as Dunn (2009) notes, the issue of human rights remains entangled within notions of the nation-state and citizenship. Human rights are conditional on citizenship, which comes with attached rights and duties. Violations (e.g., committing felony acts) can result in the diminishment of citizenship rights (e.g., voter disenfranchisement). Indeed, it is within this tradition that human rights battles for inclusion have occurred in the United States. People of color have challenged their exclusion from the full benefits of US citizenship and sought remedies. However, these remedies are conditioned by citizenship. By definition, the extraterritorial essence of the Latina/o population is a threat to the nation-state. Just as Japanese Americans were viewed during World War II as sympathetic and inextricably linked to Japan, which provided the rationale for their imprisonment, so too, and despite multiple generations of presence in the United States, is there a conflation between Mexican Americans and Mexico. Further complicating the Latina/o human rights story is that significant numbers of the US Latina/o population remain citizens of their countries of origin. Thus, the links to their homelands are still direct and, to many in the United States, threatening.

Second, the narrow framing of human rights conditioned upon citizenship has pitted Latina/o citizen against Latina/o noncitizen. The narrow targeting of, for example, immigration laws on racial grounds has resulted not only in broken families but in an "us-versus-them" mentality that has tolerated human rights violations so long as citizens are not the target (Dunn 2009). As Ngai (2004) argues, this framing of migrants as threats, together with the prolific national discourse surrounding the need to "secure our borders," provides cover for the state to engage in a variety of racist and discriminatory acts that even the Supreme Court acknowledges "would be unacceptable if applied to citizens" (Ngai 2004, 12).

Third, as articulated in the works of LatCrit theorists, the ambiguous racial category that Latinas/os inhabit renders the application of traditional human rights perspectives problematic. Fourteenth Amendment protections are predicated on race, ancestry, or national origin. This leaves most Latina/os who lack a distinct racial category or national origin without a basis for a discrimination claim. As detailed earlier, this is problematic on several fronts, including the fact that some Latina/os are Americans with deep ties to their countries of origin. The effect of both the narrow focus of the equal protection clause and the multidimensional nature of the Latina/o population has allowed for "discrimination to remain remedied" and for "the manipulation of the Latina/o image to exploit racial fears" (Trucios-Haynes 2001, 4).

The human rights perspective offers potential redress to the nation-state/citizenship-rights perspective. This perspective begins with the premise that all human beings have fundamental and inalienable human rights (Blau and Moncada 2005; Sjoberg, Gill, and Williams 2001). These rights are unconditional, universal, and, importantly, transnational. As Turner explains, these individual rights emerge as a result of our "shared vulnerabilities" (2006a, 47). This perspective provides a different frame (outside the citizenship/nation-state divide) from which to evaluate questionable policies despite their legality within the nation-state. Unfortunately, the platform for realizing these rights is relatively narrow. The UN offers a Declaration of Human Rights, but there are only weak enforcement capabilities at the global level. Thus, despite the recognition of inalienable and universal human rights, this perspective has gained little traction.

Further, as Bonilla-Silva (2008) argues, the human rights tradition suffers from its failure to recognize and incorporate race into its analysis. Bonilla-Silva asserts that "the HRT idealizes the autonomous individual who can be located within a universe of abstract rights, devoid of racially constraining social structures" (2008, 11). While the human rights perspective recognizes the inalienable rights of people, it "seems unwilling to temper this view with the fact that there are vast differences of power among individuals as individuals as well as members of social groups or nation-states" (Bonilla-Silva 2008, 12). In short, all people are not the same. Much of the story told, thus far, involves the successful efforts to marginalize the Latina/o population. Immigration laws, including the present-day variations, have been constructed along highly racialized lines with specific racial bogeymen as their target.

THE ROAD FORWARD

Despite the long presence of Latina/os in the United States and the fact that the majority of Latina/os are US born, Latina/os continue to be viewed as "perpetual foreigners" and "anticitizens." Hostilities toward Latina/os have risen over the last several decades as global forces and economic and political linkages between the United States and Latin America have uprooted many Latin Americans who have migrated to the United States. The youthfulness of the Latina/o population also portends a disproportionate growth of Latina/os in the coming decades in this country. Numerous policies have emerged throughout the country, but especially in states bordering Mexico, to stem the entrance of Latina/o immigrants and to roundup and deport those already here. While ostensibly undocumented Latina/os are the target, in reality Latina/o naturalized citizens and US-born Latina/os have also been affected by such policies.

Policies such as Arizona's SB 1070, the vigilantism that has arisen along the border in the form of the Minutemen, the militarization of the border, and the rise of detention centers have made Latina/os, regardless of citizenship status, vulnerable to a wide range of human rights violations. For example, on a daily basis, Latina/o families are being split due to the deportation of family members, while others are questioned or pulled over by law enforcement for looking Latina/o. Moreover, the militarization of the border and governmental efforts to push immigrants to enter through dangerous and treacherous terrains have resulted in the deaths of countless human beings seeking better lives in the United States. Furthermore, the militarization of the border has also occasionally resulted in the killing of Latina/os and Mexican nationals (see Brice 2010). The killing of Esequiel Hernández Jr., an eighteen-year-old high school student who was herding goats in Redford, Texas, at the time of his death at the hands of a US Marine Corps antidrug patrol, best illustrates the vulnerability that Latina/os face along the border as the US government wages war against immigrants and drug traffickers (National Drug Strategy Network 1997). Reverend Mel La Follette, a retired Episcopalian priest in Redford, aptly described the situation: "We were invaded, and one of our sons was slaughtered.... The whole community was violated" (National Drug Strategy Network 1997). Such policies and traumatic events have undone many of the gains Latina/os achieved through civil rights legislation.

Our review of the literature reveals that only recently have we seen the incorporation of human rights concerns into the study of Latina/os. We see this as a much-needed and welcome addition to scholarship on the Latina/o population. Much of the existing literature examining the plight of the Latina/o population has merely alluded to the human rights implications without delving deeply into the human rights consequences of the conditions of the population. However, there is a need to make adjustments in the human rights perspective to better capture the racialized situation of Latina/os in the United States, along with the unequal power relations between the United States and Latin American countries (Bonilla-Silva 2008). Insights from the sociology of Latina/o literature related to the racialization of Latina/os, the heterogeneity of the Latina/o population, the agency that Latina/os possess, and the transnational aspects of the lives of Latina/os are considerations that the human rights perspective must take into account to more fully address the human rights of the Latina/o population.

CHAPTER SEVEN

CHILDREN AND YOUTH

Brian K. Gran

Sociology of children and youth is a vibrant, young area of the discipline. This chapter presents key questions sociologists consider when studying young people, findings from those studies, as well as a discussion of the methods they employ and data they analyze. It then discusses potential contributions sociology of children and youth may make to human rights research and what human rights scholarship may contribute to sociology of children and youth. This chapter concludes by reviewing questions for future research arising from the intersection of human rights and sociology of children and youth.

KEY QUESTIONS

Sociology of children and youth is a young subdiscipline that is experiencing growth all over the world. In 1984, a section on children and youth was established in the Nordic Sociological Association. The American Sociological Association (ASA) Section on Children and Youth was founded in 1991 under the leadership of Professor Gertrud Lenzer, and the section of the German Sociological Association was set up in 1995. Internationally, Research Committee 53, Sociology of Childhood, of the International Sociological Association was established in 1998. Organizations that focus on sociological studies of children and youth are found all over the world, including the European Sociological Association's Research Network 4, Sociology of Children and Childhood.

Sociologists of children and youth research various questions and issues that span the discipline of sociology. One question sociologists ask is how young people's experiences and perspectives have changed over time. An additional question is how young people's experiences vary by location. Does a young person living in one community have different life chances compared to a child living in another community? Are globalization forces reducing or expanding these differences in childhood?

Of course, sociologists want to know why young people's experiences differ across time and space. Do young persons' life chances depend solely on their parents' well-being? What role does community have in how young people fare? Can laws and social-policy programs improve life chances? What factors shape young people's actions and decisions? What encourages young people to participate in their communities? If young people possess rights, what matters to whether a young person exercises those rights?

As is true for all social-science research, sociologists consider how their data-collection approaches shape their findings. A challenge for sociologists of children and youth is ensuring that a young person not only gives informed consent to participate in research but voices opinions about how social-science research is undertaken.

KEY FINDINGS

A starting point for sociology of children and youth is social construction of childhood. Referring to Aries's momentous work, *Centuries of Childhood* (1962), Corsaro (2005) describes how children have come to be seen as different from adults. Nowadays, specializations have been established that are devoted to children, such as psychology of children and sociology of children. Institutions have also developed, including age-organized educational institutions and courts devoted to young people's legal issues. Indeed, conventions on children's rights are widely accepted.

Sociologists of children and youth have demonstrated that young people's experiences have changed, sometimes remarkably, over time. Shorter (1977, 172) contends that mortality levels among young people were so high prior to the Industrial Revolution that parents sometimes did not attend their child's funeral. Turmel (2008) describes how the construction of what came to be considered "normal" changed young people's lives. For instance, public health officials demonstrated that children laboring in factories were typically shorter physically than other children. This information not only led to laws regulating child labor but was used to designate what was normal for a child's development. Across many countries, national laws now restrict young people's paid employment, and international treaties, such as the ILO's Minimum Age Convention (1973), attempt to regulate those governmental efforts.

Sociologists recognize that many factors facing children are frequently out of their control, yet these factors may strongly shape their futures. Low-birth-weight babies receive attention from sociologists because their health has a great deal to do with their parents and the environment in which they were conceived, gestated as fetuses, and now live, rather than anything the children themselves have done. Conley's work not only draws attention to critical factors contributing to births of low-birth-weight babies (Conley, Strully, and Bennett 2003) but has prompted attention to short- and long-term challenges facing these infants (Population Research Bureau 2007).

How young people spend their childhood affects their future paths. Whitbeck (2009) finds that many crucial adolescent experiences are skipped on the way to becoming an adult for young people who are homeless. Furstenberg's (2010) work demonstrates how social class affects a young person's transition to adulthood and, in turn, how those experiences shape his or her long-term experiences. Yeung and Conley's (2008) examination of the Panel Study of Income Dynamics indicates family wealth is a strong predictor of differences in test scores among US black and white students. Employing Bourdieu's ideas, Lareau's (2003) groundbreaking ethnographic study shows how parents cultivate their children's cultural capital. Compared to children from lower-class backgrounds, middle- and upper-middle-class children tend to learn how to express themselves, question authority, and navigate bureaucracy.

Sociologists have paid close attention to how changes in family homes shape young persons' experiences. In a blog posting, Raskoff (2011) notes that evidence exists not only that posttraumatic stress disorder affects many US soldiers but that its consequences are felt in the homes to which they return. She points out that this evidence has not been translated into policy changes that benefit soldiers' families. Sociologists have made significant contributions to what is known about divorces in the United States. In her study of 1998 to 1999 data, Kim (2011) finds that children whose parents have divorced are more likely to experience difficulties in formal schooling and to internalize "problem behaviors." Sociological research on children's rights has informed counseling programs for young people who have been legally separated from their families (Lenzer and Gran 2011).

Corsaro (2005, 67) notes that histories of childhood have often overlooked how children and young people are actors who influence their own circumstances. Adler and Adler (2011) chronicle how self-injury of young people has shifted from individual practice ten years ago to shared experience today. A subculture has emerged of practitioners who share values and vocabulary, partially due to ease of communication via social media.

Sociologists are studying factors leading to child-headed households and how those households fare. While expressing caution regarding their results, Ciganda, Gagnon, and Tenkorang (2010) find evidence that child-headed households in sub-Saharan countries do better in meeting some basic needs than adult-headed households. Edin and Kefalas's (2005) compelling study, *Promises I Can Keep*, shows that rather than stacking odds against themselves, the teenage women they studied made thoughtful decisions in desperate circumstances to become pregnant. Sociologists have asked how a young person comes to terms with his or her sexuality and decides to become sexually active (Myers and Raymond 2010; Regnerus 2007).

Sociologists have examined why some young people appear reluctant to leave home. In their groundbreaking book *Not Quite Adults*, Settersten and Ray (2010) rely on analyses of more than two dozen national data sets and five hundred interviews of young people to tackle how "traditional" US paths to adulthood have dramatically changed. They find that contemporary perceptions of indolent young people may be misperceptions. Instead, some young people opt to live with parents in pursuit of long-term goals, such as saving money to pay off debt and to buy their own homes.

Outside the home, in some societies, many children spend a great deal of time in schools. On the basis of case studies of East Los Angeles, Harlem, and the Bronx, Gaston et al. (2009) demonstrate in *Our Schools Suck* that students are critical of their educational opportunities, yet at the same time strongly desire the benefits they expect from their formal educations. The authors conclude a new civil rights movement is needed to secure equal educational opportunities for all American young people. The importance of education is confirmed by Hao and Pong (2008), whose research demonstrates that upward mobility of first- and second-generation US immigrants is strongly influenced by high school experiences.

In addition to education, government policies can dramatically shape young people's lives in ways that sometimes result in substantially disparate childhoods. In *Divided by Borders*, Dreby (2010) employs ethnography, interviews, and surveys to demonstrate that young people are not passive; rather, the children she studies live on their own, attending school and taking care of themselves, while their parents live and work in another country. Gonzales's (2011) study reminds us that a crucial step for many young people is their change in legal status upon reaching majority. For US "undocumented immigrants," one consequence of reaching majority is a change from legal protection as a young person to needing legal status to participate in society and the economy. Sociologists have shown that illegal status hurts young people's educational engagement and future success, as well as their cognitive development (Preston 2011).

Sociologists have explored what factors contribute to young people's feeling that they are part of their communities. In his groundbreaking study *Fitting In, Standing Out*, Crosnoe (2011) finds that young people who are marginalized experience long-term consequences as adults, including being less likely to attend college. Sociologists (Pugh 2009) have shown that parents purchase consumer goods, like computer games, to bolster their children's feelings of belonging. In *Hanging Out, Messing Around, and Geeking Out*, an innovative collection of twenty-three ethnographic studies, Ito et al. (2009) show how young people use a variety of new media, such as social media, to manage different parts of their lives, from recreation to schooling to romance. A common perception in the United States is that parents are afraid to let their children play outside without adult supervision. In *Adult Supervision Required*, Rutherford (2011) focuses on the contradiction that these days young people enjoy greater autonomy and freedom than their parents did as young people, yet there is greater fear for young people and how they use their freedoms.

In the midst of institutional and structural failures, loss of parents may be especially devastating to young people. In a special issue of *Children, Youth, and Environment*, Babugra (2008) presents her study of physical and emotional stresses young people experience during drought in Botswana. Based on interviews and participatory rural appraisals, Baburga's work shows that during and after disasters, not only do young people need to fulfill physical requirements, but family loss exacerbates their emotional, economic, and educational needs.

Institutions and social structures can not only exert strong pressures but produce conflicts in young people's lives. In his book, *When a Heart Turns Rock Solid*, Black (2010) gives a "sociological storytelling" of three brothers and their friends, whose lives are a struggle to avoid the "pull of the street." Growing up in an impoverished US neighborhood and without English as their primary language, the young men Black studied attempt to overcome weak educations and absent economic opportunities to battle drug addiction and criminal sentencing laws that automatically send people to prison without consideration of mitigating circumstances and failures of government and society. A former gang member, Victor Rios (2010) returned to his neighborhood to shadow forty young men to demonstrate how a culture of punishment pushes these young men into crime.

Young people can be compelled into activities against their will. Government can actively control young people. Margolis (1999) undertook a visual history of forced cultural assimilation among Native American children through public schooling. Other governments have imposed assimilation on indigenous children, including in Australia (van Krieken 1999).

Trafficking in young people truly is global in scope, sometimes in plain sight (Bales and Soodalter 2009). Contributors to a volume arising from a 2009 conference sponsored by the Rutgers Childhood Studies Program considered diverse experiences of children who have been forced to become soldiers and what policies and laws should be established to move to a just society where young people do not participate in armed conflict (Cook and Wall 2011).

Issues of coercion extend to bodily control. Boyle's (2002) groundbreaking work on female genital cutting (FGC) reveals conflicts between international consensuses on human rights, which calls for bans on FGC, national enforcement of those bans, and local practices and beliefs that support FGC practices. Violence against young people is a focus of sociological work that has resulted in steps to prevent and outlaw child abuse. The Family Research Laboratory of the University of New Hampshire and its codirectors, Murray Straus and David Finkelhor, are among the leading sociologists whose work on child abuse has documented significant, long-term harms resulting to children from abuse. Their work has encouraged international calls for national bans on corporal punishment of young people (endcorporalpunishment.org).

As political actors, young people have been collectively involved in producing political change. In the 1960s, young people were involved in the US civil rights movement and other collective behavior. More recently, young people have taken leadership roles in the Arab Spring. In other parts of the world, concerns are expressed about apathy among young people given that they will eventually vote, hold political office, and serve in leadership positions in government and civil society (Tisdall 2008). Sociologists have provided evidence of why young people become engaged and why many turn away from participating in mainstream institutions. Through analyses of three case studies, Rossi (2009) shows that young people make decisions to participate based on institutional characteristics and whether participation will fulfill personal and professional objectives.

Sociologists increasingly focus on how forces of globalization shape young people's lives, while social, political, and economic models and ideas cross national borders. As Western educational policies and practices sweep the world, sociologists ask whether influences of public education will be found elsewhere. A powerful globalizing social force is children's rights. As young people's rights receive greater attention, sociologists are examining whether children's rights are similar everywhere

(Gran 2010b). Sociologists are asking how institutions work to advance children's rights (Boyle 2002, 2009; Gran 2011). Thomas, Gran, and Hanson (2011) are undertaking research on organizational features of European independent children's rights institutions and how those features work in practice.

KEY METHODS

No one method is relied upon in sociological studies of children and youth. Qualitative, comparative, historical, visual, and quantitative approaches are prominently used to study young people. Indeed, many sociologists employ multiple methods in studying evidence of social phenomena affecting children and youth.

In *Gender Play*, Thorne (1993) conducted ethnographic research of children at school and on their school playground to show how young people and others are split by gender. In *A Younger Voice: Doing Child-Centered Qualitative Research*, Clark (2010) discusses what she has learned as a qualitative researcher of young people. Taking a child-centered approach, Clark has employed a variety of qualitative approaches in her work, including participant observation, focus groups, interviews, and visual methods. Some sociologists have undertaken multiyear ethnographies to study young people's lives, including Lareau (*Unequal Childhoods*, 2003), Edin and Kafelas (*Promises I Can Keep*, 2005), Pugh (*Longing and Belonging*, 2009), and Black (*When a Heart Turns Rock Solid*, 2010).

Comparative sociology of children and youth often presents useful perspectives on social problems by comparing children's experiences as well as structures shaping their lives. In comparing states in Ethiopia and the Sudan, Jalata (2005) contends that one group, the Tigrayan, make superior educational opportunities available to their young people to ensure those children eventually become leaders instead of Oromo children. Gran and Aliberti (2003) employ qualitative comparative analysis, which is based in Boolean algebra, to explore why some governments and not others have established offices of children's ombudspersons.

Tinkler's (1995) historical study examined how popular magazines shaped the adolescence of women growing up in England from the 1920s to the 1950s. Her book provides insights into how attitudes and concerns of young women were shaped over this three-decade period. In his comparative-historical, quantitative study, Carlton-Ford (2010) finds that young people start life with fewer opportunities if they grow up in countries where major armed conflict has occurred.

For sociologists of children and youth who undertake quantitative research, units of analysis range from individual children to schools to countries. In their analysis of the National Longitudinal Study of Youth for the years 1979 to 1998, Levine, Emery, and Pollack (2007) link data from young people and their mothers to find that teenage childbearing, controlling for background and other factors, has limited impacts on both mother and child. The Luxembourg Income Study (LIS), a database of twenty-five data sets, allows sociologists to compare children's experiences across countries. Contending with definitions of absolute and relative poverty affecting young people, in *Poor Kids in a Rich Country*, Rainwater and

Smeeding (2005) compare impacts of income packaging and different kinds of income, for instance, on reducing poverty among young people. An advantage of their study of Australia, Canada, the United States, and twelve European countries is that Rainwater and Smeeding can use the LIS database to examine how one country's income package would work in another country to reduce impacts of income inequality on childhood poverty.

Sociologists employing multilevel modeling have made significant inroads into understanding how context shapes young persons' experiences. Raudenbush and colleagues have used hierarchical linear models to show how classroom size can affect what young people learn at school (Shin and Raudenbush 2011) and how neighborhoods affect young people's verbal abilities, an important predictor of adult success (Sampson, Sharkey, and Raudenbush 2008). Levels, Dronkers, and Kraaykamp (2008) use a double comparative design to distinguish between impacts of an immigrant's sending country and those of the receiving country to study the mathematical performance of 7,403 children who left thirty-five different countries to live in thirteen host countries.

Visual sociologists employ visual evidence to give meanings to young people's contexts and relationships. Clark-Ibáñez (2007) has demonstrated that photo elicitation, the presentation of visual evidence to participants to elicit their viewpoints on social phenomena, empowers young people to use photographs to "teach" researchers about how their home lives affect school experiences. Jon Wagner (1999b) edited a special issue of *Visual Sociology*, "Visual Sociology and Seeing Kids' Worlds," that presented research on how children can use visual narratives to teach their physicians (Rich and Chalfen 1999), how young people understand their contexts (Wagner 1999a), including urban environments (Orrellana 1999), and how video can be used to express young people's points of view (Larson 1999).

As there are various methods, there are several sources of secondary evidence of young people's welfare and rights. Cochaired by Ben-Arieh and Goerge, the International Society for Childhood Indicators (www.childindicators.org) develops standards for data and indicators of children's well-being and rights and publishes the journal *Child Indicators Research*. UNICEF collects data on "the situation of children" and publishes reports about their welfare, including *The State of the World's Children*. It maintains ChildInfo, a website data resource. UNICEF's Innocenti Research Centre is devoted to research on children's rights and welfare and publishes reports and advises different UN agencies. A prominent cross-national database is the Organization for Economic Cooperation and Development's Programme for International Study Assessment, which consists of data from seventy countries about skills and experiences of fifteen-year-old students, particularly their preparation to participate in society as adults.

In the United States, government and nongovernment organizations collect and publish data about children and youth. The Federal Interagency Forum on Child and Family Statistics publishes an annual report, "America's Children." The nongovernmental organization Child Trends regularly updates its DataBank. Kenneth Land coordinates the Child and Youth Well-Being Index Project, a collection of US evidence of the quality of life of American young people. The US Children's

Bureau is a resource for state-level data on adoption, child abuse, and general child welfare, among other areas. The Integrated Health Interview Series makes data on child health conditions, health care, and health behaviors publicly available. Many individual states publish state- and county-level data on births, deaths, infant mortality, and low birth weights.

Other organizations tend to focus on particular questions about young people and their well-being. Established in 2009, the International Society for Longitudinal and Life Course Studies will provide a forum for life-course researchers to share data. The American Educational Research Network has set up an Institute on Statistical Analysis for Education Policy, which has the goal of enhancing access to large national and international databases involving education.

Sociologists are striving to develop databases on children's rights. Boyle (2009) was recently awarded a US National Science Foundation (NSF) grant for her study "The Cost of Rights or the Right Cost? The Impact of Global Economic and Human Rights Policies on Child Well-Being since 1989." Gran (2010a) also received NSF support to develop and replicate the Children's Rights Index for the period 1989 to 2009.

WHAT CAN HUMAN RIGHTS SCHOLARS LEARN FROM SOCIOLOGY OF CHILDREN AND YOUTH?

What can human rights scholars learn from sociology of children and youth? One important contribution is that just as childhood is socially constructed, so is adulthood. Human rights work relies on the dichotomous social construction of adult and child. This dichotomy occasionally invites conflict in human rights. Near-universal ratification of the UN Convention on the Rights of the Child (UNCRC) suggests widespread commitment to special treatment of young people. The Universal Declaration of Human Rights (UDHR) distinguishes between adults and young people in Article 25, where it directs that childhood merits "special assistance." UDHR Article 26 endows parents with the right to choose their child's education. Despite this similarity, the UDHR and UNCRC do conflict in important ways, the most important of which has to do a young person's freedom of conscience. UDHR Article 18 states, "Everyone has the right to freedom of thought, conscience and religion." Article 14 of the UNCRC, however, endows parents with the right to make decisions about a young person's religious beliefs and practices "in a manner consistent with the evolving capacities of the child." This conflict between the UDHR and the UNCRC accentuates the notion that young people are less than human.

Human rights scholars can learn from sociologists about what explains successes of institutions established to advance children's interests, including children's rights. Sociologists can demonstrate means by which the UN Committee on the Rights of the Child and other committees can monitor state implementation of children's rights instruments. Sociologists can offer insights into institutional isomorphism (Hafner-Burton, Tsutsui, and Meyer 2008) of independent institutions for children's rights and how their offices advance young people's rights (Thomas, Gran, and Hanson 2011; Gran 2011).

Human rights scholars can learn from sociologists about how local cultural practices can shape the practice of human rights. Given that adults typically mediate the rights of young people, sociologists can offer information about how human rights work for young people in communities and family homes.

Human rights scholars can learn how sociologists attempt to respect the young people they study. Working with institutions that monitor the interests of human subjects involved in research, sociologists strive to achieve informed consent of young people participating in their research while remaining cautious and aware of young people's interests. Sociologists recognize that young people often cannot and do not make decisions to participate in research.

WHAT CAN SOCIOLOGISTS OF CHILDREN AND YOUTH LEARN FROM HUMAN RIGHTS?

Human rights scholarship can teach many lessons to sociologists of children and youth. One important lesson is that the lives of children and youth take place on a vast playing field. Human rights scholars consider not only human rights treaties and organizations responsible for implementing human rights (and fighting against human rights) but barriers to and catalysts of implementation. Sociologists of young people may learn from human rights scholarship on how social-science evidence is used to monitor young people's rights.

Sociologists can learn from human rights scholars how governments respond to calls for human rights and how those responses vary by political party and form of government. Given that young people's experiences are mediated through manifold institutions, human rights scholars can provide insights into which institutions deserve attention.

Human rights are based on the notion of equality and dignity. Sociologists have examined equal access to education, even calling for a civil right to education as noted above (Gaston et al. 2009). Sociologists can consider other forms of equality important to young people's lives, how those notions of equal rights may change young people's lives, and how those rights may be attained. Important issues will be raised, such as how to implement a child's right to social security that is not based on a relationship with a parent or caretaker. Human rights scholars will provide insights into how human rights will change laws and practices governing young people's experiences with privacy.

Human rights scholars can teach sociologists how to take seriously a young person's dignity. By doing so, a host of research questions will be raised for sociologists. Human rights scholarship will lead to new sociological questions about expectations and norms involving young people, their parents, and schools.

Human rights scholarship can help sociologists rethink other ways young people can participate in research. Human rights scholars may point to new means by which young people can exert formal roles in sociological research, such as assuming council positions in the ASA section on Children and Youth.

IT'S NOT *WHAT* BUT *WHO* IS THE FUTURE

At the intersection of human rights and sociology of children and youth can be found many fascinating questions and exciting possibilities. Universal agreements do not exist on what human rights are and what childhood means. Strident disagreements are heard globally over whether young people possess rights. At their core, these differences revolve around what it means to be a child.

Young people may be able to explain what it fundamentally means to be human and to possess rights. Human rights scholars and sociologists will do well to listen to and try to take the perspectives of young people, recognizing their diverse needs, interests, and experiences. Children and youth may teach us about social qualities of human rights and what is necessary to take rights seriously.

CHAPTER EIGHT

RACE, CLASS, AND GENDER

Mary Romero

The traditional sociological lens for analyzing and conceptualizing social inequality has been dominated by class and social class. Over the last century, sociologists have also recognized race and ethnicity as significant in understanding inequality. Most early research was based on a white/black racial binary, classifying all other groups as "ethnic." Gradually scholars conceptualized the ways that legal, economic, political, and social institutional practices racially construct groups. Michael Omi and Howard Winant (1986) presented the conceptualization of racialization as a process in their classic work *Racial Formation in the United States.* Ian Haney López (1993) further developed the legal analysis of race and citizenship in *White by Law* by documenting the legal cases that defined whiteness and the history of allowing persons identified as nonwhite to be citizens. Studies in whiteness contributed an understanding of the social processes involved in categorizing groups previously labeled as nonwhite using white classifications (Roediger 1991; Ignatiev 1995). Apart from these intellectual projects, gender analyses theorized male privilege and gender discrimination. Feminist scholars interrogated the ways that male experiences dominated sociological perspectives that made the experiences of women invisible.

While these different types of social inequality were recognized and flourished as separate fields of study, the analyses of race, class, ethnicity, and gender remained separate from each other. The major consequence was a privileging of certain experiences while hiding or disguising others. Critiques of class analysis pointed to the assumption of white male as the ideal type, race analysis assumed black men, and gender analysis assumed white women (Dill 1983; Baca Zinn et al. 1986). Each of these analyses ignored women of color and assumed their lived experiences were represented by men of color or by white women. Women-of-color scholars challenged this construction of social inequality and social position by arguing that race, class, and gender must be theorized as fluid identities that operate simultaneously with racism, capitalism, and patriarchy rather than as fixed identities (Dill 1983; Baca Zinn et al. 1986; Harris 1990). Theories and research on race, class, and gender emerged from interdisciplinary fields with histories of struggle and with a social-justice agenda, such as African American studies, women's and gender studies, Latino studies, and critical race legal theory. The study of race, class, and gender in sociology continues to have an ongoing connection to interdisciplinary studies.

Race, class, and gender perspectives overlapping with human rights are most likely to turn toward critical race feminism because this intellectual project best illustrates the significance of this sociological lens in developing a human rights analysis and advocacy for women and other marginalized groups. In this chapter, I identify the key concerns and questions in the sociology of race, class, and gender and summarize key findings and methods. I then turn to a critical discussion of the contributions race, class, and gender have made to development of a human rights paradigm. I then resituate race, class, and gender within a human rights paradigm and explore new questions doing so raises. I end the chapter with a brief discussion of these new questions and the potential that resituating the field in a human rights paradigm holds for further developing the field and making contributions to understanding human rights.

KEY CONCERNS AND QUESTIONS

Recalling Sojourner Truth's words from her 1851 speech given at the Women's Convention in Akron, Ohio, "Ain't I a woman?," several women-of-color scholars picked up the mantle and began theorizing a race, class, and gender analysis that was inclusive rather than exclusionary (Dill 1983; Baca Zinn et al. 1986; King 1988; Romero 1988; Segura 1989; Brewer 1993). Theorizing race, class, and gender arose out of the scholarship of women of color who found their voices silenced by a single-axis analysis and instead represented by men of color and white women. Traditional lenses for analyzing social inequality defined women of color in mutually exclusive ways that either completely separated them from men of color and white women or emphasized conflicting agendas and blurred paths toward social justice. Women-of-color scholars turned their inquiry toward explaining how and why individuals located at the juncture of multiple marginalizations were invisible. As sociologists attended to racial formation and to the social construction of race, the fluidity of gendered and class-based racial experiences became visible. Rather than examining social inequality by centering on the lives of relatively privileged individuals as the norm, the focus became the lived experiences of women of color. Incorporating a race, class, and gender analysis challenged previous ways of studying inequality because each no longer could each be treated as a static variable representing all conditions.

Concern that theorizing identities as social identities would lead to essentialism emerged in the interdisciplinary fields of African American studies, Asian Pacific American studies, women's and gender studies, queer studies, disability studies, and other intellectual projects. Alongside political struggles for equal rights, each constituency began to carve out an identity agenda for advocacy and failed to search for points of intersection for coalition building. As each began to encounter more diversity within its group identity, the single axis of oppression was challenged as essentialism and, more importantly, as exclusionary. Identity categories were acknowledged as multidimensional. "Anti-essentialists feared that descriptions of identity often falsely homogenized the experiences of different group members" (Levit 2002, 228). Therefore, not all blacks in the United States are citizens, not all LGBTs are white and middle-class, not all the unemployed are poor workers of color, and not all prisoners convicted for drugs are Latino or black men. To be inclusive of all black people in the United States, fighting racism needs to include immigrants of color. Blacks are not racialized in the same way at different times in history or in different contexts. To be inclusive of black gays and lesbians, racism must also be addressed in developing advocacy programs. Similarly, stereotypes about the sexuality of women are not universal and differ by age, race, ethnicity, and religion. Consequently, sexual harassment cases may not be solely based on gender discrimination and can only be understood by recognizing the multilayered aspects.

Avoiding essentialism involved being inclusive and understanding the complexity of oppression, as well as the privileges that social positions have at certain times and in certain contexts. In analyzing *Degraffenreid v. General Motors*, Kimberlé Crenshaw (1991) described the need for an intersectional approach. White women were hired in the front office, and industrial jobs hired black men. However, no black women were hired in either the front office or industrial jobs. The court found that gender discrimination did not occur because women were hired in the front office and race discrimination did not occur because blacks were hired in industrial jobs. Since the court defined race and gender discrimination as group based and exclusive rather than multifaceted, black women were unable to make a case for either gender or race discrimination. As a result, Crenshaw developed the metaphor of intersectionality to capture analyses that incorporate race, class, and gender. Focusing on power relations, Patricia Hill Collins (1993) introduced the metaphor of interlocking oppressions to highlight the link to structural relations of domination. Other concepts used to capture the complexity of inequality are the matrix of domination (Collins 1990; Baca Zinn and Dill 1994), multiple consciousness (King 1988), interlocking systems of oppression and privilege (Collins 1993), "integrative" (Glenn 1999), race, class, and gender (Pascal 2007), and complex inequality (McCall 2001). Intersectionality aims to address the complexity of social positions as lived experiences rather than static, one-dimensional social conditions. The fluidity of social positions reflects the significance of time and context in analyzing oppression and privilege (King 1988).

Using an inclusive framework for examining social inequalities constantly moves scholars toward identifying additional axes of domination, such as citizenship, age, sexuality, and disability (Glenn 1999; Razack 1998). We might think of intersectionality analysis as akin to working with a Rubik's cube. By turning the axis, we see distinct social locations depending on which position the block is moved to in relationship to the other blocks. After examining a social position as a lived experience (Collins 2000; Jordan-Zachary 2007), the next step is to understand the connection to interlocking oppressions of racism, patriarchy, and capitalism (Collins 2000; Smith 1987; Acker 2006).

KEY FINDINGS

Researchers recognized that individual experiences are concrete and that there are real consequences in the form of privilege and oppression. Race, class, and gender are not static but fluid social positions that take on unique forms of privileges and oppressions in various contexts and in the presence of different social identities. A variety of identities shape and influence social positions, but all are linked to race, class, and gender. Both social and political processes maintain, reinforce, or modify consequences. This is further enhanced by having these processes embedded in the everyday practices of social institutions, such as the law, media, economy, and schools. Structures of power are organized around intersections of race, class, and gender. No single dimension of the axis of domination either captures social reality as experienced by everyone or completely accounts for social inequality. The type of oppression identified may fall under one or more of the following rubrics: exploitation, marginalization, powerlessness, cultural imperialism, or violence (Young 1990). Privilege and oppression are gained or lost in social situations, social institutions, and social structures. Gains or losses in privilege depend on which axis is most salient—race, class, or gender—in a specific context. While race, class, and gender are experienced simultaneously, all three are not necessarily salient in each situation, encounter, or institution.

Rather than essentializing race, class, and gender, intersectional analysis identifies the distinct features in overlapping social positions. Intersectionality avoids an essentialist perspective and does not perceive identities as stable, homogeneous, and undifferentiated. White middle-class feminists identified the home and family as women's work and a universal experience; however, not all women experience care work as unpaid labor or gaining employment outside the home as liberating. A major criticism of essentialism is that the perspective characterizes other cultures as inferior or backward and assumes an evolutionary social process (Narayan 1998; Goodhard 2003).

Intersectionality uses a similar conceptualization as standpoint theory in locating groups' and individuals' position of subordination and/or privilege. Emphasis on lived experiences becomes central in understanding "the relations of ruling" (Smith 1987), as well as moving beyond abstract concepts and understanding real and complex social positions. Identifying the process of power and privilege in social institutions and social interaction is central to understanding how whiteness, maleness, heterosexuality, and middle- and upper-class status are normalized in everyday activities. Recognizing everyday practices that reinforce, maintain, and reproduce privileges based on race, class, and gender illuminates the link between the micro and macro structures. "The form of discrimination experienced by Black women is not related to some 'immutable' characteristic(s) inherent in Black women (skin color for example), but rather, it is a form of discrimination arising because of society's stereotyping of black women, its historical treatment of them" (Aylward 2010, 17). Self-ascriptions are less significant as socially designated labels in understanding processes of subordination and domination (Hulko 2009).

Oppression and privilege are systems that operate in tandem with racism, patriarchy, and capitalism, which mutually reinform each other. Understanding how racism, patriarchy, and capitalism are systems of privilege and oppression that operate in tandem is central to intersectionality.

KEY METHODS

Having an interdisciplinary history that challenged previous scientific knowledge as failing to incorporate race, class, and gender, the field rejects traditional empirical methodology accepted within mainstream sociology. Consequently, a major social science criticism is the emphasis on theorizing lived experiences previously invisible in the prototypes of their respective identity groups (Purdie-Vaughs and Eiback 2008) and the absence of a clearly defined empirical methodology (Nash 2008).

The weakness of intersectionality becomes more obvious when it is applied to empirical analysis: its implications for empirical analysis are, on the one hand, a seemingly insurmountable complexity and, on the other, a fixed notion of differences. This is because the list of differences is endless or even seemingly indefinite. It is impossible to take into account all the differences that are significant at any given moment (Ludvig 2006, 246).

Intersectionality cannot be understood or explained by using an "add-on" approach. The black lesbian experience is not "racism + sexism + homophobia." Instead, an intersectional framework recognizes that various combinations of identities produce substantively distinct experiences. "The facts of identity are 'not additive,' but instead 'indivisible,' operating simultaneously in people's daily experiences" (Levit 2002, 230). Therefore, additional identities are not treated as an accumulated burden or compounded discrimination but recognized as a unique experience produced as a result of various combinations of burdens and discriminations.

Feminist researchers working from an interdisciplinary perspective have primarily used humanistic methodological approaches to avoid the problems arising in past empirical quantitative methodology. They advocate for value-free research, recognizing that all research is influenced by the researcher's questions, conceptual frameworks, and selected methods for collecting and analyzing data. Feminists advocate for socially engaged research in analyzing the intersectionality of race, class, gender, and other structural features. In an effort to avoid essentialism, feminists collect and analyze data about lived experiences. "Everyday life" provides the means to contextualize discrimination and social inequality. In an effort to avoid misrepresenting different cultures, participatory action research is frequently incorporated into the methodology (Harding and Norberg 2005). Recent quantitative research has started to pave the way for new methods for intersectional analyses (Landry 2007).

INTERSECTIONALITY'S CONTRIBUTIONS TO A HUMAN RIGHTS PARADIGM

Intersectionality is fairly absent in human rights with the exception of human rights for women. In response to the criticism that gender is not included, the UN human rights leadership committed to a gender-sensitive perspective, and gender mainstreaming became an accepted practice (UN 2000, 2001, 2009; Riley 2004).

This approach called for considering the implications for women and men in all actions, legislation, policy, and programs. For many human rights organizations already working closely with women, the gender-sensitive mandate was interpreted as a call to recognize gender discrimination as impacting other social identities, such as race, class, skin color, age, ethnicity, religion, language, ancestry, sexual orientation, culture, geographic location, and status as citizen, refugee, or migrant (Satterthwaite 2005). Intersectionality is not a one- or two-dimensional approach that privileges certain conditions and denies the existence of others. This interpretation requires a concerted effort to avoid homogeneity of identity or experience by recognizing patterns of "domination and resistance along geopolitical and geoeconomic lines" (Reilly 2004, 83). More recently, time and context have been added to the list of significant features in comprehending interlocking oppressions (Hulko 2009). Intersectionality functions to highlight the way that certain rights are relegated to the margins, particularly when traditional analysis is used and individuals' identities are fragmented into separate categories.

Several human rights documents incorporate an intersectional analysis in articulating a human rights platform. For instance, Point 69 of the declaration of the World Conference against Racism, Racial Discrimination, Xenophobia, and Related Intolerance states,

> We are convinced that racism, racial discrimination, xenophobia and related intolerance reveal themselves in a differentiated manner for women and girls, and can be among the factors leading to a deterioration in their living conditions, poverty, violence, multiple forms of discrimination, and the limitation or denial of their human rights. We recognize the need to integrate a gender perspective into relevant policies, strategies and programmes of action against racism, racial discrimination, xenophobia and related intolerance in order to address multiple forms of discrimination. (2001, 13)

The Committee on the Elimination of Racial Discrimination, General Recommendation 25, Gender Related Dimensions of Racial Discrimination, states,

> The Committee notes that racial discrimination does not always affect women and men equally or in the same way. There are circumstances in which racial discrimination only or primarily affects women, or affects women in a different way, or to a different degree than men. Such racial discrimination will often escape detection if there is no explicit recognition or acknowledgment of the different life experiences of women and men, in areas of both public and private life. (2000)

One of the strongest statements advocating intersectionality in human rights is made by the Association for Women's Rights in Development:

> As a theoretical paradigm, intersectionality allows us to understand oppression, privilege and human rights globally. It helps us to build arguments for substantive equality from women's histories and community case studies (that

is, women writing/speaking from their experiences of specific, interesecting identities) by extracting theoretical statements and overarching principles. This allows us to see that the claims women are making for their equal rights are not merely an instance of a self-interested group promoting its own interests, but instead fundamental to achieving the promise of human rights for all. Interesectionality, therefore, is a tool for building a global culture of human rights from the grassroots to the global level. (Symington 2004, 3)

The Ontario Human Rights Commission refers to an intersectional approach to discrimination as a "contextualized approach":

An intersectional approach takes into account the historical, social and political context and recognizes the unique experience of the individual based on the intersection of all relevant grounds." Applying a contextual analysis involves examining "the discriminatory stereotypes; the purpose of the legislation, regulation or policy; the nature of and or situation of the individual at issue, and the social, political and legal history of the person's treatment in society. (2001, 3)

Incorporating intersectionality into human rights highlights the significance of social, political, and historical context; makes multiple marginalizations visible; and establishes programs and policies that treat social positions as fluid identities operating simultaneously.

Ethnographic research methodology dominates intersectional research and is perceived by many human rights scholars as the most useful tool for obtaining data, particularly in collecting descriptive data. For instance, in her work on women migrant workers, Margaret Satterthwaite advocates ethnography to capture "women's own 'sense of entitlement' concerning their lives, bodies, and futures" (2005, 65) rather than the state's interests. Furthermore, she argues that "human rights advocates could then use an intersectional approach to formulate claims anchored within existing rights standards but which respond to the multiple forms of discrimination making up the limits on women's lives. Moving such claims to the center of advocacy efforts would honor the agency of the women migrant workers whose experiences have so far been described and analyzed only through existing legal norms" (Satterthwaite 2005, 65).

Intersectionality is a recognized tool and conceptual framework for developing advocacy programs and human rights policy because the approach emphasizes the need to identify multiple types of discriminations and to understand how different social locations shape one's access to rights and opportunities. Intersectionality provides an approach for addressing central questions of universalism versus cultural particularism, human nature, and the nature of rationality, to name a few. NGOs advocating for an intersectional approach recognize that narrowly defined laws and human rights statements can only address a single form of discrimination and are not contextualized to address the various economic, social, political, and cultural lived experiences. The approach of understanding antisubordination and privilege involves a participative, dialogic progress engaged in (re)interpretation and (re)definition that is grounded in concrete concerns defined by women's lived experiences (Reilly 2004). Using intersectionality to identify and link organizational power may assist in developing new organizational forms that reduce existing obstacles to human rights and expand our understanding of power dynamics and social reproduction of inequality. Experience has demonstrated that added protection for marginalized groups does not affect the rights of the majority but brings issues facing otherwise isolated groups to the forefront of the global rights agenda.

RESITUATING INTERSECTIONALITY WITHIN A HUMAN RIGHTS PARADIGM

A major challenge of intersectionality is moving beyond the abstract to concrete lived experiences. Too often intersectionality becomes viewed only as a metaphor rather than as lived experience. Identity categories and various concepts such as axis of domination, interlocking oppression, and even intersectionality itself can become blinders to recognizing and analyzing emerging themes. A human rights paradigm may be useful in grounding intersectionality in real issues and problems and assist in further developing an intersectionality-type analysis that includes both the micro and macro. While confusion still arises in the literature over distinctions between identities, social position, intersectionality, and interlocking oppressions, there is growing agreement that there is a distinction between identity categories (race and gender), processes (racialization and gendering), and systems of oppression (racism, patriarchy, and capitalism) (Dhamoon 2010; Hulko 2009). A general consensus exists that there is a "systemic interplay of patriarchal, capitalist, and racist power relations" and a need for intersectionality as "a commitment to cross-boundaries dialogue, networking, and social criticism" (Reilly 2007, 184). Indivisible and interdependent tools are used to facilitate an intersectional analysis in human rights and assist in antiessentialist understanding of the self as complex and dynamic (Crooms 1997). These understandings of intersectionality offer clarity to its use in the field of race, class, and gender.

Several human right scholars have criticized intersectionality as including an endless number of social categories and conflating the structural differences between race, class, and gender (i.e., Butler 1990, 182–183). Others argue that specific historical situations create different social divisions that are meaningful and position groups along economic, political, and social hierarchies. In the case of human rights, the focus of analysis needs to identify the points of intersection for political struggle (Yuval-Davis 2006a). The reflective process is "integral to contesting false universalization and neo-imperialist manifestations of supposedly cosmopolitan values" (Reilly 2004, 86). As Johanna Bond iterates,

> Intersectional analysis provides a vehicle for recognizing all the relevant human rights that are violated in given situation along multiple axes of oppression, rather than merely those rights violations that stem from a singular approach to human rights that focuses on racism or sexism to the exclusion of other identity categories. By recognizing all relevant human rights in a given situation and the multiple systems of oppression that lead to rights violations, qualified universalism actually promotes the concept of "universal" human rights.

> International intersectionality provides a more complete picture and analysis
> of human rights, one that ultimately leads to a more complete or "universal"
> recognition of human rights. (2003, 156)

Human rights activists recognize both the strength of and the challenges posed by developing a platform based on intersectional analysis.

Critics of intersectional analysis argue that there is an overemphasis on victimization and little if any attention paid to acts of resistance. This is particularly a problem in constructing the "third world" victim because this image is frequently used to justify "imperialist interventions" (Kapur 2002, 2). Focusing on how race, gender, and class interact to create a particular form of discrimination and oppression turns attention to institutional and procedural practices rather than the characteristics of certain groups. Instead of compartmentalizing types of discrimination, intersectionality recognizes that "individuals experience the complex interplay of multiple systems of oppression operating simultaneously in the world" (Bond 2003, 77). This approach empowers instead of reinscribes victimhood, which is significant in rethinking human rights law and policies. Here the questions are not simply framed to understand individual or group oppression; rather, researchers pose questions from the standpoint of organizations in an attempt to understand abuses of organizational power. Margaret Satterthwaite argues that "shifting the focus from only articulating forms of discrimination to also identifying protections" will "uncover human rights norms that already exist, and which could be called upon to fight the subordinating practices made clear through intersectional descriptions of violations" (2005, 12).

Resituating intersectionality within a human rights paradigm pushes the methodological approach to analyze social issues more fully to identify convergences that can be used as effective interventions and that will advocate more inclusive coalition building among groups. Antisubordination analysis redirects efforts to highlight only differences and begins to address questions concerning the ways that individuals and groups are not subordinated by conditions or made dependent. Most intersectionality approaches, including antiracism, aim for the lowest denominator of "tolerance" rather than equal respect and dignity for all. Focusing on the end product of engaging in aid and human rights work may be extremely useful in developing a more clearly defined intersectionality methodology (Yuval-Davis 2006b). Human rights advocates of an intersectional approach strongly recommend moving beyond merely theorizing and applying scholarship to human rights problems (Bond 2003).

LOOKING FORWARD: IDENTIFYING NEW QUESTIONS AND NEW POSSIBILITIES FOR BOTH THE AREA AND HUMAN RIGHTS REALIZATIONS

In analyzing the contributions of international intersectionality to understanding and advocating human rights for women, Bond (2003) points to the need for all laws and policies to embrace intersectionality. The campaign to mainstream gender in human rights laws resulted in an add-on approach that made sure women were included. For many issues not directly identified as gender-specific problems, gender mainstreaming became a "gender-plus" analysis. However, the goal of an international intersectionality approach requires rethinking human problems by considering the salient social categories impacting people's lives in specific situations, which may be age, sexuality, caste, religion, or citizenship. This approach needs to be used to address all populations—migrants, prisoners, refugees, and children. The lack of intersectonality is not only found at the United Nations but common among issue-specific NGOs. If one plays a crucial role as watchdog in representing human rights violations internationally, incorporating an intersectionality approach is central as a human rights practice. Bond notes the inconsistent use of intersectionality in Human Rights Watch (HRW) reports on women. For example, in 1995 HRW produced a report on violence against women in South Africa that identified the role of apartheid in women's decision not to report domestic violence and risk further violence by the state. However, in the case of US prisons, "the report failed to explore the impact of intersecting human rights violations based both on gender and sexual orientation or, in some cases, on race, gender, and sexual orientation" (Bond 2003, 151). As a matter of practice, according to Bond, NGOs need to ask, "How does this type of violation affect different categories of people along multiple axes of oppression, including *inter alia* race, class, ethnicity, gender, religion, and sexual orientation?" (2003, 152). Only through an acceptance of intersectionality in all human rights issues can women or any other group be completely served by laws, policies, and programs.

In my own research, intersectionality is central in framing circumstances Latinos face in an era of nativist anti-immigrant sentiment. Without a recognition of the racialized notions of citizenship and mixed-status families, the range of human rights violations that Latino communities experience during immigration raids and at the hands of law enforcement are minimized. Human rights violations result from militarization of the border, militarized tactics used in immigration raids, indefinite detention of minors and others migrating to the United States, policies that result in migrants' deaths, the terrorizing of low-income Latino communities, conducting raids and using law-enforcement practices without regard for human life or minors' safety, and denial of public services on the basis of race and ethnicity (Romero 2006, 2011).

Bringing human rights and intersectionality together moves us forward in developing an adequate set of universal human rights principles, rights, practices, and methods. Working together by reconceptualizing discourses is a step toward recognizing the legitimacy of more than one agenda and developing an integrated approach that values human dignity as universal. As researchers, we need to move our analysis beyond naming intersections and toward identifying processes for the eradication of discrimination and celebration of diversity. Similarly, researchers and human rights activists can begin to observe ways "in which individuals and communities are engaged in active resistance" (Bond 2003, 159).

CHAPTER NINE

SEXUALITIES

Mary Bernstein

This chapter addresses two themes in the sociology of sexualities that are relevant to the study of human rights. First, the sociology of sexualities challenges the assumption that sexuality is "essentialist," a property of individuals, something that has its own truth and exists outside social forces, that is somehow presocial and biologically driven or perhaps divinely ordained. In contrast, sexuality is socially constructed. As Gayle Rubin explains, "Desires are not preexisting biological entities, but rather ... they are constituted in the course of historically specific social practices" (1984, 276). Second, sociologists of sexualities theorize the ways in which sexuality serves as an axis of domination and is part of every major social institution. As a result of studying how sexuality both influences and is influenced by major institutions, theorists reconceptualize the concept of power to understand how culture and discourse are constitutive of dominant institutions and produce new forms of knowledge and power that organize and regulate sexuality and provide sites of resistance. Thus, how we understand sexuality, what we define as normal or abnormal, and the types of sexual identities that exist in a given society are influenced by culture and discourse, institutions, and power. Understanding sexuality as an axis of domination and a site of resistance thus expands our study of human rights struggles.

THE SOCIOLOGY OF SEXUALITIES

CHALLENGING ESSENTIALISM: THE BODY, GENDER, AND SEXUALITY

Sociologists of sexualities challenge essentialism by illustrating that our very understandings of what constitutes male and female bodies are socially constructed. Notions of what bodies should look like and the extent to which they should experience pleasure are used to justify regulating and disciplining them. Scholars also find that gender and age structure expectations about what is appropriate sexual activity.

THE BODY

Control over appropriate sexuality is linked to what Ponse termed "the principle of consistency" (1978)—that is, a view that biological sex (genes, genitals, hormones, secondary sex characteristics) is linked to gender (masculinity or femininity) and sexual orientation (whether one is attracted to men or women) in a straightforward manner, so that one is biologically male, masculine, and attracted to women or female, feminine, and attracted to men. Yet, in practice, these do not always align easily, as in the case of gay men, lesbians, bisexuals, and transgender people. Furthermore, control over this alignment starts from birth with the policing of genitals. In the early twentieth century, male circumcision was seen as a way to reduce the male sexual drive. Yet others see circumcision as a means to enhance, rather than reduce, male sexual pleasure (Ross 2009). Jewish rites of male circumcision are tied to men's covenant with god—a patriarchal rite from which women are excluded (Kimmel 2001). In short, views of appropriate genitals for men are bound to views of masculinity, male sexuality, and whether or not sexual pleasure is viewed as problematic, in need of reining in, or in need of enhancement.

Intersexed people who have "ambiguous genitals" are regulated as infants through surgical procedures designed to make their genitals appear to be either male or female (often accompanied later by hormonal treatment). Rather than chromosomes, whether or not a penis is big enough for sexual intercourse determines whether the child is surgically altered. Parents are instructed to socialize their child into the gender that matches the surgically altered genitals. Thus, appropriate views of sexuality and gender are used to justify medically unnecessary surgery on infants in order to support society's sex/gender system (Fausto-Sterling 2000a; Kessler 1990; Preeves 2003).

The desire to control adult sexuality and police gender is also apparent in cultures that practice female genital mutilation. These cultures place a strong value on virginity at marriage and do not believe in a woman's right to sexual agency or sexual pleasure. Thus, with removal of the clitoris and, in some places, the practice of infibulation, girls' bodies are irrevocably altered in ways that ensure they remain virgins and cannot enjoy sexual pleasure as adults (Hosken 1993). While debates over men's bodies concern enhancing male pleasure and sometimes reducing (but never eliminating) it, the assumption is that men will and should enjoy sexuality. Groups simply differ on how best to achieve this goal.

Whereas intersex infants are subjected to surgery without their consent, transgender people who wish to transition surgically are only allowed to do so after receiving a mental-illness diagnosis of gender identity disorder. Although this diagnosis, which is influential globally (GID Reform Advocates 2008), is useful for those whose insurance will pay for hormones and sex-reassignment surgery, others argue that the diagnosis contributes to societal stigma and harms the quest for legal rights and protection. Some transgender activists argue for reform of the diagnosis, facilitating access to surgery and hormones. Others avoid the issue of insurance coverage, advocating removal of the diagnosis coupled with acceptance of "genderqueer" individuals whose gender and physical body may not line up (Burke 2010).

Gender

Gendered expectations about sexuality result in a double standard for sexual behavior. Studies of US teenagers illustrate that girls' reputations suffer more damage than boys' due to their having sex and that girls are more likely to be condemned and considered "easy" for carrying a condom than boys are (Hynie and Lydon 1995; Levine 2002; Vanwesenbeeck 1997). In Mexico, González-López (2005) finds that a young woman's virginity provides her with a "capital feminino" that can be exchanged for social status for the family. Research in the United States also finds gendered differences in negotiations around sex. Boys initiate sex far more often than girls. As a result, the responsibility for saying no to sex falls disproportionately on girls. Beneke (1983) argues that this pattern of behavior, where boys are responsible for initiating sex and escalating sexual encounters, results in the development of a rape-like mentality among boys and men, so that boys learn not to listen when girls say no. Both boys and girls believe that a girl risks the loss of her relationship if she refuses to have sex with her boyfriend (Gavey, McPhillips, and Doherty 2001). In addition, boys are far less likely to raise the issue of safer sex than girls are (Holland et al. 1998; Kaiser Family Foundation 2002).

In explaining gendered differences in sexuality, sociologists challenge essentialist explanations. Essentialist models drawing on hormonal studies, brain studies, and sociobiology are methodologically flawed (Schwartz and Rutter 1998; Fausto-Sterling 2000b). Essentialist arguments also make analogies from animal behavior to explain human behavior such as violence, rape, and male dominance. But animals engage in a wide variety of sexual and social behavior, including homosexual behavior, anal and oral sex, and promiscuous sex (Bagemihl 2000), making it problematic to infer what does or does not constitute "normal" sexual behavior in humans. Furthermore, human behavior is based more on learning than on instinct, casting doubt on such analogies.

Instead, sociologists of sexualities posit a combination of factors to account for gender differences in sexuality. For example, fewer women masturbate than men because of the cultural messages they get about what is appropriate sexually for women. As a result, they may not know their bodies. Even for women who know what pleases them sexually, communication between partners may be poor, leading to less satisfaction for women (Schwartz and Rutter 1998). The sexual double standard inhibits women from developing their full sexual potential. Socioeconomic conditions and rural/urban differences also explain sexualized gender inequality (González-López 2005).

Sexualities scholars also study heterosexuality as a social institution that has its own rules and norms that pattern behavior. Heterosexuality as an institution disadvantages heterosexual women, lesbians, and gay men. Ingraham (2008) argues that a romanticized view of heterosexuality symbolized by the big white wedding masks the gendered inequality that takes place within marriage. Others contend that heterosexuality is not only an institution but compulsory. Rich's (1980) concept of compulsory heterosexuality illustrates the ways in which men control female sexuality through physical force, economic inequality, punishment for lesbian sexuality, strictures against masturbation, and stronger punishments for female adultery than for male adultery, which makes women more financially dependent on men, leading women to marry for physical and financial protection (Eisenstein 1983).

SEXUALITY AS AN AXIS OF DOMINATION

Sexualities scholars study the ways in which sexuality is entwined with larger systems of domination. In this section, I examine heteronormativity—that is, "the institutions, structures of understanding and practical orientations that make heterosexuality seem not only coherent—that is, organized as a sexuality—but also privileged" (Berlant and Warner 1998, 548)—through a discussion of sexual orientation, sex education, sexual health, and sex work. I also discuss how colonialism and racial and ethnic inequality are justified through understandings of appropriate (hetero)sexuality and gender.

Sexual Orientation

Psychologists dominate the study of homophobia (Adam 1998), defining it as an irrational fear of lesbians and gay men. These studies find that those who are older, less educated, single, or male tend to be more homophobic than those who are younger, more educated, married, or female (Britton 1990; Yang 1998). The few studies that examine race suggest that African Americans are more homophobic than white Americans (Herek and Capitanio 1996), though that may be related to higher levels of religiosity among African Americans (Egan and Sherrill 2009). Bernstein, Kostelac, and Gaarder (2003) find that African Americans are typically more supportive of civil liberties for lesbians and gay men than are white Americans. Explanations for these relationships stress that lesbians and gay men may threaten one's psychological sense of self in terms of sexuality, masculinity, and group identity. These approaches also stress the importance of contact with lesbians and gay men as a factor that minimizes prejudice and maximizes intergroup cooperation (Herek and Glunt 1993; Jordan 1997; Yang 1998).

Recent sociological approaches (Bernstein and Kostelac 2002; Bernstein, Kostelac, and Gaarder 2003; Bernstein 2004) pay closer attention to the interplay between the social construction of minorities and the role that organized groups play in fostering those constructions. Gay-rights opponents express status concerns when faced with lesbian and gay demands for equality. Dynamic interactions between diverse groups that have a stake in maintaining homophobia influence a group's sense of its proper position. From the group-position perspective, certain religions and social movements based on particular religious interpretations may indicate a commitment to group status based on self-interest as much as on psychological factors.

Sexuality scholars also examine the ways in which LGBT people of color may experience "secondary marginalization" (Cohen 1999) within the broader LGBT movement as well as within communities of color (Bennett and Battle 2001; Takagi 1994). This research is particularly important in examining the complex ways in which race, class, culture, and sexual identity influence the experience of sexuality, negotiations around sexuality, and family relations (Bernstein and Reimann 2001; Asencio 2009; Battle 2009).

Sexuality scholars also debate whether social movement strategies, identities, and goals challenge or support heteronormativity. For example, scholars question the value of the institution of marriage and debate the wisdom of pursuing same-sex marriage as a goal of the LGBT movement (Walters 2001; Warner 2000). For lesbian and gay rights activists, extending the right to marry to same-sex couples would simply give them the same rights and legitimacy as different-sex couples. In contrast, queer activists view extending the right to marry to same-sex couples as expanding current conceptions of what is normal to include same-sex married couples. Marriage equality would not ultimately challenge the very notions of normality that define LGBT people as other and would offer no support to people with nonnormative family structures.

Historical research on the emergence of the categories "lesbian," "gay," and "bisexual" finds that these categories, which are supposed to represent fixed sexual identities, are historically and culturally specific ways of organizing erotic desire and behavior. Even defining people in terms of sexual identity is a recent phenomenon (Katz 2007; Foucault 1978). Research on non-Western cultures finds that there are multiple ways of organizing same-sex desire and gender/transgender behavior. For example, sexual relations may be differentiated by biological sex, gender, and age (Herdt 1994, 1997; Drucker 2000). Western sexual and gender categories cannot be mapped onto non-Western configurations, such as the *aravani* or *hijras* of India (Herdt 1994; Waites 2009) or the *nahdle* of the Navajo/Dine culture, who are considered to belong to a third gender.

Studies of LGBT movements in the developing world show that homosexuality is often constructed as "Western," something that is not indigenous but is instead a colonial imposition (Adam, Duyvendak, and Krouwel 1999). These arguments are used as a way to deny basic human rights protection for intimate sexual behavior and other rights based on sexual orientation and point to the significance of discourse, culture, and colonialism for explaining inequality based on sexual orientation.

Sex Education and Sexual Health

In the United States, heteronormativity structures contemporary sex-education programs and research on sexual health. Rather than addressing how to empower women within sexual relations, research on sexual health and behavior focuses on sexuality as a social problem. As a result, such research centers on explaining what contributes to unwed motherhood, sexually transmitted infections (STIs), and adolescent sexuality with its presumed negative consequences, such as pregnancy, disease, and poor mental health. This is also reflected in battles over sex education (Irvine 2002; Luker 2006).

The United States has supported abstinence-only sex education since 1981. According to SIECUS (2010), "Moreover, many abstinence-only-until-marriage programs rely on fear, shame, and guilt to try to control young people's sexual behavior. These programs include negative messages about sexuality, distort information about condoms and STDs, and promote biases based on gender, sexual orientation, marriage, family structure, and pregnancy options." Sexualities research has shown consistently that abstinence-only education is ineffective in changing rates of vaginal intercourse or number of sexual partners (Underhill, Montgomery, and Operario 2007). In contrast, comprehensive sex-education programs present information on methods of birth control and discuss STIs, but these programs nonetheless present sexuality in terms of fear of pregnancy and risk of diseases. Ignored are discussions of how to empower girls around sexuality to say both no and yes. In other words, even comprehensive sex education fails to acknowledge that sexuality can be pleasurable, operating instead from the perspective of risk and fear. More recent work has focused on understanding "sexual subjectivity" (Horne and Zimmer-Gembeck 2005)—that is, on girls and women as sexual agents who can experience entitlement to sexual desire and pleasure (Tolman 1994; Martin 1996). In 2010, the United States dedicated money for comprehensive sexuality education. States may also choose to apply for funding for abstinence-only-until-marriage programs (SIECUS 2010).

The Sex Industry

Debates over the sex industry generally rest on the view that sex workers are either victims of male domination or are romanticized as the "happy hooker" (Weitzer 2000). Sociologists contend that neither view is correct. Instead, scholars examine the extent to which sex workers have agency in constructing their lives and work choices. By viewing sex work as an occupation, one can examine differences in terms of social status (e.g., street versus indoor prostitution), control over working conditions (e.g., the ability to choose or refuse clients, access to resources for safety and protection, independence or dependence on managers or pimps, and the ability to leave sex work), and experiences at work (prevalence of rape and assault and the risk of STIs) (Weitzer 2000). While some women may have more control over their working conditions in the sex industry, others may have no control, as in women who are victims of "sex trafficking," "a modern-day form of slavery in which a commercial sex act is induced by force, fraud, or coercion, or in which the person induced to perform such an act is under the age of 18 years" (US Department of Health and Human Services 2010).

Race, Ethnicity, and Sexuality

Sociologists of sexualities argue that sexuality is intimately linked to racialized systems of domination. For example, cross dressing and homosexual relations were commonplace among many indigenous peoples in the Americas (Terl 2000). European colonizers exported their views on such practices to the Americas as they worked to eradicate sodomy among indigenous people through terror and extermination. Viewed as an offense to their Christian god, the colonizers embarked on a campaign of mass destruction and appropriation of Native land, carried out partially in the name of abolishing sin (Fone 2000).

Slavery in the United States depended on sexualized and racialized stereotypes that provided whites with a convenient means of justifying exploitation. For example, stereotypes that Africans were overly sexual provided white slaveholders with a way to justify the rape of black women. Not only did this constitute sexual exploitation, but the children born of these rapes were considered slaves, thus providing an economic benefit to the slaveholder. This became particularly important economically after the transatlantic slave trade was abolished and reproduction became the only way to produce new slaves. Other racialized sexual stereotypes served to keep African and African American men in line. Viewing African and African American men as overly sexual and predatory justified lynching black men who even looked at a white woman or were simply accused of doing so. These stereotypes also served to keep white women afraid and dependent on white men for protection (Dowd 1993). Collins describes a series of sexual stereotypes of black women rooted in slavery that have "been essential to the political economy of domination fostering Black women's oppression" (2000, 67). Other sexual stereotypes linked to ethnicity are an integral part of nationalist discourse, colonization, sex tourism, and globalization (Nagel 2003).

Scholars of sexuality find that sexuality is linked to immigration. For example, Cantú (2009) examines why Mexican men who have sex with men (MSM) immigrate to the United States. Most research on immigration assumes that people immigrate for financial reasons but ignores the ways in which socioeconomic structures are linked to inequalities like sexuality, race, and gender. Men who have sex with men are marginalized and suffer discrimination and prejudice, which constrains their socioeconomic opportunities. MSMs who do not create a heteronormative family unit as an adult are subject to more discrimination. And thus, for some MSMs, sexuality contributes to a lack of financial opportunities, which pushes them to immigrate.

STUDYING SEXUALITIES

The early study of sexualities was dominated by psychiatrists using the case-study approach, which was limited by not having control groups of people in nonclinical settings. Alfred Kinsey was the first researcher to conduct sexuality research on a large scale. However, his study did not employ random sampling techniques, likely skewing his findings (Kinsey, Pomeroy, and Martin 1948). In the mid-1950s, William Masters and Virginia Johnson conducted a major study of sexual physiology to measure exactly what human bodies do during sexual encounters. However, they limited their study to volunteers who were orgasmic and had experience masturbating and ignored the meaning of sexuality to the participants. The result is that sexual dysfunction, including diagnosis in the American Psychiatric Association's *Diagnostic and Statistical Manual of Mental Disorders*, is related to the failure of body parts to work appropriately. This has led to a view of sexuality that is not representative of female experience and ignores emotional attachment, which far more women than men define as key to their sexual satisfaction (Tiefer 2004).

Laumann et al. (2000) launched the National Health and Social Life (NHSL) Survey in the 1990s using a national random sample of adults and face-to-face interviews. Their study found Americans to be rather conservative in terms of sex. However, the accuracy of these findings has been questioned, based on the idea that respondents may "lie, or fudge, or misremember, or leave things out" and the fact that the study was done at a point in the AIDS scare where people were afraid that sex with the wrong partner could kill them (Adelson 2001, 63).

Large-scale, quantitative sociological research on adolescent sexuality emerged in a conservative context with public concern over teen pregnancy, the spread of STIs, and the reproduction of those deemed "undeserving," namely, the poor, immigrants, and racial minorities. For example, early incarnations of the National Longitudinal Study of Adolescent Health (Add Health) assumed that race and class differences, as well as biological factors such as hormones, accounted for differences in sexuality. Recent versions of Add Health focus on explaining teen sexual activity by looking at the impact of peers, family, religion, community, and schools (Cavanagh 2007; Wilkinson and Pearson 2009; Harding 2007; Bearman and Bruckner 2001). While important, these studies lack attention to the meaning of sexual activity and assume a framework of sexuality as harm. Some recent quantitative work, in contrast, has examined positive effects of sexuality as well as what contributes to female sexual empowerment (Horne and Zimmer-Gembeck 2005).

Sexuality research is difficult to fund, and it is always political (DiMauro 1995; Ericksen and Steffen 2001). The US government has canceled funding for many sexuality studies, including the NHSL survey, which was ultimately funded by private donors. There is a fear that simply asking people about sexual behavior or reporting on what others do will lead them to engage in those sexual acts and that findings will challenge some people's moral and religious views (Adelson 2001).

Qualitative research on sexuality typically focuses on the meaning of sexual activity, sexual development, and experience (Diamond 2006). Ethnography, in-depth interviews, discourse, and content analysis are also important staples of sexuality scholarship. These methods provide insight into the symbolic meaning that sexual activity may hold for respondents and may uncover new sexual scripts (Bogle 2008) that develop in response to broader demographic and cultural trends. Many of these works question the universality of the categories that are used in the contemporary West to define gender and sexual orientation (Valentine 2007; Katz 2007). One of the most important implications of this work is that care must be paid when utilizing the categories "sexual orientation" and "gender identity" in international human rights advocacy and law.

WHAT CAN THE HUMAN RIGHTS PARADIGM LEARN FROM THE STUDY OF SEXUALITIES?

Sexualities research illustrates that the categories used to describe sexual orientation (gay, lesbian, and bisexual) and gender (male, female, transgender, gender identity) in the West are socially constructed. Scholars also illustrate that sexuality can be understood as fluid rather than fixed. While same-sex erotic behavior and attraction exist in every culture across time, how they are organized and whether they are used to define categories of persons is historically contingent (Rupp 2009; Greenberg 1988). Similarly, many cultures have had ways of instituting transgender behavior that differs from Western models (Kulick 1998). Therefore, human rights scholars and activists can work to identify indigenous forms of same-sex erotic behavior in order to sever the link that conservatives often make between "being gay" and the imperialism and excesses of Western bourgeois culture. As Waites (2009) points out, we must have a language to use, but care must be taken to ensure that "sexual orientation" and "gender identity" are understood in diverse ways.

Human rights activists have created a list of principles designed to protect people on the basis of sexual orientation and gender identity. The Yogyakarta Principles also outline the deleterious consequences that people suffer because of their sexual orientation or gender identity: "They include extra-judicial killings, torture and ill-treatment, sexual assault and rape, invasions of privacy, arbitrary detention, denial of employment and education opportunities, and serious discrimination in relation to the enjoyment of other human rights" (Corrêa and Muntarbhorn 2007, 6).

The sociology of sexualities also shows how practices such as female genital mutilation and surgery on intersexed children are rooted in views about appropriate genitals, bodily integrity, and sexual fulfillment. Surgeries on intersexed children and female genital mutilation often impair later sexual functioning, can curtail the ability to experience sexual pleasure, and can result in other health complications. Human rights groups opposed to male circumcision, female genital mutilation, and surgery on intersexed infants argue for children's rights to bodily integrity and to be free from unnecessary medical procedures.

Studies of sexual negotiations and sex education point human rights scholars toward understanding that strategies for preventing unwanted pregnancy and reducing the spread of STIs and HIV are linked not only to providing access to condoms, birth control, and education about safer sex but to women's becoming empowered in sexual encounters. If girls and women continue to be charged with saying no in sexual encounters, then old sexual scripts that perpetuate male dominance will linger.

The push for same-sex marriage and parental rights shows the importance of equality for those who want to enter into the institution of marriage, but the debate has also shown that the traditional family structure is not the only one deserving of state support. Human rights scholars and activists must push for recognition of a variety of family forms and policies that support the economic, emotional, and caretaking needs of all people.

WHAT HAPPENS WHEN WE CENTER THE HUMAN RIGHTS PARADIGM ON SEXUALITIES RESEARCH?

Centering the human rights paradigm pushes the sexual health literature away from focusing on models of disease and pregnancy prevention to ask more questions about sexual empowerment and control and how that is linked to basic issues of human rights and dignity. A human rights perspective should help sexuality scholars focus on how eliminating economic disparities between men and women will facilitate greater equality of power in negotiating sexual encounters.

Sociologists of sexualities need to incorporate a more global perspective on sexualities and incorporate human rights perspectives into their research. While it is important to be aware of how the goals of the LGBT movement may reinforce heteronormativity, as in the case of same-sex marriage, or reinstantiate the closet, as in the case of decriminalizing homosexuality based on a right to privacy, scholars must be aware that, according to the International Lesbian and Gay Human Rights Commission, "over 80 countries currently have sodomy laws or other legal provisions criminalizing homosexuality" (IGLHRC 2011). In such contexts, challenging heteronormativity may be neither desirable nor realistic. Obtaining basic human rights protections may be paramount.

In other ways, many sexualities scholars have already begun to link issues of sexual rights to the broader project of seeking fundamental human dignity. All too often, those who advocate rights for sex workers and those who advocate the abolition of sex work are speaking past each other, not acknowledging the variation that exists in the experience of sex workers. Chapkis (2000) offers a middle position, arguing that the best way to help women in the sex industry is by giving all women greater economic opportunities to do other types of work and by working to ensure that those who choose to be in the sex industry have control over their working conditions. So rather than take an abolitionist approach, human rights activists should work to improve conditions for all sex workers, eliminate forced sexual slavery, and increase economic opportunities for women and those who are transgendered, many of whom only turn to sex work as a means of survival. Sexuality scholars can also do much to link broader patterns of militarization to the sexual exploitation of women and global economic inequality that fosters sex tourism.

CHAPTER TEN

ANIMALS AND SOCIETY

Victoria Johnson and John Sanbonmatsu

What is the relationship between human rights and animal rights? Is the notion of human rights, as a protected domain of universal moral and legal rights, premised on the exclusion of nonhuman animals from that domain? Does the systemic exploitation and killing of other conscious beings by human beings indicate instability or incoherence in the notion of universal rights? What are the social implications of the fact that our mass killing of other animals continues to be rationalized on the basis of discourses implicated in genocide—in presumptions of biological difference and worthlessness, lack of intelligence, or simply weakness?

Although some scholars and activists have sought to distance human rights from animal rights, the two are historically and conceptually intertwined. The question of animal rights intersects the question of human rights in at least four ways. First, historically, animal rights developed at the same time as human rights and on the basis of a similar set of moral and social concerns. Second, the social institutions, ideologies, and practices that lead to the oppression and dehumanization of human beings derive in part from the structures, beliefs, and practices used by human beings to control, dominate, and kill nonhuman animals. Third, and conversely, systems of human oppression that justify the conquest of nature confound attempts to protect members of both vulnerable human groups and other species from exploitation and violence. Fourth, the notion of human rights itself rests on unexamined anthropocentric assumptions about human superiority and nonhuman inferiority based on biological difference. This chapter explores these and related questions.

WHAT IS THE SCOPE OF ANIMAL RIGHTS?

Various philosophers and critics over the centuries, among them Pythagoras, Plutarch, Montaigne, David Hume, Jeremy Bentham, Arthur Schopenhauer, Leo Tolstoy, and Henry Salt, opposed human violence and cruelty against other animals and advocated for their protection (Walters and Portness 1999; Steiner 2010). While there are premodern antecedents for the protection of other animals from human cruelty, the concept of animal rights as such is a modern notion, one closely tied to the earliest development of modern human and civil rights (West 1841). By the late eighteenth century, ethical vegetarianism had become a serious intellectual current in the British isles (Stuart 2006), and by 1822, the British parliament had enacted the first of many subsequent animal-cruelty laws (Shevelow 2008).

Despite these and other developments, however, it was not until the early 1970s, especially with the publication of Peter Singer's book defending animal interests, *Animal Liberation* (2005), that the question of animal rights as such entered popular discourse. In the 1970s, the work of analytic moral philosophers such as Singer, Tom Regan, and Mary Midgley and a handful of sympathetic legal scholars firmly established animal rights theory as a recognized subfield of contemporary moral theory (Midgley 1995). Today, the animal rights movement is a significant international social movement, and animal studies is a growing field of interdisciplinary study involving thousands of academics working in dozens of different fields.

If there is consensus among animal studies scholars, it is that the long-neglected "animal question" is one of the most important questions of the twenty-first century. Because human exploitation of animals is so deeply woven into the fabric of human cultures—with billions being killed for their flesh and skin, used in scientific laboratories, and incorporated in myriad rituals, from Islamic animal sacrifice to Thanksgiving dinner to the lamb shank bone on Jewish seder plates—the range of possible scholarly concerns is overwhelming. Scholars are now asking questions about the relationship between human and nonhuman animals that simply have not been asked before.

One implication of the existing research is that human approaches to knowledge need to be rethought in a truly fundamental way. Over the past few decades, scientific research has demonstrated far more evolutionary and ontological similarities among humans and other animals—including nonmammalian species—than had been previously thought, at least in modern times. There is no longer any clear or distinct line separating humans from nonhuman animals vis-à-vis such traditional measures of human distinction as tool use, transmission of culture, intelligence, emotion, or even language (Armstrong and Botzler 2008; Stamp Dawkins 2006; Beckoff 2002; Rogers 1998). What we think we know about ourselves as a species turns out to be grounded in deeply embedded ideologies of supremacy that justify the exploitation and killing of those who are perceived to be lacking in reason. As a result, scholars are finding it necessary to revise traditional categories of human understanding, ontology, and science. If the animal rights critique turns out to be justified—that is, if we determine that there are good reasons to reject the exploitation, killing, and domination of other sentient beings and even to proscribe such behaviors by law—then the moral, legal, and economic organization of existing human societies must be found to be deeply flawed and in need of change.

HOW DO ANIMAL RIGHTS INTERSECT WITH HUMAN RIGHTS?

The current animal rights movement derives from the same historical and cultural context as the modern human rights movement—specifically, the bourgeois democratic revolutions of the late eighteenth century that legitimated and codified the belief in natural and inalienable rights. These rights, originally secured for propertied European males, have through popular struggles over time been expanded to include (at least formally) men of color and women. Now animal rights activists and scholars seek to extend legal protections to sentient nonhuman animals—beings capable of suffering and of experiencing the world.

The human rights template has been criticized for its origins in a European Enlightenment tradition that privileges reason (Kennedy 2002). Since the 1990s, a growing number of critical theorists have attacked the very notion of human rights, suggesting that the invocation of "rights" in fact serves to obscure the social inequalities and power differentials that produce international violence and inequality (Žižek 2005). In a similar vein, self-described posthumanist scholars in animal studies have drawn on poststructuralist thought to express skepticism toward animal rights too, effectively seeing rights as an epiphenomenon of state repression. However, other scholars have sought to expand the language of rights to include other sentient beings (Regan 2004; Wise 2005; Francione 2000; Jamieson 2003).

Animal rights scholars thus draw upon the human rights template to gain legal status for nonhuman animals as "moral subjects." But human rights scholars also stand to gain from animal rights scholarship, for example, in helping them gain a better understanding of the ways in which discourses operate to exclude entire categories of subjects. The scholarship in animal studies also reveals some of the underlying contradictions within human rights theory itself. For example, current definitions of human rights have been codified through the United Nations' 1945 Universal Declaration of Human Rights proposing that human beings be granted inalienable rights due to their "reason" and "conscience." Article 1 states, "All human beings are born free and equal in dignity and rights. They are endowed with reason and conscience and should act toward one another in a spirit of brotherhood" (UN 2010).

A variety of animal rights critics, however, have argued that neither moral concern nor legal equality should be contingent upon reason or reasonableness. Peter Singer, for example, pointedly observes that criteria such as the ability to reason or to use language would place not only (some) animals, but also human babies and severely mentally disabled human beings, outside the realm of moral consideration. (We could add the mentally ill and some categories of the human elderly to Singer's list as well.) The current codified justification for human rights in the Universal Declaration of Human Rights therefore excludes most animals from the domain of universal rights and some categories of human beings as well. This problematic logic poses a particular challenge to critics who express skepticism that animals can or should have "rights" at all on grounds that rights bearers must first be capable of knowledgeably entering into a social contract with others in a rights-granting community, which other animals cannot (Cohen 1986; Scruton 2000; Nobis 2004).

Animal rights studies contribute to the analysis of human rights in other ways as well. Historically, particularly in Kantian moral theory, philosophical concern about the human mistreatment of other species was seen as a problem only insofar as sadism and violence toward other animals could lead to abuse of humans

(Regan 2004). However, if it is true, as the psychological and sociological evidence suggests, that causing harm to nonhumans paves the way for the abuse of human beings (Bierne 2009; Linzey 2009; Fitzgerald, Kalof, and Dietz 2009), the reverse may hold true as well: that is, human social hierarchies and forms of power that are anathema to universal human rights, often involving ideologies that justify the conquest over "nature," are also related to enslaving and hurting other sentient beings closely identified with them.

Some animal studies critics maintain that we can better understand the processes of capitalist exploitation and environmental destruction through the lens of animal domination. In *Animal Rights/Human Rights*, for example, David Nibert (2002) shows how the exploitation of workers and animals is mutually reinforcing within capitalist relations. Subsequent scholars have further elaborated on the coconstitution of international capital and animal industries, both at the level of material production and semiosis (Shukin 2009; Torres 2007). Meanwhile, substantial scientific and sociological literatures now address the role of meat production in the global ecological crisis. Factory farming is one of the leading causes of anthropogenic climate change (global warming) and a major polluter of freshwater resources (UNFAO 2006). The international trade in animal flesh has meanwhile led to massive deforestation in the "third world" and to the impoverishment and political oppression of rural workers in Latin America (Nibert 2009). The oppression of other animals is thus intertwined with the oppression of vulnerable human populations.

One recent branch of research has taken up the controversial parallels between human mass extermination of other animals and genocide, including the Holocaust (Patterson 2002; Derrida 2004; Coetzee 1999). Critics ask whether there is a relationship between the beliefs and practices that justify the exploitation and murder of animals and the wholesale extermination of human groups. The common reply to the question of what gives humans the right to dominate and kill billions of other animals is that other species are our inferiors. Specifically, our superiority and right to domination are justified by reference to a precategorical and unchanging "nature." When applied to human beings, however, such beliefs are recognizably fascist and provide schemas for the "animalization" of different human groups (Johnson 2011).

As we see, then, in recent decades animal rights scholarship has begun to push questions about the treatment of nonhuman animals from the philosophical margins to the center of debates about social inequalities, human rights, the origins of violence, and environmental policy. An eclectic community of activists and scholars has posed challenging questions about the relationship of animal domination to racial, gender, disability, and other modes of domination. In *The Dreaded Comparison: Human and Animal Slavery*, Marjorie Spiegel (1988) delineates some of the many overlapping ideological and cultural practices that link human domination of animals with human social domination, that is, slavery. In 1990, Carol Adams focused feminist attention on the overlapping institutional and semiotic structure of patriarchy, the domination of nature, and speciesism in *The Sexual Politics of Meat*. She and other feminist scholars have since extended this critique (Donovan and Adams 1995, 2007). Diverse cultural understandings of human/animal relationships of love and hate and the processes through which we reify formerly conscious beings as "meat" are being analyzed by scholars through new theoretical lenses that illuminate cultural contradictions within human relationships with nonhuman animals (Oliver 2009; Vialles 1994). New questions and perspectives continue to emerge.

THE ANIMAL RIGHTS/HUMAN RIGHTS DIVIDE

The human rights paradigm seems ambiguous or unstable so long as it cannot find a way to incorporate the "other" upon which it has constituted its own identity as a discourse of liberation. By definition, the discourse of human rights evokes a universal claim concerning both the nature of human beings as possessing reason and conscience and the normative juridical and civil framework that such an ontological assertion entails. However, by defining the human against the nonhuman—that is, against beings presumed not to be reasonable or not to have a conscience (or to be self-conscious), hence not to have inherent rights to be free—the discourse re-creates the very conditions of violent exclusion it would undo. The solution to this problem is therefore perhaps to be sought in a "third term" between animal and human rights, or perhaps in a new conception in which the human/animal divide is dissolved altogether. The disambiguation of "human rights" thus stands as one of the greatest challenges facing contemporary theorists.

Despite the many similarities between the animal rights cause, social movements, and human rights campaigns—for example, struggles against the exploitation and oppression of devalued beings, unjust practices of torture and mass killing, and so on—activists in other movements have largely greeted the animal rights movement with skepticism, if not outright hostility. Most of the objections stem from the perception that taking animal interests seriously would "trivialize" human rights and social justice by implicitly drawing an analogy between humans and animals. However, as John Sorenson (2011) points out, such objections, voiced with equal fervor on the political left and right of the spectrum, rest firmly on an irrational speciesist ideology whose starting premise—that other animals simply do not matter—is rooted solely in prejudice against beings perceived to be so fundamentally and biologically different from ourselves that they fall completely outside the sphere of our moral concern.

Too often critics of animal rights scholarship and activism propose a false dichotomy between human or animals rights. It seems obvious that just as the interests of human individuals and groups clash with one another, we might expect human interests to clash with nonhuman ones, particularly in the context of increasing natural resource scarcity and widening habitat destruction due to unchecked human expansion. In fact, in a small number of cases animal rights seem to be in tension with some important human ones—consider, for example, past efforts by animal rights activists to end some seal hunts and whaling by Native peoples. However, few if any scholars today believe that the vast majority of existing human practices of domination and violence toward other animals can be justified on grounds of necessity. Gary Francione rightly observes that of the myriad practices we engage in at the expense of our fellow creatures, "most of the suffering that we impose on animals is completely unnecessary *however* we interpret" the notion of necessity itself (2000, xxiv).

Like the women's movement and the gay rights movement before it, the animal rights movement has been charged with being "bourgeois" or privileged—remaining a predominantly white, middle-class, Western phenomenon. Such characterizations obscure two important points, however. First, the identity of the individuals advancing a particular moral or political claim bears no necessary relation to the underlying validity of that claim. Thus, the fact that many of the leaders of the American abolition movement were white, propertied men was irrelevant to the essential justness of the antislavery cause. Second, it is well established within the social-movements literature that lacking resources, movements do not get very far (McCarthy and Zald 1977; McAdam 1999). Having social privilege can in fact free individuals in ways that enable them more readily to organize into social movements and dedicate their labor and resources to activism. The civil rights movement was organized by the African American middle class, the moderate and radical branches of the women's liberation movement came from middle-class backgrounds, and skilled, employed workers played a pivotal role in the making of the modern labor movement. Perhaps the more relevant point, taking into consideration the intersection of race, gender, and class, concerns the ways in which social location narrows or opens the scope of possibilities and commitments. It should come as no surprise that people of color and the poor (with the majority of the poor being women) may gravitate toward social issues of more immediate material and political concern to them than animal rights.

In fact, however, many animal rights activists and scholars are women, and a significant number of animal rights scholars and activists appear to come from working-class backgrounds. Furthermore, the animal rights issue has recently received more sympathetic attention from communities of color (Harper 2010). Vegans of Color, for example, a new movement organization located in Oakland, California, affirms its commitment to a variety of social causes—"Because we don't have the luxury of being single issue"—a nod to the ways in which identities of race and gender intersect with animal rights (Vegans of Color 2011). Many activists and scholars concerned with animal rights themselves come from diverse research and activist backgrounds that enable them to connect the oppression of other animals to other forms of inequality and injustice.

Finally, the charge that animal rights is solely a "first world" phenomenon ignores the fact that any number of religious and spiritual traditions in regions we now associate with the "third world" have highlighted our moral duties toward other animals for many centuries, including Mahayana Buddhism, Jainism, and Hinduism. While the multiple branches and sects of these religious traditions vary in their doctrinal beliefs toward nonhuman beings, with some advocating vegetarianism and some not, they all defend the principle of practicing nonharm toward other sentient beings, citing both the integrity of the animals themselves and the detrimental impact of killing and eating nonhuman animals on the spiritual development of human societies (Gandhi 2002; Shah 1998).

NEW QUESTIONS AND FUTURE DIRECTIONS

Three broad trends can be discerned in the field. First is the convergence between humanities scholarship and the biological sciences (particularly cognitive ethology, or the study of animal mind) concerning the complexity and phenomenology of nonhuman consciousness and experience, as well as the ethical implications of the new scientific research. Second, there has been increasing politicization of the field in the form of renewed interest in the intersection of speciesism with other forms of social inequality and violence, including capitalism, colonialism, gender oppression, and racism. In recent years, a determined group of activist intellectuals has endeavored to redefine the field as critical animal studies. The Institute of Critical Animal Studies, founded in 2001, now sponsors conferences, publishes an online journal, and has embarked on an international book series. Unifying this approach is the so-called critical theoretical tradition—broadly speaking, the radical, or "left," and feminist traditions in social and political thought. Drawing on, for example, Marx's critique of capital or on contemporary anticolonial theories of race, such critics emphasize the political, social, and historical dimensions of speciesism. They also affirm the traditional critical understanding of theory as a form of praxis for revealing truth and changing social reality (Sanbonmatsu 2011). By the same token, such critics (or a portion of them) emphasize that overcoming speciesism will in turn ultimately require the dissolution of inegalitarian social institutions and modes of development, including patriarchy and capitalism.

A third development is the marked professionalization of the field, which can be seen in the growing number of international conferences, peer-reviewed journals such as *Animal Law,* credentialed courses, and specialized degree-granting programs in the area (including some at the graduate level), as well as the formation of professional societies such as the American Sociological Association's Animals and Society Section (2011) and the online Society and Animals Forum. As in other instances where an advocacy movement has entered academia, however, tensions have emerged over the proper relationship between scholarly inquiry and activist praxis. As an increasingly legitimate and expansive field of scholarly research, animal studies may face the same dilemma or historical crisis confronting similar academic fields that owe their original impetus to social-movement activity: political irrelevance. The academic incorporation and professionalization of the women's movement, for example, came after that movement had crested and gone into decline. Animal studies faces a similar danger that it may refine the instruments of analysis and inquiry but play little role in the actual reform of society and social institutions. However, while some researchers have called for a more "disinterested" approach, the majority of scholars appear to identify their work as contributing to animal rights and social change, and those involved in critical animal studies continue to build bridges between activist and academic communities, with some success.

In any event, the greater challenge for animal rights is not academic irrelevance, per se, but speciesism itself as a mode of production, or way of producing and reproducing human societies. On the one hand, activists and scholars continue to make meaningful headway in extending the idea of rights, with its implicit notion of the dignity and inviolability of the person, to other sentient beings. On the other hand, the economic incentives for maintaining and indeed expanding the global system of species exploitation are stronger than they have ever been. Meanwhile, the cultural and ideological systems reinforcing speciesism show great resilience. Like other social movements for emancipation, then, the animal rights movement faces daunting obstacles in the years ahead, including an inhospitable organizing environment overdetermined by resource scarcity; the social, political, and economic pressures of neoliberalization; global warming; regional war; massive socioeconomic inequality; and the residue of thousands of years of cultural practices that treat the exploitation of nonhuman animals as natural and right.

Yet these social forces also have the potential to spark new scholarly research and ignite movements to explain and challenge the inequitable global distribution of resources, including unsustainable agricultural practices involving "meat" production. While the problem of world hunger is not yet a problem of scarcity but rather one of distribution and production, animal agriculture, as a grossly inefficient and ecologically damaging form of agriculture, has greatly amplified economic inequality and exacerbated the food crisis. Wealthy nations where "meat" consumption is the highest rely heavily on cattle-export economies in the "third world" that utilize agricultural practices that result in deforestation, displaced rural communities, and loss of land for local food production. Mitigating ecological crisis in the twenty-first century will require that "first world" nations phase out cattle-export practices, while also providing the resources for poorer nations to have options to change practices toward animals and the environment. In other words, solving the growing problems of global poverty and environmental destruction in the twenty-first century will require scholars, activists, and citizens to rethink philosophies, religions, and historical practices in very different ways, thereby creating a transformative potential to minimize the suffering and expand the rights of both human and nonhuman animals.

CHAPTER ELEVEN

DISABILITY AND SOCIETY

Jean M. Lynch

One thing is perfectly clear with respect to disability: for a long time there has been an empty seat at the human rights table. Compared to other minority groups, and with respect to related issues of inequality, disability has received very little attention from sociologists and human rights activists. What about disability—compared to other human rights issues, such as sex and gender, labor and labor movements, and the sociology of emotion—leads us so often to disregard it as an issue worthy of our attention? Disability as a human rights issue is simply ignored.

DISABILITY SCHOLARSHIP

Two competing models offer radically different conceptualizations of and perspectives on disability. Each model conceptualizes disability by outlining the causes of and appropriate responses to disability, shapes public perceptions, determines media images, and subsequently suggests the roles and scripts that the able-bodied and the disabled should assume in their interactions with each other. But they do so very differently.

THE MEDICAL MODEL OF DISABILITY

The traditional model, the medical/essentialist/individualist model, is the one primarily subscribed to by medical professionals. It emphasizes individualism. In the medical model, able-bodiedness is a normative ideal against which disability is compared (Switzer 2003). The goals of cure and rehabilitation are paramount (Silvers 1998b); it is assumed that the disabled want, and should want, to become as physically and mentally similar to able-bodied individuals as possible.

In the medical model, disability becomes the person's sole, salient identity; the focus is on the inability to function and individual reliance on others for care (Evans, Assadi, and Herriott 2005). It is assumed that there are no other relevant statuses (e.g., occupational, parental) occupied by those with disabilities, or if there are, they are not important. The person is infantilized and subject to others' perceptions and judgments (Longmore 2003). The true experts, the disabled themselves, remain almost totally excluded from the discourse! In this model, individuals should comply with medical prescriptions regarding treatment plans and goals whether or not they agree with these plans, consider them in their best interest, or perceive them as aligned with their life goals. The power of the professional is paramount, so much so that professionals can exercise social control, including denial of services, if the patient fails to comply with the professionals' directives (Adkins 2003; Barnes and Mercer 2010). Problematically, even decisions about types of medical equipment, definitions of the quality of life, and issues surrounding euthanasia—when based on empirical data—typically derive from data collected from able-bodied respondents (Silvers 1998a; Timmermans 2001). In a society where public perceptions rest on stereotypic assumptions about the disabled, the findings from such questionable data-collection procedures frequently yield policies and programs that further the exclusion and disadvantages already levied against this group (Silvers 1998a).

Indeed, the vast majority of media images are based on the medical model. These images present disability as an individual flaw and a personal tragedy due entirely to natural causes. Living with a disability is a "fate worse than death" (Fleischer and Zames 2001; Longmore 2003). Normalization depicts the disabled as "other," as the victims of an arbitrary fate who, if they attend to and comply with medical directives, can overcome their inferiority (Fleischer and Zames 2001). The disabled person is responsible for managing or controlling the consequences of the disability. The patient is exhorted to "psychologically manage" the disease, minimizing the effects of the disability as much as possible (Barnes and Mercer 2010).

Among many other things, the medical model fails to consider external sources that impact disability and does not attend to the conflicts embedded in the social relations between the disabled and the able-bodied; the focus is on changing the individual, not on modifying the environment—an environment that typically reflects only the dominant group's preferences (Silvers 1998a). The medical model fails to capture the experience of disability, including the goals of many with disability who focus on objectives other than cure. No attention is paid to the social, economic, and physical barriers that limit the opportunities of the disabled or to the conflicts embedded in the social relations between the disabled and the able-bodied (Silvers 1998a).

THE SOCIAL MODEL OF DISABILITY

The alternative model is the social model, which views disability as a creation of society. This model emphasizes inclusion and accessibility through modification of the environment (Switzer 2003). Social models of disability propose that disability is socially constructed and that the barriers to disability can be matters of physical accessibility or created by negative attitudes of the able-bodied toward those with disability. The impact of these barriers can only be reduced through social change

(Adkins 2003). Unlike the medical model, in which the individual is responsible for the disability and for failures that result from it, in the social model, society is at fault for the problems those with disability confront (Pfeiffer 2001).

In the social model, the professional is not the expert; nor are the able-bodied considered a normative ideal. The experts are those who are disabled, and their voices and experiences are central. The social model encourages arrangements that promote maximum mainstream social and economic participation. Rather than a focus on cure, maximizing the potential and life satisfaction of individuals in accordance with their own preferences is paramount (Asch 2001; Barnes 1996; Barnes and Mercer 2010; Silvers 1998b). The social model recognizes that people with disability are stigmatized and negatively labeled. Such recognition justifies the need for disability to be included in broader human rights conversations.

Recently, the limitations of the social model have been recognized within disability studies (Barnes and Mercer 2010; Shakespeare and Watson 2001). The social-constructionist model originally provided advantages over the medical model—primarily in making the voices of the disability community central to the conversation on disability. However, the model ultimately excludes much of what is essential to the lived experience of disability. For example, the model ignores impairment (physical or mental abnormalities or functional loss), recognizing only disability (the result of the former; a restriction or lack of an ability considered "normal" for a typical person [Barbotte, Guillemin, and Chau 2002]). There are other limitations in using the social model as the sole perspective on disability. The model does not lend itself to empirical observation as the concepts are not easily operationalized. It fails to recognize that those with disabilities are a heterogeneous group—for instance, in creating a solution to one person's issues we might create additional obstacles for another individual (Barnes and Mercer 2010; Shakespeare and Watson 2001). Perhaps most significantly, the model does not lend itself to the development of policy resolutions or strategies of resistance.

Despite these limitations, the social model shifts attention away from the individual and explicitly emphasizes social responsibility. It suggests an important alternative to the perception of disability as a tragic, individual phenomenon and instead emphasizes a recognition of social responsibility. Most importantly, it helps mobilize the disability community (Barnes and Mercer 2010), which hopefully will result in the community's ability to resist discrimination and to demand essential human rights.

RESEARCH ON DISABILITY

Disability studies differ across cultural contexts. For example, in Britain, disability studies were originally located within sociology, whereas in the United States disability scholarship originated in literature and rhetoric (Gordon and Rosenblum 2001). These beginnings have impacted future concerns with disability, including which models predominated then—and now. Since sociologists emphasize the social-constructionist model in considering minority groups (e.g., race, gender, sex, and age) and variations in privilege, it is surprising when people with disabilities are not included as a minority group. At least in the United States, disability is still frequently presented under the medical model and conceptualized as an individual rather than a social experience.

Space constraints prevent an exhaustive review of research findings; however, we can briefly present key findings from areas in which the most research has been completed. First, there has been a plethora of studies (e.g., Keller and Siegrist 2010; Leasher, Miller, and Gooden 2009; Ouellette-Kuntz et al. 2010; Scheid 2005) on attitudes toward persons with disabilities in a variety of settings (e.g., employment, educational institutions) and among different populations (e.g., college students). These studies provide specific understandings of how people perceive people with disability. For example, younger and more educated individuals hold more positive attitudes toward those with intellectual disabilities (Ouellette-Kuntz et al. 2010). People who like other people have more positive perceptions of people with physical disabilities; the reverse is true for those who believe in a just world (Keller and Siegrist 2010). We know that direct experiences, indirect experiences, and the attitudes of one's primary social group toward people with disabilities are central to an individual's attitude formation (Farnell and Smith 1999; Keller and Siegrist 2010). In addition, studies indicate that the amount of control we have over contact with people with disabilities and the amount of information we possess about disability both influence our attitudes (Krahe and Altwasser 2006; Pettigrew and Tropp 2006; Yuker 1994). For example, the less control we exert over an interaction, the more negative our attitudes, and the more intimate the contact situation, the less positively we feel about it. The more knowledge we have about disability, the more positive our attitudes (Berry and Jones 1991; Evans, Assadi, and Herriott 2005; Krahe and Altwasser 2006).

Second, there is a substantial amount of literature on specific types of disabilities (e.g., learning disabilities). These studies are of use to individuals diagnosed with those disabilities, their allies, and professionals who are invested in those particular disabilities (Dudley-Marling 2004; Phemister and Crewe 2004). Unfortunately, these findings offer little understanding in general about the lives of those with disability and how best to advance our knowledge of disability as a human rights issue.

Third, a moderate amount of literature describes the disability movement over time. Some of these findings provide an historical overview of the growth of the community and demonstrate the ways in which the disability community attempts to advance its cause (Dowse 2001; Foster-Fishman et al. 2007; Pfeiffer 1993). Fourth, the Americans with Disabilities Act has received a fair amount of attention, including evaluations of how it has influenced certain types of cases (e.g., employment cases) and how it has helped or hindered the disability community (e.g., Blau and Moncada 2006; Colker 2005; Fleischer and Zames 2001; Switzer 2003). Recent scholarship describes the changes made to the Americans with Disabilities Act to alleviate some of the initial drawbacks it posed for the disability community (Long 2008).

Two additional categories of literature have received significant attention and offer interesting insights for disability and the human rights agenda. First are content analyses of various genres. This work ranges from images of disability in children's books (Matthews 2009) to the presentations of disability in films (Black and Pretes 2007) and in the news (Haller, Dorries, and Rahn 2006). Second, euthanasia and eugenics have received a disproportionate share of attention, at least considering the scant amount of such scholarship that has been conducted within disability studies or by those with expertise in disability studies (Shakespeare 2006). Rather, these studies often rely on a medical perspective and are conducted by members of the able-bodied population (Grue 2010).

DISABILITY RESEARCH AND CONTENT ANALYSIS

One of the most popular kinds of sociological research on disability is content analyses of various media genres. These studies (e.g., Black and Pretes 2007; Safran 2001; Switzer 2003) are particularly instructive because they demonstrate how the social construction of disability occurs. Content analysis examines one or more media genres looking for recurring words or themes; after analyzing a sample of a particular genre, the researcher combines similar words or themes into categories that provide an overall picture of the images that depict a particular type of person, issue, event, and so on. Content analyses of media are instructive, as they can tell us about public perceptions and public attitudes. It is through the media and most often through films that the public is provided with what is often their only experience with disability. Safran, who analyzed six Academy Award–winning films that featured disability and war, argues that films "project representations of how individuals fit into a nation's social and political landscape" (2001, 223). These images are consistent with the medical model portrayal of disability; they depict disability as tragic (Switzer 2003) and the disabled as frequently incapable of adjusting to these tragedies and in need of help from the able-bodied to adapt, to provide care, or to access cures (Longmore 2003). The disabled are cast as unidimensional and rarely seen as anything but their disability; they rarely live successfully, whether success is measured occupationally, educationally, or through the ability to create or maintain intimate relationships (Black and Pretes 2007). Worse, the media provides many audiences with what may be their only socialization into relationships between the able-bodied and the disabled. Incapable of adjusting to their own life circumstances, the disabled must depend on the able-bodied, who are shown as emotionally, intellectually, and socially superior.

Some images that are perceived as positive by the able-bodied are considered by many members of the disability community as evidence of stereotypes and detrimental to the community and to persons with disabilities. One such image is the "supercrip." Often portrayed in fictional films and presented in news stories as well, supercrips are individuals who not only live very successfully with a disability (a fate worse than death) but also accomplish some spectacular feat (e.g., climb Mount Everest, play the violin with their tongue) (Black and Pretes 2007). This is comparable to Horatio Alger stories about people who pull themselves up by their bootstraps and attain enormous success and wealth despite being raised in an environment of extreme poverty. The ideology behind these messages is clear:

disabilities can be overcome if one simply works at it hard; those who fail to do so are just not trying enough.

Unfortunately, such imagery does disservice to the disabled. First, these presentations bear little connection to the experiences and the lives of the majority of those who live with disabilities. Second, these images provide the public with unrealistic standards that are then used to downplay the very real obstacles and barriers that do confront those with disabilities. Third, they also provide the able-bodied public with an "out," an image that they can assume would reflect their reality were they to become disabled.

With respect to the social construction of disability, the media is used to perpetuate ableist images of disability and send messages to the audience about what disability is like, what the lives of those with disability are about, how those with disability should behave and live, and how those who are able-bodied should perceive and treat the disabled. The function of these images is to absolve able-bodied individuals of any responsibility for the disabled and for the obstacles and barriers that confront individuals with disability.

Certain images of disability are particularly prevalent and becoming more frequent over time (Black and Pretes 2007). These images communicate the message that death through suicide or other means is an intelligent and responsible solution to the problem of living with a disability, one that a reasonable individual would choose. Increasingly films depict individuals with disabilities as wanting and fighting for the right to die. In a recent content analysis of films, almost half contained attempted, successful, or assisted suicide, and many included the "right to die" as a major theme (Black and Pretes 2007); media portrayal of disability as a fate worse than death is quite common (Black and Pretes 2007; Fleischer and Zames 2001; Longmore 2003). This evokes the fear in the disability community that the "right to decide to live and die may become a duty to die" (Mackelprang and Mackelprang 2005, 323). In reality, the disabled find themselves in situations where they need to fight for the "right to live." Although most people with disability may experience a brief period during which adjusting to the disability is difficult, research on the lives of the disabled and memoirs demonstrate the majority of those with disability lead happy and successful lives and would not choose suicide as an option.

EUTHANASIA AND EUGENICS

Recent questions posed by bioethicists include, What is a life of quality? Are there life situations not of value? Should this life be saved? These questions have intruded into the scholarship on disability, particularly that which considers eugenics and euthanasia (Asch 2001; Koch 2004). Exploring what is meant by human rights, Blau and Moncada (2005) speak as if euthanasia only exists in cultures removed from our own. Furthermore, they argue that in discussions of human rights, the focus is "everyday rights," not "human rights violations *in extremis*." Issues such as euthanasia and eugenics are not typically tied to human rights; yet for people with disability, they are very much aligned with their human rights. The suggestion that the lives of those with disabilities might be of lesser value than those of the able-bodied must be considered under the human rights umbrella. Many disability-studies scholars and some sociologists (e.g., Gordon and Rosenblum 2001; Grue 2010; Jotkowitz, Glick, and Gesundheit 2008; Koch 2004) claim that threats of euthanasia and eugenics are increasingly encroaching on the lives of those with disability.

Recent scholars suggest that contemporary thoughts about euthanasia and disability are not unlike the perspectives seen during the Nazi regime (Grue 2010; Jotkowitz, Glick, and Gesundheit 2008). Grue (2010) claims that we pacify ourselves by asserting that the German euthanasia programs and ideologies of eugenics disappeared after World War II, but she admonishes that there is little difference between our culture and Germany of the past, or between the physicians involved in genocide then and our own present-day physicians who support assisted suicide and link decisions about euthanasia to disability.

Research demonstrates that our evaluation of the value of a person's life is influenced by the fact of his or her disability (Fleischer and Zames 2001). For example, Mackelprang and Mackelprang (2005) indicate that favorable judgments are more likely to be handed down in right-to-die cases when the individual who requests the "right to die" is disabled. It is not that individuals should not be able to choose whether to live or to die; it is that our responses should not be tied to whether a person is disabled.

Many contemporary decisions about euthanasia rely on quality-of-life measures; yet these are not valid operationalizations of the will to live. Asch (2001) reports that persons with disabilities who seek to terminate their lives are typically recently disabled. Having lived in a world where media images portray disability as tragic and the lives of those with disability as miserable, is it any wonder that the onset of disability is accompanied by a wish to commit suicide? Given time, adjustments in accessibility, new learning, and attitude changes, most persons with disabilities quickly change their mind and choose to live. Most persons with disabilities describe their lives as happy and successful, a description most medical professionals and the public do not envision, given the lack of images that portray such a perspective (Asch 2001). Our reluctance to consider persons with disabilities as experts on living with a disability and our overreliance on physicians' views and on public perceptions of disability do not bode well for the future of euthanasia of the disabled.

Timmermans (2001) found that hospital medical staff typically consider certain patients as socially dead; although biologically alive, they are treated as if they were corpses. In resuscitation attempts, disabled patients are much more likely to be defined as socially dead than are able-bodied patients and more likely to be the recipients of passive euthanasia. In interviews with medical staff, attitudes toward the value of life for those with disability parallel public perceptions of disability (Timmermans 2001).

Although many persons with disability support issues of choice, there is a legitimate fear that the "right to die" will become a "duty to die" (Mackelprang and Mackelprang 2005). Already such pressure is placed on people with disabilities (Fleischer and Zames 2001). Under the capitalist system, the disabled are presumed to be living in nonexploitable and therefore valueless bodies. There is little hope that the public, holding the negative attitudes they do, will lend support if (or when) cost-benefit analyses are applied to life-and-death choices about the disabled. Hockenberry (1995) argues that much more effort is put into cure than into integrating persons with disabilities into society and suggests that the disabled are made to feel that if they cannot be cured, they have a civic responsibility to die.

The same issues exist in the area of eugenics. The fact that we have tests that allow people to ensure that they will not bear children with certain conditions can be perceived either as progress or as encouragement to eventually produce a purely able-bodied society. The assumption is that such a society would be a good one. There is no discussion about diversity; nor is there suggestion of the benefits that the disabled provide to society. The message to the public and to the disability community is clear: having individuals with disabilities is something to be avoided at all costs.

I believe we cannot discuss eugenics or euthanasia in any morally responsible way until we first disseminate accurate, realistic, and complete information about disability. Presently, decision-makers' views are informed by media images that fail to depict any objective view of what life with a disability is like and, instead, rely on public perceptions of disability and medical professionals' views. These perceptions generate unrealistic fears of disability. Severely lacking are the perceptions of those who live with a disability and accurate recognition of the social, economic, and environmental barriers they confront. It is one thing to decide not to have a child with a disability based on illusions and incomplete and misguided information. It is another decision entirely when one has been privy to complete objective, scientific, and experiential testimony and knowledge that includes both positive and negative information about the reality of that disability.

Singer's claim that "killing a disabled infant is not morally equivalent to killing a person; very often is not morally wrong at all" (1993, 191) is typical of the thinking that accompanies decisions about eugenics and euthanasia. If we replaced the phrase "disabled infant" with another identity or group, there would be moral outrage. Yet we live in a world where we allow decisions that reinforce the medical model and support the notion that it is disability, not discrimination against persons with disabilities, that we should eliminate. Whether eugenics or euthanasia is morally justifiable is beyond the confines of this chapter. It is essential, however, to consider whether we can tie eugenics and euthanasia to the fact of a person's disability or any other minority status. Making a decision about quality of life, especially when the majority of the information is based on possibly questionable operationalizations of such (if any at all), cannot be justified.

WHAT HUMAN RIGHTS OFFER DISABILITY STUDIES

As noted above, we lack a model that captures the experience of disability. The medical model is clearly deficient, but recently the disability community has recognized that the social-constructionist model has outlived its usefulness (Barnes and Mercer 2010). Originally the latter helped to mobilize the disability community; however, it is not a comprehensive model in that it fails to include significant aspects of being disabled, most notably impairment.

One way in which human rights scholarship benefits disability studies is the capabilities approach. This model suggests that human capabilities are universal and that people have the right, and therefore must be afforded opportunities, to develop their capabilities (Sen 1999b). Burchardt (2004) suggests that the capabilities model offers a useful complement to (not a replacement for) the social-constructionist approach. The strength of the capabilities approach is its focus on ends and opportunities rather than on means and the "typical" or actual. That is, the model suggests that mobility and accessibility are important; less important are the means through which those are achieved. It matters little whether mobility is achieved by walking or that accessibility is possible through sight; what is significant is that each equal human being, disabled or able-bodied, is afforded opportunities for accessibility and mobility (Blau and Moncada 2009).

It is difficult to discuss what else human rights offers disability since disability is so rarely considered under the human rights banner. One possibility is that human rights has much to offer people with disability—as for all minority groups—yet, because of its exclusion, it is difficult to identify specific aspects of the human rights agenda and its implications for studying persons with disabilities. One obvious priority is to include disability in the human rights conversation and for human rights advocates to place people with disabilities and the disability movement on an equal footing with other rights movements. People with disabilities must be seen as suffering not from an individual tragedy but from the ways in which disability has been socially constructed and people with disability have been denied opportunities to develop their capabilities and to participate equally in social, economic, and political life. We rely on human rights activists to promote human rights; yet they seem loath to include those with disability among the litany of groups for whom they advocate. Even though people with disability are clearly the "other," the activists who should know better ignore disability and avoid the "messiness" that accompanies it. We need to figure out why and what to do about this.

THE FUTURE OF DISABILITY AND HUMAN RIGHTS

The most pressing issue that faces disability as a human rights issue is to ensure that people who consider themselves human rights activists understand how and in what way disability is a human rights issue, along with gender, sex, poverty, race, age, and other identity characteristics that are routinely denied privilege. Currently, disability is an afterthought in human rights conversations and considerations. Some suspect this is because disability is one of the only statuses that can be entered at any moment without warning. Why it is avoided matters less than the fact of its avoidance and the necessity of rendering this avoidance obsolete.

We need to encourage human rights advocates to become allies to people with disabilities. Allies are "members of dominant social groups who are working to end the system of oppression that gives them greater privilege and power based on their social-group membership" (Broido 2000, 3). The ally identity is a unique status chosen by dominant group members who work for social justice, who believe in a society based on equity and justice. According to scholarship on the adoption of an ally identity, working as an ally, realizing and helping to break down the system that benefits dominant groups and disadvantages minority groups, liberates everyone (Bell 1997; Edwards 2006). As Freire (2000) and Brod (1987) argue, members of both minority groups and the dominant group suffer from participation in systems of oppression. History instructs us that most struggles for civil rights have been accomplished through the coordinated efforts of the "other" and their allies. Successful movements and achievements along the way owe much to the efforts and struggles of allies who had and offered the resources, power, and privilege to help groups denied privilege and human rights.

More research needs to be conducted on issues of disability. So much of the extant work was conducted from a medical-model perspective rather than from a social-constructionist or capabilities model. As a result, we have little substantive information regarding the social, environmental, and economic barriers that produce difficulties for people with disabilities. Nor do we know the ways in which interaction and systems of oppression are created and maintained between people with disabilities and people who are able-bodied. We need to know much more about how disability is socially constructed and why. We need to discover how to provide opportunities for people to realize their capabilities and opportunities. Disability deserves a seat at the human rights table as these discussions evolve.

Discussion Questions and Additional Resources

Chapter 1: Sex and Gender

- What are the connections among intersectionality, human rights, sex, and gender?
- How does a human rights approach change our understanding of essentialism and the social construct?
- If public-private is a false dichotomy, how should we think of our social lives as gendered and sexed people?
- What are the needs of women and girls as women and girls?
- How can we acknowledge both the universality of human rights and the particularity of local cultures to promote human rights for women and girls?

Additional Resources for Chapter 1:

- *Half the Sky* (documentary) and Half the Sky Movement. Accessible online at http://www.halftheskymovement.org/
- United Nations' Committee on the Elimination of Discrimination against Women. Accessible online at http://www.ohchr.org/EN/HRBodies /CEDAW/Pages/CEDAWIndex.aspx
- *The Line* (documentary) and Where Is Your Line. Accessible online at www .whereisyourline.org.
- Women Watch. Accessible online at http://www.un.org/womenwatch /directory/human_rights_of_women_3009.htm

Chapter 2: Aging and the Life Course

- How does a human rights approach change our understanding of the life course?
- Do an individual's human rights change as they age?
- Why do some societies provide greater support of human rights at different stages of the life course? Should they?
- Are some types of human rights more important depending on a person's age? Why?

Additional Resources for Chapter 2:

- GlobalAging. Accessible online at http://www.globalaging.org/elderrights /world/index%202012.html
- Protecting the Rights of Older People. Accessible online at http://www.helpageusa .org/what-we-do/rights/rights-policy/un-openended-working-group-on-aging /protecting-the-rights-of-older-people/
- Elder Abuse and Neglect. Accessible online at http://www.ohrc.on.ca/en /time-action-advancing-human-rights-older-ontarians/elder-abuse-neglect
- International Federation on Ageing. Accessible online at http://www.ifa-fiv .org/

Chapter 3: Mental Health and Human Rights

- How will human rights–centered institutions differ from existing institutions for mental health care?
- Why has mental health not been connected to human rights in sociology?
- How do inequality and mental illness underscore the importance of a human rights lens?
- What does vulnerability to mental distress among those whose human rights are not protected suggest about society and human rights?
- What are challenges to the *universality* of human rights uncovered by considering mental health?
- How can human rights protect the self-determination and agency of the mentally ill?
- Do we need to regard mental illness from an essentialist view or as a social construct? Which one enables better human rights protections?

Additional Resources for Chapter 3:

- The World Health Organization—Resources on Mental Health. Accessible online at http://www.who.int/mental_health/en/
- World Federation for Mental Health. Accessible online at http://wfmh.com/
- *Breaking the Chains* (documentary). Accessible online at http://movie-ment .org/breaking-the-chains/
- Citizens Commission on Human Rights. Accessible online at http://www .cchr.org/

Chapter 4: Racial and Ethnic Minorities

- What are the three strands of research on racial and ethnic minorities? How do human rights add to each strand?
- Why do the authors state that the study of race and ethnic minorities must be the study of oppression and resistance?
- Do you agree that social scientists are obligated to explore the nature of moral commitments within their disciplines? Why or why not?

- What is the authors' view of a sociology of human rights? Please give evidence from the chapter. What do you feel they missed?

Additional Resources for Chapter 4:

- International Convention on the Elimination of All Forms of Racial Discrimination. Accessible online at https://treaties.un.org/Pages /ViewDetails.aspx?src=TREATY&mtdsg_no=IV-2&chapter=4&lang=en
- *The Black Power MixTape: 1967–1975* (documentary). Accessible online at http://www.pbs.org/independentlens/black-power-mixtape
- Human Rights Education Association—Rights of Ethnic and Racial Minorities. Accessible online at http://www.hrea.org/index.php?base_id=142
- American Civil Liberties Union—Racial Justice. Accessible online at https:// www.aclu.org/human-rights/racial-justice

CHAPTER 5: ASIA AND ASIAN AMERICA

- The authors raise the issue of cultural relativism and human rights. What is "cultural relativism"? What are the pros and cons of the cultural relativist argument in the study, understanding, recognition, and implementation of human rights?
- Who "owns" human rights? The West? Developed nations? What evidence exists to answer these questions in the case of Asia and Asian America?
- In the chapter, the authors state that Confuscianism has the principles of human rights embedded within its philosophy. How so? What other philosophic, religious, and other cultural systems might we look to for understanding grounded human rights?
- What is the difference between human rights and political and civil rights in the case of Asian and Asian Americans' struggles for equality?

Additional Resources for Chapter 5:

- 1993 Bangkok Declaration. Accessible online at http://www.hurights.or.jp /archives/other_documents/section1/1993/04/final-declaration-of-the -regional-meeting-for-asia-of-the-world-conference-on-human-rights.html
- Center for Asian American Media—Human Rights Documentaries. Accessible online at http://caamedia.org/buy-caam-films/browse-by-subject/#Human /Civil%20Rights
- Asian Human Rights Commission. Accessible online at http://www .humanrights.asia/

CHAPTER 6: LATINA/O SOCIOLOGY

- Why do the authors spend so much time on the racialization of Latina/os? How is this related to understanding human rights?

- What does it mean that all humans have a human right to (im)migration? What lessons have been learned from the sociology of Latina/os that may help ensure these human rights?
- The authors describe the experiences of Latina/os as "creat[ing] a gray area between the human and citizenship rights paradigms." What does this mean? What does this gray area illuminate for us? Obscure from us?
- What is "diversity"? How do the lives and experiences of Latina/os teach us about this term?

Additional Resources for Chapter 6:

- Derechos Humanos en América Latina. Accessible online at http://www.derechos.org/nizkor/
- The Project Disappeared/El Proyecto Desaparecidos. Accessible online at http://www.desaparecidos.org
- SIPAZ (Chiapas Human Rights). Accessible online at http://www.sipaz.org/
- Liberdad Latina. Accessible online at http://www.libertadlatina.org/

CHAPTER 7: CHILDREN AND YOUTH

- What are three contributions human rights scholarship can make to sociology of children and youth?
- What are three contributions sociology of children and youth can make to human rights scholarship?
- Think of a person older than you. How did human rights matter to your childhoods? Do your experiences differ?

Additional Resources for Chapter 7:

- Campaign for U.S. Ratification of the Convention on the Rights of the Child International Society for Child Indicators. Accessible online at https://www.isci.chapinhall.org
- UNICEF Innocenti Research Center. Accessible online at www.unicef-irc.org
- African Charter on the Rights and Welfare of the Child. Accessible online at http://acerwc.org/the-african-charter-on-the-rights-and-welfare-of-the-child-acrwc/
- United Nations Convention on the Rights of the Child. Accessible online at https://treaties.un.org/Pages/ViewDetails.aspx?src=TREATY&mtdsg_no=IV-11&chapter=4&lang=en

CHAPTER 8: RACE, CLASS, AND GENDER

- What are "binaries"? What is "essentialism"? How are these concepts related to studying, understanding, and realizing human rights?
- What is "intersectionality"? How does one study intersectionally? How does this approach relate to human rights recognition and advocacy?

- The author highlights the role of resistance in human rights research, understanding, and activism. Why is resistance an important concept?
- How does this chapter differ from the other chapters in the book?

Additional Resources for Chapter 8:

- The Intersection of Human Rights Violations and Multiple Grounds of Discrimination. Accessible online at http://www.snis.ch/call-projects-2013_6086_intersectionality-human-rights-violations-and-multiple-grounds-discriminatio
- Framing Issues on Intersectionality—Human Rights Network. Accessible online at http://www.ushrnetwork.org/resources-media/framing-questions-intersectionality
- InLawGrrls. Accessible online at http://www.intlawgrrls.com/2010/09/intersectionality-and-un-special.html

CHAPTER 9: SEXUALITIES

- Human rights violations occur in the name of heteronormativity and due to our concepts of the body and gender. How can society respond? How can we as individuals respond?
- How do human rights challenge heteronormativity?
- Examine sexuality from an intersectionality perspective. What are vectors of oppression and privilege? What other vectors may impact the level of oppression or privilege that an individual experiences?
- How is sexuality related to human dignity?
- How do you experience benefits due to the normative conceptions of the body, gender, and sexuality?
- How do you experience harms due to the normative conceptions of the body, gender, and sexuality?

Additional Resources for Chapter 9:

- Envisioning Global LGBT Human Rights. Accessible online at http://envisioninglgbt.blogspot.com/
- The Human Rights Campaign. Accessible online at http://www.hrc.org/resources/entry/sexual-orientation-and-gender-identity-terminology-and-definitions
- International Gay and Lesbian Human Rights Commission. Accessible online at http://www.iglhrc.org/
- *God Loves Uganda* (documentary). Accessible online at http://www.godlovesuganda.com/

CHAPTER 10: ANIMALS AND SOCIETY

- Does the very category of "human rights" serve to reinforce our sense of ourselves as different from, and superior to, the other animals?

- Does affirming animal rights weaken or strengthen the notion of human rights?
- What morally justifies the exploitation of animal bodies for human use as food and clothes?
- Is there a relationship between the reasons used to justify human exploitation of animals and the conquest and exploitation of human groups?
- Does the celebration of hunting, bull fighting, and other rituals of animal conquest have implications for cultural values about nature and women?

Additional Resources for Chapter 10:

- Breeze Harper's website. Accessible online at http://sistahvegan.com
- Breeze Harper at Human Rights Are Animal Rights Conference (YouTube). Accessible online at http://search.yahoo.com/search?ei=utf-8&fr=aaplw &p=human+rights+are+animal+rights+and+youtube+and+breeze+harper
- Carol Adams, Sexual Politics of Meat. Accessible online at http://www .caroljadams.com/contact.html
- Animal Rights: The Abolitionist Approach. Accessible online at www .abolitionistapproach.com/video/#.UvP0tDnWqJs
- Artist Sue Coe's website :http://www.graphicwitness.org/coe/enter.htm

CHAPTER 11: DISABILITY AND SOCIETY

- When thinking of human rights, why has disability been ignored?
- What can the sociology of human rights learn from studying disability?
- How do human rights change the medical and social models?
- What human rights may be essential to implementing the capabilities approach?
- Discuss how an ally can employ a human right to benefit everyone. What human right would you recommend employing?

Additional Resources for Chapter 11:

- Convention on the Rights of Persons with Disabilities. Accessible online at https://treaties.un.org/Pages/ViewDetails.aspx?src=TREATY&mtdsg _no=IV-15&chapter=4&lang=en
- Human Rights Watch—Disability. Accessible online at http://www.hrw.org /topic/disability-rights
- Disability Rights Blog. Accessible online at http://www.ahrcblog.com/
- *Fixed: The Science/Fiction of Human Enhacement* (documentary). Accessible online at http://www.newday.com/films/fixed.html

Acronyms

ASA   American Sociological Association
CEDAW   Committee on the Elimination of Discrimination against Women
FGC   female genital cutting
HRW   Human Rights Watch
ILO   International Labour Organization
LGBT   lesbian, gay, bisexual, and transgender
LIS   Luxembourg Income Study
MSM   men who have sex with men
NAFTA   North American Free Trade Agreement
NGO   nongovernmental organization
NHSL   National Health and Social Life
NIA   National Institute on Aging
NICHD   National Institute of Child Health and Human Development
NSF   National Science Foundation
SALC   sociology of age and the life course
STD   sexually transmitted disease
STI   sexually transmitted infection
SWS   Sociologists for Women in Society
UDHR   Universal Declaration of Human Rights
UN   United Nations
UNCRC   United Nations Convention on the Rights of the Child
UNICEF United Nations International Children's Emergency Fund
WHO   World Health Organization

REFERENCES

Achenbaum, Andrew W. 1978. *Old Age in the New Land: The American Experience since 1790.* Baltimore: Johns Hopkins University Press.

——. 2009. "A Metahistorical Perspective on Theories of Aging." In *Handbook of Theories of Aging*, edited by V. L. Bengston, D. Gans, N. M. Putney, and M. Silverstein. 2nd ed. New York: Springer Publishing.

Acker, Joan. 2006. "Inequality Regimes: Gender, Class and Race in Organizations." *Gender and Society* 20: 441–464.

Adam, Barry D. 1998. "Theorizing Homophobia." *Sexualities* 1: 387–404.

Adam, Barry D., Dan Willem Duyvendak, and André Krouwel. 1999. *The Global Emergence of Gay and Lesbian Politics: National Imprints of a Worldwide Movement.* Philadelphia: Temple University Press.

Adams, Carol. 1990. *The Sexual Politics of Meat.* New York: Continuum Press.

Adams, Vincanne. 1998. "Suffering the Winds of Lhasa: Politicized Bodies, Human Rights, Cultural Difference, and Humanism in Tibet." *Medical Anthropology Quarterly* 12: 74–102.

Adelson, Joseph. 2001. "Sex among the Americans." In *Speaking of Sexuality: Interdisciplinary Readings*, edited by J. Kenneth Davidson Sr. and Nelwyn B. Moore, 57–63. Los Angeles: Roxbury Publishing.

Adkins, W. 2003. "The Social Construction of Disability: A Theoretical Perspective." Paper presented at the annual meeting for the American Sociological Association, Atlanta, Georgia, 1–31.

Adler, Patricia A., and Peter Adler. 2011. *The Tender Cut: Inside the Hidden World of Self-Injury.* New York: New York University Press.

Albritton, Robert B. 2005. "Thailand in 2004: The 'Crisis in the South.'" *Asian Survey* 45: 166–173.

Alexander, M. Jacqui, and Chandra Talpade Mohanty. 1997. "Introduction." In *Feminist Genealogies, Colonial Legacies, Democratic Future*, edited by M. Jacqui Alexander and Chandra Talpade Mohanty, xiii–xlii. New York: Routledge.

Allen, Beverly. 1996. *Rape Warfare: The Hidden Genocide in Bosnia-Herzegovina and Croatia.* Minneapolis: University of Minnesota Press.

Alwin, Duane F., Scott M. Hofer, and Ryan J. McCammon. 2006. "Modeling the Effects of Time: Integrating Demographic and Developmental Perspectives." In *Handbook of Aging and the Social Sciences*, edited by R. H. Binstock and L. K. George, 20–41. 6th ed. Amsterdam: Elsevier.

American Sociological Association (ASA). 2011. "Animals and Society Section." ASA. www2.asanet.org /sectionanimals (accessed March 1, 2011).

Amirthalingam, Kumaraligam. 2005. "Women's Rights, International Norms, and Domestic Violence: Asian Perspectives." *Human Rights Quarterly* 27: 683–708.

Ancheta, Angelo N. 1998. "Race, Rights, and the Asian American Experience." *Journal of Asian American Studies* 1: 293–297.

Aries, Philippe. 1962. *Centuries of Childhood.* New York: Vintage.

Arington, Michele. 1991. "English Only Laws and Direct Legislation: The Battle in the States over Language Minority Rights." *Journal of Law and Politics* 7: 325–352.

Armstrong, Susan J., and Richard G. Botzler, eds. 2008. *The Animal Ethics Reader.* 2nd ed. London and New York: Routledge.

Asch, A. 2001. "Disability, Bioethics, and Human Rights." In *Handbook of Disability Studies*, edited by G. L. Albrecht, K. D. Seelman, and M. Bury, 297–326. Thousand Oaks, CA: Sage.

Asencio, Marysol. 2009. *Latina/o Sexualities: Probing Powers, Passions, Practices, and Policies.* New Brunswick, NJ: Rutgers University Press.

Ashar, Sameer. 2003. "Immigration Enforcement and Subordination: The Consequences of Racial Profiling after September 11." *Immigration and National Law Review* 23: 545–560.

Aylward, Carol A. 2010. "Intersectionality: Crossing the Theoretical and Praxis Divide." *Journal of Critical Race Inquiry* 1: 1–48.

Baars, Jan, Dale Dannefer, Chris Philipson, and Alan Walker. 2006. *Aging, Globalization, and Inequality: The New Critical Gerontology.* Amityville, NY: Baywood Publishing Company.

Babugura, Agnes A. 2008. "Vulnerability of Children and Youth in Drought Disasters: A Case Study of Botswana." *Children, Youth, and Environments* 18, no. 1: 126–157.

Baca Zinn, Maxine, and Bonnie Thornton Dill. 1994. "Difference and Domination." In *Women of Color in U.S. Society*. Philadelphia: Temple University Press.

———. 1996. "Theorizing Difference from Multiracial Feminism." *Feminist Studies* 22: 321–331.

Baca Zinn, Maxine, Lynn Weber Cannon, Elizabeth Higginbotham, and Bonnie Thornton Dill. 1986. "The Costs of Exclusionary Practices in Women's Studies." *Signs: Journal of Women in Culture and Society* 11: 290–303.

Baden, Sally, and Anne Marie Goetz. 1997. "Who Needs [Sex] When You Can Have [Gender]? Conflicting Discourses on Gender at Beijing." In *Women, International Development, and Politics*, edited by Kathleen Staudt, 37–58. Philadelphia: Temple University Press.

Bagemihl, Bruce. 2000. *Biological Exuberance: Animal Homosexuality and Natural Diversity*. New York: St. Martin's Press.

Baker, Carrie N. 2007. *The Women's Movement against Sexual Harassment*. New York: Cambridge University Press.

Bales, Kevin, and Ron Soodalter. 2009. *The Slave Next Door: Human Trafficking and Slavery in America Today*. Berkeley: University of California Press.

Baltrušaitytė, G. 2010. "Psychiatry and the Mental Patient: An Uneasy Relationship." *Culture and Society* 1. http://culturesociety.vdu.lt/wp-content/uploads/2010/11/G.-Baltrusaityte-Psychiatry-and-the-Mental -Patient-An-Uneasy-Relationship1.pdf (accessed January 22, 2012).

Barbotte, E., F. Guillemin, and N. Chau. 2002. "Prevalence of Impairments, Disabilities, Handicaps and Quality of Life in the General Population: A Review of Recent Literature." *Bulletin of the World Health Organization* 79: 1047–1055.

Barham P. 1992. *Closing the Asylum*. London: Penguin Books.

Barnes, C. 1996. "Theories of Disability and the Origins of the Oppression of Disabled People." In *Disability and Society: Emerging Issues and Insights*, edited by L. Barton, 43–60. London: Longman.

Barnes, C., and G. Mercer. 2010. *Exploring Disability*. 2nd ed. Cambridge, UK: Polity Press.

Battle, Juan. 2009. *Black Sexualities: Probing Powers, Passions, Practices, and Policies*. New Brunswick, NJ: Rutgers University Press.

Bearman, Peter S., and Hannah Bruckner. 2001. "Promising the Future: Virginity Pledges and First Intercourse." *American Journal of Sociology* 106: 859–912.

Becker, Anne E. 1994. "Nurturing and Negligence: Working on Others' Bodies in Fiji." In *Embodiment and Experience: The Existential Ground of Culture and Self*, edited by Thomas J. Csordas, 100–115. Cambridge, UK: Cambridge University Press.

Beckoff, Marc. 2002. *Minding Animals: Awareness, Emotions, and Heart*. New York: Oxford.

Bell, Daniel. 2000. *East Meets West: Human Rights and Democracy in East Asia*. Princeton, NJ: Princeton University Press.

Bell, L. A. 1997. "Theoretical Foundations for Social Justice Education." In *Teaching for Diversity and Social Justice: A Sourcebook*, edited by M. Adams, L. A. Bell, and P. Griffin, 3–15. New York: Routledge.

Beneke, Timothy. 1983. *Men on Rape: What They Have to Say about Sexual Violence*. New York: St. Martin's Press.

Bengston, Vern L., Daphna Gans, Norella M. Putney, and Merril Silverstein, eds. 2009a. *Handbook of Theories of Aging*. 2nd ed. New York: Springer Publishing.

———. 2009b. "Theories about Age and Aging." In *Handbook of Theories of Aging*, edited by Vern L. Bengston, Daphna Gans, Norella M. Putney, and Merril Silverstein, 3–24. 2nd ed. New York: Springer Publishing.

Bennett, Michael, and Juan Battle. 2001. "'We Can See Them, but We Can't Hear Them': LGBT Members of African American Families." In *Queer Families, Queer Politics: Challenging Culture and the State*, edited by Mary Bernstein and Renate Reimann, 53–67. New York: Columbia University Press.

Beresford, P., and A. Wilson. 2002. "Genes Spell Danger: Mental Health Service Users/Survivors, Bioethics and Control." *Disability and Society* 17: 541–553.

Berlant, Lauren, and Michael Warner. 1998. "Sex in Public." *Critical Inquiry* 24: 547–566.

Bernstein, Mary. 2004. "Paths to Homophobia." *Sexuality Research and Social Policy* 1: 41–55.

Bernstein, Mary, and Constance Kostelac. 2002. "Lavender and Blue: Attitudes about Homosexuality and Behavior toward Lesbians and Gay Men among Police Officers." *Journal of Contemporary Criminal Justice* 18: 302–328.

Bernstein, Mary, Constance Kostelac, and Emily Gaarder. 2003. "Understanding 'Heterosexism': Applying Theories of Racial Prejudice to Homophobia Using Data from a Southwestern Police Department." *Race, Gender and Class* 10: 54–74.

Bernstein, Mary, and Renate Reimann, eds. 2001. *Queer Families, Queer Politics: Challenging Culture and the State*. New York: Columbia University Press.

Berry, J. G., and W. H. Jones. 1991. "Situational and Dispositional Components of Reaction towards Persons with Disabilities." *Journal of Social Psychology* 131: 673–684.

Best, Joel. 2007. *Social Problems*. New York: W. W. Norton and Company.

Beyrer, Chris. 1998. "Burma and Cambodia: Human Rights, Social Disruption, and the Spread of HIV/AIDS." *Health and Human Rights* 2: 84–97.

Bhabha, Homi K. 2004. *RC Series Bundle: The Location of Culture*. 2nd ed. London: Routledge.

Bierne, Piers. 2009. *Confronting Animal Abuse: Law, Criminology, and Human-Animal Relationships*. Lanham, MD: Rowman & Littlefield.

Binion, Gayle. 1995. "Human Rights: A Feminist Perspective." *Human Rights Quarterly* 17: 509–526.

Binstock, Robert H. 2007. "The Doomsters Are Wrong: What's Needed Are Policies Aimed at Several Generations." *AARP Bulletin* 48, no. 3: 33.

Binstock, Robert H., Linda K. George, Stephen J. Cutler, Jon Hendricks, and James H. Schultz. 2006. *Handbook of Aging and the Social Sciences*. Amsterdam: Elsevier.

———. 2011. *Handbook of Aging and the Social Sciences*. Amsterdam: Elsevier.

Binstock, Robert H., and Stephen G. Post. 1991. *Too Old for Health Care? Controversies in Medicine, Law, Economics, and Ethics*. 6th ed. Baltimore: Johns Hopkins University Press.

Birren, J. E., ed. 1959. *Handbook of Aging and the Individual: Psychological and Biological Aspects*. Chicago: University of Chicago Press.

Black, R. S., and L. Pretes. 2007. "Victims and Victors: Representation of Physical Disability on the Silver Screen." *Research and Practice for Persons with Severe Disabilities* 32: 66–83.

Black, Timothy. 2010. *When a Heart Turns Rock Solid: The Lives of Three Puerto Rican Brothers on and off the Streets*. New York: Vintage.

Blair, T., and M. Minkler. 2009. "Participatory Action Research with Older Adults: Key Principles in Practice." *Gerontologist* 49: 651–662.

Blau, J., and A. Moncada. 2005. *Human Rights: Beyond the Liberal Vision*. Lanham, MD: Rowman & Littlefield.

———. 2006. *Justice in the United States: Human Rights and the U.S. Constitution*. London: Rowman & Littlefield.

———. 2009. *Human Rights: A Primer*. Boulder, CO: Paradigm Publishers.

Bogle, Kathleen. 2008. *Hooking Up: Sex, Dating, and Relationships on Campus*. New York: New York University Press.

Bond, Johanna E. 2003. "International Intersectionality: Theoretical and Pragmatic Exploration of Women's International Human Rights Violations." *Emory Law Journal* 52: 71–187.

Bonilla-Silva, Eduardo. 2003. *Racism without Racists: Color-Blind Racism and the Persistence of Racial Inequality in the United States*. Lanham, MD: Rowman & Littlefield Publishers.

———. 2008. "'Look, a Negro': Reflections on the Human Rights Approach to Racial Inequality." In *Globalization and America*, edited by A. J. Hattery, D. G. Embrick, and E. Smith, 9–22. Lanham, MD: Rowman & Littlefield Publishers.

Bonnin, Debbie. 1995. "Road to Beijing." *Agenda* 27: 74–77.

Border Network for Human Rights (BNHR). 2003. *Two–US/Mexico Border Reports*. BNHR. http://www.bnhr.org/reports/u-s-mexico-border-reports-2000-2005 (accessed July 17, 2012).

Bottomore, T. B. 1963. *Karl Marx: Early Writings*. New York: McGraw-Hill.

Bourgois, Philippe. 1990. "Confronting the Ethics of Ethnography: Lessons from Fieldwork in Central America." In *Ethnographic Fieldwork: An Anthropological Reader*, edited by Antonius C. G. M. Robben and Jeffery A. Sluka. Malden, MA: Blackwell Publishing.

Boyle, Elizabeth Heger. 2002. *Female Genital Cutting: Cultural Conflict in the Global Community*. Baltimore: Johns Hopkins University Press.

———. 2009. "The Cost of Rights or the Right Cost? The Impact of Global Economic and Human Rights Policies on Child Well-Being since 1989." NSF Grant, Law and Social Science Program.

Brabeck, Kalina, and Qingwen Xu. 2010. "The Impact of Detention and Deportation on Latino Immigrant Children and Families: A Quantitative Exploration." *Hispanic Journal of Behavioral Sciences* 32: 341–361.

Bradshaw, W., D. Roseborough, and M. Armour. 2006. "Recovery from Severe Mental Illness: The Lived Experience of the Initial Phase of Treatment." *International Journal of Psychosocial Rehabilitation* 10: 123–131.

Brewer, Rose. 1993. "Theorizing Race, Class and Gender: The New Scholarship of Black Feminist Intellectuals and Black Women's Labor." In *Theorizing Black Feminisms: The Visionary Pragmatism of Black Women*, edited by Stanlie M. James and Abena P. A. Busia, 13–30. New York: Routledge.

Brice, Arthur. 2010. "Mexico Asks for Probe into Teen's Shooting Death by U.S. Border Agent." CNN News. June 10. http://articles.cnn.com/2010-06-08/us/texas.border.patrol.shooting_1_ciudad-juarez-fbi-agent?_s=PM:US (accessed March 23, 2011).

Britton, Dana M. 2003. *At Work in the Iron Cage: The Prison as Gendered Organization*. New York: New York University Press.

Brod, H. 1987. *The Making of Masculinities: The New Men's Studies*. Boston, MA: Allen and Unwin.

Broido, E. M. 2000. "The Development of Social Justice Allies during College: A Phenomenological Investigation." *Journal of College Student Development* 41: 3–17.

Brown, Tony N., Sherrill L. Sellers, Kendrick T. Brown, and James S. Jackson. 1999. "Race, Ethnicity, and Culture in the Sociology of Mental Health." In *Handbook of the Sociology of Mental Health,* edited by Carol S. Aneshensel and J. C. Phelan, 167–182. New York: Springer.

Brückner, H., and K. U. Mayer. 2005. "De-Standardization of the Life Course: What It Might Mean? And if It Means Anything, whether It Actually Took Place." In *The Structure of the Life Course: Standardized? Individualized? Differentiated?,* edited by R. Macmillan, 27–54. Advances in Life Course Research 9. Amsterdam: JAI Elsevier.

Brush, Lisa D. 2002. *Gender and Governance.* Lanham, MD: AltaMira Press.

Bunch, Charlotte. 1990. "Women's Rights as Human Rights: Toward a Re-Vision of Human Rights." *Human Rights Quarterly* 12: 486–498.

Bunch, Charlotte, and Susana Fried. 1996. "Beijing '95: Moving Women's Human Rights from Margin to Center." *Signs* 22: 200–204.

Burchardt, T. 2004. "Capabilities and Disability: The Capabilities Framework and the Social Model of Disability." *Disability and Society* 19: 735–751.

Burke, Mary C. 2010. "Transforming Gender: Medicine, Body Politics, and the Transgender Rights Movement." PhD diss., University of Connecticut, Storrs.

Busfield, J. 1996. *Men, Women and Madness: Understanding Gender and Mental Disorder.* London: Macmillan Press.

Bush, Roderick. 2000. *We Are Not What We Seem: Black Nationalism and Class Struggle in the American Century.* New York: New York University Press.

Bustamante, Jorge A. 1972. "The Wetback as Deviant: An Application of Labeling Theory." *American Journal of Sociology* 77: 706–718.

Butler, Judith. 1990. *Gender Trouble: Feminism and the Subversion of Identity.* New York: Routledge.

Butler, R. 2002 [1972]. *Why Survive? Being Old in America.* Baltimore: Johns Hopkins.

Buvinic, Mayra. 1998. "Women in Poverty: A New Global Underclass." Women in Politics. http://www.onlinewomeninpolitics.org/beijing12/womeninpoverty.pdf (accessed April 11, 2011).

Cagatay, Nilufur. 2001. *Trade, Gender, and Poverty.* New York: United Nations Development Program.

Cahill, Sean. 2009. "The Disproportionate Impact of Antigay Family Policies on Black and Latino Same-Sex Couple Households." *Journal of African American Studies* 13: 219–250.

Callahan, D. 1987. *Setting Limits: Medical Goals in an Aging Society.* New York: Simon and Schuster.

Carlton-Ford, Steve. 2010. "Major Armed Conflicts, Militarization, and Life Chances: A Pooled Time Series Analysis." *Armed Forces and Society* 36: 864–889.

Carpenter, M. 2000. "'It's a Small World': Mental Health Policy under Welfare Capitalism since 1945." *Sociology of Health and Illness* 22: 602–620.

Castel, R. 1988. *The Regulation of Madness: The Origins of Incarceration in France.* Oxford: Blackwell.

Cavanagh, Shannon E. 2007. "The Social Construction of Romantic Relationships in Adolescence: Examining the Role of Peer Networks, Gender, and Race." *Sociological Inquiry* 77: 572–600.

Cerna, Christina M. 1995. "East Asian Approaches to Human Rights: Proceedings of the Annual Meeting." *American Society of International Law* 89: 152–157.

Césaire, Aimé. 2001. *Discourse on Colonialism.* New York: Monthly Review Press.

Chapkis, Wendy. 2000. "Power and Control in the Commercial Sex Trade." In *Sex for Sale: Prostitution, Pornography, and the Sex Industry,* edited by Ronald Weitzer, 181–202. New York: Routledge.

Chavez, Leo R. 2008. *The Latino Threat: Constructing Immigrants, Citizens, and the Nation.* Stanford, CA: Stanford University Press.

Chow, Esther Ngan-ling. 1996. "Making Waves, Moving Mountains: Reflections on Beijing '95 and Beyond." *Signs* 22: 185–192.

Chudacoff, H. 1989. *How Old Are You? Age Consciousness in America.* Princeton, NJ: Princeton University Press.

Ciganda, Daniel, Alain Gagnon, and Eric Tenkorang. 2010. "Child and Young Adult Headed Households in the Context of the AIDS Epidemic in Zimbabwe, 1988–2006." PSC Discussion Papers Series 24, no. 4: 1–17.

Clapham, Andrew. 2007. *Human Rights: A Very Short Introduction.* New York: Oxford University Press.

Clark, Cindy Dell. 2010. *A Younger Voice: Doing Child-Centered Qualitative Research.* New York: Oxford University Press.

Clark-Ibáñez, Marisol. 2007. "Inner-City Children in Sharper Focus: Sociology of Childhood and Photo-Elicitation Interviews." In *Visual Research Methods: Image, Society, and Representation,* edited by Gregory C. Stanczak, 167–196. Thousand Oaks, CA: Sage Publications.

Cohen, Carl. 1986. "The Case for the Use of Animals in Biomedical Research." *New England Journal of Medicine* 315: 865–870.

Cohen, Cathy. 1999. *The Boundaries of Blackness: AIDS and the Breakdown of Black Politics.* Chicago: University of Chicago Press.

Cohn, Marjorie. 2001. "The World Trade Organization: Elevating Property Interests above Human Rights." *Georgia Journal of International and Comparative Law* 29: 427–440.

Coleman, Matthew. 2007. "Immigration Geopolitics beyond the Mexico-U.S. Border." *Antipode* 39: 54–76.

Colker, R. 2005. *The Disability Pendulum the First Decade of the Americans with Disabilities Act.* New York: New York University Press.

Collins, Patricia Hill. 1990. *Black Feminist Thought: Knowledge, Consciousness, and the Politics of Empowerment.* New York: Routledge, Chapman and Hall.

———. 1993. "Toward a New Vision: Race, Class, and Gender as Categories of Analysis and Connection." *Race, Sex and Class* 1: 25–45.

———. 1994. "Shifting the Center: Race, Class, and Feminist Theorizing about Motherhood." In *Representations of Motherhood*, edited by Donna Basin and Margaret Honey, 56–74. New Haven, CT: Yale University Press.

Coltraine, Scott, and Michelle Adams. 2008. *Gender and Families.* Lanham, MD: AltaMira Press.

Committee on the Elimination of Racial Discrimination. 2000. "General Recommendation 25, Gender Related Dimensions of Racial Discrimination." University of Minnesota, Human Rights Library. http://www1.umn.edu/humanrts/gencomm/genrexxv.htm (accessed September 6, 2012).

Conley, Dalton, Kate W. Strully, and Neil G. Bennett. 2003. *The Starting Gate: Birth Weight and Life Chances.* Berkeley: University of California Press.

Connell, Raeyn. 1987. *Gender and Power: Society, the Person, and Sexual Politics.* Stanford, CA: Stanford University Press.

Cook, Daniel T., and John Wall, eds. 2011. *Children and Armed Conflict.* Hampshire, UK: Palgrave Macmillan.

Cook, J. A., and E. R. Wright. 1995. "Medical Sociology and the Study of Severe Mental Illness: Reflections on Past Accomplishments and Directions for Future Research." *Journal of Health and Social Behaviour* 35: 95–114.

Corrêa, S., and V. Muntarbhorn. 2007. "The Yogyakarta Principles on the Application of International Human Rights Law in Relation to Sexual Orientation and Gender Identity." The Yogyakarta Principles. http://www.yogyakartaprinciples.org/principles_en.htm (accessed July 21, 2010).

Corsaro, William A. 2005. *The Sociology of Childhood.* Newbury Park, CA: Pine Forge Press.

Cox, Oliver Cromwell. 1948. *Caste, Class, and Race: A Study in Social Dynamics.* New York: Monthly Review Press.

Crenshaw, Kimberlé. 1991. "Mapping the Margins: Intersectionality, Identity Politics, and Violence against Women of Color." *Stanford Law Review* 43: 1241–1299.

Crooms, Lisa. 1997. "Indivisible Rights and Intersectional Identities or 'What Do Women's Rights Have to Do with the Race Convention?'" *Howard Law Journal* 40: 620–640.

Crosnoe, Robert. 2011. *Fitting In, Standing Out: Navigating the Social Challenges of High School to Get an Education.* New York: Cambridge University Press.

Crosnoe, Robert, and Glen H. Elder Jr. 2004. "From Childhood to the Later Years: Pathways of Human Development." *Research on Aging* 26, no. 6: 623–654.

Currah, Paisley, Richard M. Juang, and Shannon Price Minter. 2006. *Transgender Rights.* Minneapolis: University of Minnesota Press.

Dallaire, Bernadette, Michael McCubbin, Paul Morin, and David Cohen. 2000. "Civil Commitment Due to Mental Illness and Dangerousness: The Union of Law and Psychiatry within a Treatment-Control System." *Sociology of Health and Illness* 22: 679–699.

Daniels, Roger. 2004. *Guarding the Golden Door: American Immigration Policy and Immigrants since 1882.* New York: Hill and Wang.

Dannefer, Dale. 1984. "Adult Development and Social Theory: A Paradigmatic Reappraisal." *American Sociological Review* 49: 1.

Dannefer, Dale, and P. Uhlenberg. 1999. "Paths of the Life Course: A Typology." In *Handbook of Theories of Aging*, edited by V. Bengtson and K. W. Schaie, 306–327. New York: Springer.

Dannefer, Dale, and Chris Phillipson, eds. 2010. *International Handbook of Social Gerontology.* London: Sage.

Dannefer, Dale, and Robin Shura. 2007. "The Second Demographic Transition, Aging Families, and the Aging of the Institutionalized Life Course." In *Social Structures: Demographic Changes and the Well-Being of Older Persons*, edited by K. Warner Schaie and Peter Uhlenberg, 212–229. New York: Springer.

———. 2009. "Experience, Social Structure and Later Life: Meaning and Old Age in an Aging Society." In *International Handbook of Population Aging*, edited by P. Uhlenberg, 747–755. Dordrecht, the Netherlands: Springer.

De Genova, Nicholas. 2005. "In Re: Rodriguez." In *The Oxford Encyclopedia of Latinos and Latinas in the United States*, edited by S. Oboler and D. J. González, 2:380–382. New York: Oxford University Press.

Derrida, Jacques. 2004. "The Animal that I Am." In *Animal Philosophy: Essential Readings in Continental Thought*, edited by Peter Allerton and Matthew Calarco: 113–128. New York: Continuum.

Dhamoon, Rita. 2010. *Identity/Difference Politics: How Difference Is Produced, and Why It Matters.* Vancouver: University of British Columbia.

Diamond, Lisa. 2006. "Careful What You Ask For: Reconsidering Feminist Epistemology and Autobiographical Narrative in Research on Sexual Identity Development." *Signs* 31: 471–491.

Dill, Bonnie Thornton. 1983. "Race, Class, and Gender: Prospects for an All-Inclusive Sisterhood." *Feminist Studies* 9: 131–150.

DiMauro, Diane. 1995. *Sexuality Research in the United States: An Assessment of the Social and Behavioral Sciences.* New York: Social Sciences Research Council.

Donnelly, Jack. 1982. "Human Rights and Human Dignity: An Analytic Critique of Non-Western Conceptions of Human Rights." *American Political Science Review* 76, no. 2: 303–316.

——. 2003. *Universal Human Rights in Theory and Practice.* 2nd ed. Ithaca, NY: Cornell University Press.

Donovan, Josephine, and Carol Adams, eds. 1995. *Animals and Women: Feminist Theoretical Explorations.* Durham, NC: Duke University Press.

——, eds. 2007. *The Feminist Care Tradition in Animal Ethics.* New York: Columbia University Press.

Douglas, Karen Manges, and Rogelio Sáenz. 2010. "The Making of 'Americans': Old Boundaries, New Realities." In *Teaching and Studying the Americas: Cultural Influences from Colonialism to the Present,* edited by A. B. Pinn, C. F. Levander, and M. O. Emerson, 139–156. New York: Palgrave Macmillan.

Dowd, Jacquelyn Hall. 1993. *Revolt against Chivalry.* New York: Columbia University Press.

Dowse, L. 2001. "Contesting Practices, Challenging Codes: Self Advocacy, Disability Politics and the Social Model." *Disability and Society* 16: 123–141.

Doyal, Lesley. 1995. *What Makes Women Sick: Gender and the Political Economy of Health.* London: Macmillan.

——. 2001. "Sex, Gender, and Health: The Need for a New Approach." *British Medical Journal* (November 3): 323–331.

Dreby, Joanna. 2010. *Divided by Borders.* Berkeley: University of California Press.

Dreier, J. 2004. "Decision Theory and Morality." In *The Oxford Handbook of Rationality,* edited by A. Mele and P. Rawling, 156–181. Oxford: Oxford University Press.

Drucker, Peter. 2000. *Different Rainbows.* London: Gay Men's Press.

Du Bois, W. E. B. 1983. *Dusk of Dawn: An Essay toward an Autobiography of a Race Concept.* Piscataway, NJ: Transaction Publishers.

——. 2010 [1899]. *The Philadelphia Negro.* New York: Cosimo Classics.

Dudley-Marling, C. 2004. "The Social Construction of Learning Disabilities." *Journal of Learning Disabilities* 37: 482–489.

Dunn, Timothy J. 2001. "Border Militarization via Drug and Immigration Enforcement: Human Rights Implications." *Social Justice* 28: 7–30.

——. 2009. *Blockading the Border and Human Rights: The El Paso Operation that Remade Immigration Enforcement.* Austin: University of Texas Press.

Dunn, Timothy J., Ana Maria Aragones, and George Shivers. 2005. "Recent Mexican Migration in the Rural Delmarva Peninsula: Human Rights versus Citizenship Rights in a Local Context." In *New Destinations: Mexican Immigration in the United States,* edited by V. Zúñiga and R. Hernández-León, 155–183. New York: Russell Sage.

Eaton, W. W. 1980. "A Formal Theory of Selection for Schizophrenia." *American Journal of Sociology* 86: 149–158.

Edin, Kathryn, and Maria Kefalas. 2005. *Promises I Can Keep: Why Poor Women Put Motherhood before Marriage.* Berkeley: University of California Press.

Edwards, C., S. Staniszweska, and N. Crichton. 2004. "Investigation of the Ways in Which Patients' Reports of Their Satisfaction with Healthcare Are Constructed." *Sociology of Health and Illness* 26: 159–183.

Edwards, K. E. 2006. "Aspiring Social Justice Ally Identity Development: A Conceptual Model." *NASPA Journal* 43: 39–60.

Egan, Patrick J., and Kenneth Sherrill. 2009. *California's Proposition 8: What Happened, and What Does the Future Hold?* San Francisco: Evelyn and Walter Haas Jr. Fund and the National Gay and Lesbian Task Force Policy Institute.

Eisenstein, Hester. 1983. *Contemporary Feminist Thought.* Boston: G. K. Hall.

Elder, Glen H., Jr. 1999 [1974]. *Children of the Great Depression: Social Change in Life Experience.* 25th anniv. ed. Boulder, CO: Westview Press.

Elder, Glen H., Jr., Elizabeth Colerick Clipp, J. Scott Brown, Leslie R. Martin, and Howard S. Friedman. 2009. "The Life-Long Mortality Risks of World War II Experiences." *Research on Aging* 30, no. 4: 391–412.

End Corporal Punishment. http://www.endcorporalpunishment.org.

England, Paula. 2005. "Gender Inequality in Labor Markets: The Role of Motherhood and Segregation." *Social Politics* 12: 264–288.

Enloe, Cynthia. 1990. *Bananas, Beaches, and Bases: Making Feminist Sense of International Politics.* Berkeley: University of California Press.

——. 2000. *Maneuvers: The International Politics of Militarizing Women's Lives.* Berkeley: University of California Press.

——. 2007. *Globalization and Militarism: Feminists Make the Link.* Boulder, CO: Rowman & Littlefield.

Ericksen, Julia A., with Sally A. Steffen. 2001. *Kiss and Tell: Surveying Sex in the Twentieth Century.* Cambridge, MA: Harvard University Press.

Eschbach, Karl, J. Hagan, N. Rodriguez, R. Hernandez-Leon, and S. Bailey. 1999. "Death at the Border." *International Migration Review* 33: 430–454.

Estes, C. L., S. Goldberg, S. Shostack, K. Linkins, and R. Beard. 2006. "Implications of Welfare Reform for the Elderly: A Case Study of Provider, Advocate, and Consumer Perspectives." *Journal of Aging and Social Policy* 19, no. 1: 41–63.

Eurobarometer. 2010. "Mental Health. Part One: Report." Special Eurobarometer 345/Eurobarometer 73.2. http://ec.europa.eu/health/mental_health/docs/ebs_345_en.pdf (accessed April 20, 2011).

Evans, N. J., J. L. Assadi, and T. K. Herriott. 2005. "Encouraging the Development of Disability Allies." *New Directions for Student Services* 110: 67–79.

Evans, Tony. 2001b. *The Politics of Human Rights.* London: Pluto Press.

Fakhoury, W., and S. Priebe. 2002. "The Process of Deinstitutionalization: An International Overview." *Current Opinion in Psychiatry* 15: 187–192.

Fanon, Frantz. 2005. *The Wretched of the Earth.* New York: Grove Press.

——. 2008. *Black Skin, White Masks.* Revised. New York: Grove Press.

Farnall, O., and K. A. Smith. 1999. "Reactions to People with Disabilities: Personal Contact versus Viewing of Specific Media Portrayal." *Journalism and Mass Communication Quarterly* 76: 659–672.

Fausto-Sterling, Anne. 2000a. "The Five Sexes Revisited." *Sciences* 40: 18–23.

——. 2000b. *Sexing the Body: Gender Politics and the Construction of Sexuality.* New York: Basic Books.

Feagin, Joe R. 2006. *Systemic Racism: A Theory of Oppression.* New York: Routledge.

——. 2010. *The White Racial Frame: Centuries of Racial Framing and Counter-Framing.* New York: Routledge.

Feagin, Joe R., and Hernan Vera. 2008. *Liberation Sociology.* 2nd ed. Boulder, CO: Paradigm Publishers.

Ferguson, Kathy E. 1991. "Interpretation and Genealogy in Feminism." *Signs: Journal of Women in Culture and Society* 16: 322–339.

Fink, Leon. 2003. *The Mayan of Morganton.* Chapel Hill: University of North Carolina Press.

Fitzgerald, Amy, Linda Kalof, and Thomas Dietz. 2009. "Slaughterhouses and Increased Crime Rates: An Empirical Analysis of Spillover from 'The Jungle' into the Surrounding Community." *Organization and Environment* 22: 158–184.

Fix, Michael, and Wendy Zimmermann. 2001. "All under One Roof: Mixed-Status Families in an Era of Reform." *International Migration Review* 35: 397–419.

Fleischer, D. A., and F. Zames. 2001. *The Disability Rights Movement: From Charity to Confrontation.* Philadelphia: Temple University Press.

Flippen, Chenoa Anne. 2004. "Unequal Returns to Housing Investments? A Study of Real Housing Appreciation among Black, White, and Hispanic Households." *Social Forces* 82: 1523–1551.

Fone, Byrne. 2000. *Homophobia: A History.* New York: Metropolitan Books.

Foner, A. 1974. "Age Stratification and Age Conflict in Political Life." *American Sociological Review* 39, no. 2: 187–196.

Forman, Tyrone A., and Amanda E. Lewis. 2006. "Racial Apathy and Hurricane Katrina: The Social Anatomy of Prejudice in the Post–Civil Rights Era." *Du Bois Review: Social Science Research on Race* 3: 175–202.

Foster-Fishman, Pennie, Tiffany Jimenez, Maria Valenti, and Tasha Kelley. 2007. "Building the Next Generation of Leaders in the Disabilities Movement." *Disability and Society* 22: 341–356.

Foucault, Michel. 1978. *The History of Sexuality: An Introduction.* Vol. 1. New York: Vintage Books.

——. 1995 [1971]. *Madness and Civilization: A History of Insanity in the Age of Reason.* London: Tavistock.

Fox, Mary Frank. 1995. "From the President." *SWS Network News,* 2.

Franck, Thomas M. 2001. "Are Human Rights Universal?" *Foreign Affairs* 80: 191–204.

Frankenberg, Ruth. 1993. *White Women, Race Matters: The Social Construction of Whiteness.* London: Taylor and Francis.

Franklin, James C. 2008. "Shame on You: The Impact of Human Rights Criticism on Political Repression in Latin America." *International Studies Quarterly* 52: 187–211.

Freedman, M. 2007. *Prime Time: How Baby Boomers Will Revolutionize Retirement and Transform America.* Cambridge, MA: Perseus Books.

Freeman, Marsha. 1999. "International Institutions and Gendered Justice." *Journal of International Affairs* 52: 513–533.

Freire, Paulo. 2000. *Pedagogy of the Oppressed.* New York: Continuum International.

Fry, C. L. 2007. "Demographic Transitions, Age, and Culture." In *Social Structures: Demographic Changes and the Well-Being of Older Persons,* edited by K. W. Schaie and P. Uhlenberg, 283–300. New York: Springer Publishing Co.

Fukumura, Yoko, and Martha Matsuoka. 2002. "Redefining Security: Okinawa Women's Resistance to U.S. Militarism." In *Women's Activism and Globalization: Linking Local Struggles and Transnational Politics*, edited by Nancy A. Naples and Manisha Desai, 239–263. New York: Routledge.

Furstenberg, Frank. 2010. "On a New Schedule: Transitions to Adulthood and Family Change." *Transition to Adulthood* 20, no. 1: 68–87.

Gaer, Felice. 1998. "And Never the Twain Shall Meet? The Struggle to Establish Women's Rights as International Human Rights." In *The International Human Rights of Women: Instruments of Change*, edited by Carol Lockwood et al., 41–69. Washington, DC: American Bar Association Section of International Law and Practice.

Gamson, William A. 1988. "Review: [untitled]." *American Journal of Sociology* 94: 436–438.

Gandhi, Mahatma. 2002. *The Essential Gandhi: An Anthology of His Writings on His Life, Work and Ideas*. New York: Vintage Publishers.

Garfinkel, Harold. 1967. *Studies in Ethnomethodology*. Englewood Cliffs, NJ: Prentice Hall.

Gaston, Alonso, Noel Anderson, Celina Su, and Jeanne Theoharis. 2009. *Our Schools Suck: Students Talk Back to a Segregated Nation on the Failures of Urban Education*. New York: New York University Press.

Gavey, N., K. McPhillips, and M. Doherty. 2001. "'If It's Not On, It's Not On'—Is It? Discursive Constraints on Women's Condom Use." *Gender and Society* 15: 917–934.

Gerhardt, U. 1989. *Ideas about Illness: An Intellectual and Political History of Medical Sociology*. New York: New York University Press.

GID Reform Advocates. 2008. "GID Reform Advocates." Transgender Forum. http://www.transgender.org/gird (accessed November 11, 2011).

Gill, Aisha K., and Anitha Sundari. 2011. *Forced Marriage: Introducing a Social Justice and Human Rights Perspective*. Boston: Zed Books.

Glenn, Evelyn Nakano. 1999. "The Social Construction and Institutionalization of Gender and Race: An Integrative Framework." In *Revisiting Gender*, edited by Myra Marx Ferree, Judith Lorber, and Beth B. Hess, 3–43. New York: Sage.

Goffman, Erving. 1959. *The Presentation of Self in Everyday Life*. 1st ed. Garden City, NY: Anchor.

——. 1961. *Asylums: Essays on the Social Situation of Mental Patients and Other Inmates*. New York: Anchor Books.

——. 1986. *Frame Analysis: An Essay on the Organization of Experience*. Boston: Northeastern University Press.

Golash-Boza, Tanya. 2009. "The Immigration Industrial Complex: Why We Enforce Immigration Policies Destined to Fail." *Sociology Compass* 3: 295–309.

Goldberg, David Theo. 1990. *Anatomy of Racism*. Minneapolis: University of Minnesota Press.

Gonzales, Roberto G. 2011. "Learning to Be Illegal." *American Sociological Review* 76: 602–619.

González-López, Gloria. 2005. *Erotic Journeys: Mexican Immigrants and Their Sex Lives*. Berkeley: University of California Press.

Goodhard, Michael. 2003. "Origins and Universality in the Human Rights Debates: Cultural Essentialism and the Challenge of Globalization." *Human Rights Quarterly* 25: 935–964.

Goodyear-Smith, F., and S. Buetow. 2001. "Power Issues in the Doctor-Patient Relationship." *Health Care Analysis* 9: 449–462.

Goonesekere, Savitri. 2000. "Human Rights as a Foundation for Family Law Reform." *International Journal of Children's Rights* 8: 83–99.

Gordon, B. O., and K. E. Rosenblum. 2001. "Bringing Disability into the Sociological Frame: A Comparison of Disability with Race, Sex, and Sexual Orientation Statuses." *Disability and Society* 16: 5–19.

Gramsci, Antonio. 1971. *Selections from the Prison Notebooks*. New York: International Publishers Co.

Gran, Brian K. 2010a. "A Comparative-Historical Analysis of Children's Rights." NSF Grant, Law and Social Science Program.

——. 2010b. "Comparing Children's Rights: Introducing the Children's Rights Index." *International Journal of Children's Rights* 18, no. 1: 1–17.

——. 2011. "The Roles of Independent Children's Rights Institutions in Implementing the CRC." In *Children's Rights: From 20th Century Visions to 21st Century Implementation?*, 219–237. Surrey, UK: Ashgate Publishing Group.

Gran, Brian K., and Dawn M. Aliberti. 2003. "The Office of Children's Ombudsperson: Children's Rights and Social-Policy Innovation." *International Journal of the Sociology of Law* 31, no. 2: 89–106.

Greenberg, David F. 1988. *The Construction of Homosexuality*. Chicago: University of Chicago Press.

Grewal, Inderpal, and Caren Kaplan, eds. 1994. *Scattered Hegemonies: Postmodernity and Transnational Feminist Practices*. Minneapolis: University of Minnesota Press.

——. 2000. "Postcolonial Studies and Transnational Feminist Practices." *Jouvert: A Journal of Postcolonial Studies* 5. http://social.chass.ncsu.edu/jouvert/v5i1/con51.htm (accessed September 6, 2012).

Grossberg, Lawrence. 1992. *We Gotta Get Out of This Place: Popular Conservatism and Postmodern Culture*. 1st ed. London: Routledge.

Grue, L. 2010. "Eugenics and Euthanasia—Then and Now." *Scandinavian Journal of Disability Research* 12: 33–45.

Gubrium, Jaber. 1997. *Living and Dying and Murray Manor.* Charlottesville: University Press of Virginia.

Hafner-Burton, Emilie. 2005. "Right or Robust? The Sensitive Nature of Repression to Globalization." *Journal of Peace Research* 42: 679–698.

Hafner-Burton, Emilie M., and Kiyoteru Tsutsui. 2005. "Human Rights in a Globalizing World: The Paradox of Empty Promises." *American Journal of Sociology* 110: 1373–1411.

Hafner-Burton, Emilie M., Kiyoteru Tsutsui, and John W. Meyer. 2008. "International Human Rights Law and the Politics of Legitimation: Repressive States and Human Rights Treaties." *International Sociology* 23, no. 1: 115–141.

Hagestad, Gunhild O. 2008. "The Book-Ends: Emerging Perspectives on Children and Old People." In *Families and Social Policy: Intergenerational Solidarity in European Welfare States,* edited by C. Saraceno, 20–37. London: Edward Elgar Publishing.

Hagestad, Gunhild O., and Peter Uhlenberg. 2005. "The Social Separation of Old and Young: A Root of Ageism." *Journal of Social Issues* 61: 343–360.

——. 2006. "Should We Be Concerned about Age Segregation? Some Theoretical and Empirical Explorations." *Research on Aging* 28: 638–653.

——. 2007. "The Impact of Demographic Changes on Relations between Age Groups and Generations: A Comparative Perspective." In *Social Structures: Demographic Changes and the Well-Being of Older Persons,* edited by K. W. Schaie and P. Uhlenberg, 239–261. New York: Springer Publishing Co.

Hagestad, Gunhild O., and Dale Dannefer. 2001. "Concepts and Theories of Aging: Beyond Microfication in Social Science Approaches." In *Handbook of Aging and Social Sciences,* edited by R. Binstock and L. George. 5th ed. San Diego: Academic Press.

Haiken, Elizabeth. 1999. *Venus Envy: A History of Cosmetic Surgery.* Baltimore: Johns Hopkins University Press.

Hall, G. B., and G. Nelson. 1996. "Social Networks, Social Support, Personal Empowerment, and the Adaptation of Psychiatric Consumers: Survivors: Path Analytic Models." *Social Science and Medicine* 43: 1743–1754.

Hall, Stuart. 1986. "Gramsci's Relevance for the Study of Race and Ethnicity." *Journal of Communication Inquiry* 10: 5–27.

Haney, Lynn. 2000. "Feminist State Theory: Applications to Jurisprudence, Criminology, and the Welfare State." *Annual Review of Sociology* 26: 641–666.

Hao, Lingxin, and Suet-ling Pong. 2008. "The Role of School in Upward Mobility of Disadvantaged Immigrants' Children." *Annals of the American Academy of Political and Social Sciences* 620, no. 1: 62–89.

Harding, David J. 2007. "Cultural Context, Sexual Behavior, and Romantic Relationships in Disadvantage." *American Sociological Review* 72: 341–364.

Harding, Sandra, and K. Norberg. 2005. "New Feminist Approaches to Social Science Methodologies: An Introduction." *Signs: Journal of Women in Culture and Society* 30: 2009–2015.

Harper, A. Breeze, ed. 2010. *Sistah Vegan: Black Female Vegans Speak on Food, Identity, Health, and Society.* New York: Lantern Books.

Harris, Angela. 1990. "Race and Essentialism in Feminist Legal Theory." *Stanford Law Review* 42: 581–616.

Herdt, Gilbert. 1994. *Third Sex, Third Gender.* New York: Zone Books.

——. 1997. *Same Sex, Different Cultures: Exploring Gay and Lesbian Lives.* Oxford: Westview.

Herek, Gregory M., and John P. Capitanio. 1996. "'Some of My Best Friends': Intergroup Contact, Concealable Stigma, and Heterosexuals' Attitudes toward Gay Men and Lesbians." *Personality and Social Psychology Bulletin* 22: 412–424.

Herek, Gregory M., and Eric K. Glunt. 1993. "Interpersonal Contact and Heterosexuals' Attitudes toward Gay Men: Results from a National Survey." *Journal of Sex Research* 30: 239–244.

Hershock, Peter D. 2000. "Dramatic Intervention: Human Rights from a Buddhist Perspective." *Philosophy East and West* 50: 9–33.

Hesse-Biber, Sharlene Nagy. 2006. *The Cult of Thinness.* New York: Oxford University Press.

Heyman, Josiah. 2002. "U.S. Immigration Officers of Mexican Ancestry as Mexican Americans, Citizens, and Immigration Police." *Current Anthropology* 43: 479–507.

——. 2010. "Human Rights and Social Justice Briefing 1: Arizona's Immigration Law—S.B. 1070." Society for Applied Anthropology. http://www.sfaa.net/committees/humanrights/AZImmigrationLawSB1070.pdf (accessed July 17, 2012).

Hill, Jane H. 2008. *The Everyday Language of White Racism.* Malden, MA: Wiley-Blackwell.

Hlaing, Kyaw Y. 2005. "Myanmar in 2004: Another Year of Uncertainty." *Asian Survey* 45: 174–179.

Hoang, Nghia. 2009. "The 'Asian Values' Perspective of Human Rights: A Challenge to Universal Human Rights." Social Science Research Network. http://ssrn.com/abstract=1405436 (accessed July 17, 2012).

Hockenberry, J. 1995. *Moving Violations: War Zones, Wheelchairs, and Declarations of Independence.* New York: Hyperion.

Holland, J., C. Ramazanoglu, S. Sharpe, and R. Thomson. 1998. *The Male in the Head: Young People, Hetero-sexuality and Power*. London: The Tufnell.

Hollingshead, A. B., and F. C. Redlich. 1958. *Social Class and Mental Illness*. New York: Wiley.

Holstein, James A., and Jaber F. Gubrium. 1999. *The Self We Live By: Narrative Identity in a Postmodern World*. 1st ed. New York: Oxford University Press.

Horne, Sharon, and Melanie J. Zimmer-Gembeck. 2005. "Female Sexual Subjectivity and Well-Being: Compar-ing Late Adolescents with Different Sexual Experiences." *Sexuality Research and Social Policy* 2: 25–40.

Hosken, Fran P. 1993. *The Hosken Report: Genital and Sexual Mutilation of Females*. 4th ed. Lexington, MA: Women's International Network News.

Howard, Judith, and Carolyn Allen. 1996. "Reflections on the Fourth World Conference on Women and NGO Forum '95: Introduction." *Signs* 22: 181–185.

Huda, S. 2006. "Sex Trafficking in South Asia." *International Journal of Gynecology and Obstetrics* 94: 374–381.

Hughs, Alex, and Ann Witz. 1997. "Feminism and the Matter of Bodies: From de Beauvoir to Butler." *Body and Society* 3: 47–60.

Hulko, Wendy. 2009. "The Time- and Context-Contingent Nature of Intersectionality and Interlocking Oppressions." *Affilia: Journal of Women and Social Work* 24: 44–55.

Hynie, M., and J. E. Lydon. 1995. "Women's Perceptions of Female Contraceptive Behavior: Experimental Evidence of the Sexual Double Standard." *Psychology of Women Quarterly* 19: 563–581.

Ignatiev, N. 1995. *How the Irish Became White*. New York: Routledge.

Ingraham, Chrys. 2008. *White Weddings: Romancing Heterosexuality in Popular Culture*. New York: Routledge.

International Gay and Lesbian Human Rights Commission (IGLHRC). 2011. "Our Issues." IGLHRC. http://www.iglhrc.org/cgi-bin/iowa/theme/1.html (accessed November 11, 2011).

International Labour Office. 1973. Minimum Age Convention. http://www.ilocarib.org.tt/projects/cariblex/conventions_6.shtml (accessed September 6, 2012).

Irvine, Janice M. 2002. *Talk about Sex: The Battles over Sex Education in the United States*. Berkeley: University of California Press.

Ito, Mizuko, Sonja Baumer, Matteo Bittanti, Danah Boyd, Rachel Cody, Becky Herr-Stephenson, Heather A. Horst, Patricia G. Lange, Dilan Mahendran, Katynka Z. Martinez, C. J. Pascoe, Dan Perkel, Laura Robinson, Christo Sims, and Lisa Tripp, with Judd Antin, Megan Finn, Arthur Law, Annie Manion, Sarai Mitnick, David Scholssberg, and Sarita Yardi. 2009. *Hanging Out, Messing Around, and Geeking Out*. Cambridge, MA: Massachusetts Institute of Technology Press.

Jalata, Asafa. 2005. "State Terrorism and Globalization: The Cases of Ethiopia and Sudan." *International Journal of Comparative Sociology* 46, no. 1–2: 79–102.

James, Helen. 2006. "Myanmar in 2005: In a Holding Pattern." *Asian Survey* 46: 162–167.

Jamieson, Dale. 2003. *Morality's Progress: Essays on Humans, Other Animals, and the Rest of Nature*. London: Oxford University Press.

Jayasree, A. K. 2004. "Searching for Justice for Body and Self in a Coercive Environment: Sex Work in Kerala, India." *Reproductive Health Matters* 12: 58–67.

Jo, Moon Ho. 1984. "The Putative Political Complacency of Asian Americans." *Political Psychology* 5: 583–605.

Johnson, E. Patrick. 2003. *Appropriating Blackness: Performance and the Politics of Authenticity*. Durham, NC: Duke University Press.

Johnson, Victoria. 2011. "Everyday Rituals of the Master Race: Fascism, Stratification, and the Fluidity of 'Animal' Domination." In *Critical Theory and Animal Liberation*, edited by John Sanbonmatsu, 203–218. Lanham, MD: Rowman & Littlefield.

Jordan, Kathleen Casey. 1997. "The Effect of Disclosure on the Professional Life of Lesbian Police Officers." PhD diss., City University of New York.

Jordan-Zachary, Julia S. 2007. "Am I a Black Woman or a Woman Who Is Black? A Few Thoughts on the Meaning of Intersectionality." *Politics and Gender* 3: 254–263.

Jotkowitz, A., S. Glick, and B. Gesundheit. 2008. "A Case against Justified Non-Voluntary Active Euthanasia (The Groningen Protocol)." *American Journal of Bioethics* 8: 23–26.

Kaiser Family Foundation. 2002. *Sex Smarts Survey: Gender Roles*. Menlo Park, CA: Kaiser Family Foundation.

Kang, Miliann. 2003. "The Managed Hand: The Commercialization of Bodies and Emotions in Korean Immigrant-Owned Nail Salons." *Gender and Society* 17: 820–839.

Kapur, Ratna. 2002. "The Tragedy of Victimization Rhetoric: Resurrecting the 'Native' Subject in International/Post-Colonial Feminist Legal Politics." *Harvard Law School Human Rights Journal of Law* 15: 1–38.

Katz, Jonathan. 2007. *The Invention of Heterosexuality*. Chicago: University of Chicago Press.

Kausikan, Bilahari. 1995. "An East Asian Approach to Human Rights." *Buffalo Journal of International Law* 2: 263–283.

Keller, C., and M. Siegrist. 2010. "Psychological Resources and Attitudes toward People with Physical Disabilities." *Journal of Applied Social Psychology* 40: 389–401.

Kennedy, David. 2002. "Boundaries in the Field of Human Rights: The International Human Rights Movement: Part of the Problem?" *Harvard Law School Human Rights Journal* 15: 101–25.

Kessler R. C., and J. McLeod. 1984. "Sex Differences in Vulnerability to Undesirable Life Events." *American Sociological Review* 49: 620–631.

Kessler, Suzanne J. 1990. *Lessons from the Intersexed.* New Brunswick, NJ: Rutgers University Press.

Kim, Hyun Sik. 2011. "Consequences of Parental Divorce for Child Development." *American Sociological Review* 76, no. 3: 487–511.

Kimmel, Michael S. 2001. "The Kindest Un-Cut: Feminism, Judaism, and My Son's Foreskin." *Tikkun* 16, no. 1. http://www.cirp.org/pages/cultural/kimmel1/ (accessed September 6, 2012).

———. 2005. *Manhood in America: A Cultural History.* New York: Oxford University Press.

Kincaid, Jamaica. 2000. *A Small Place.* 1st ed. New York: Farrar, Straus and Giroux.

King, Deborah K. 1988. "Multiple Jeopardy, Multiple Consciousnesses: The Context of a Black Feminist Ideology." *Signs: Journal of Women in Culture and Society* 14: 42–72.

Kinsey, Alfred, Wardell B. Pomeroy, and Clyde E. Martin. 1948. *Sexual Behavior in the Human Male.* Philadelphia: W. B. Saunders Company.

Koch, T. 2004. "The Difference that Difference Makes: Bioethics and the Challenge of 'Disability.'" *Journal of Medicine and Philosophy* 29: 697–716.

Kohli, M., and J. W. Meyer. 1986. "Social Structure and Social Construction of Life Stages." *Human Development* 29, no. 3: 145–149.

Kohli, Martin. 1986. "Social Organization and Subjective Construction of the Life Course." In *Human Development and the Life Course,* edited by A. Sorensen, F. Weinert, and L. Sherrod, 271–292. Cambridge, MA: Harvard University Press.

———. 2007. "The Institutionalization of the Life Course: Looking Back to Look Ahead." *Research in Human Development* 4, no. 3–4: 253–271.

Kohn, Melvin L. 1981. "Social Class and Schizophrenia: A Critical Review and a Reformulation." In *The Sociology of Mental Illness: Basic Studies,* edited by O. Grusky and Pollner M. Holt, 127–143. New York: Rinehart and Winston.

Koven, Seth, and Sonya Michel, eds. 1993. *Mothers of a New World: Maternalist Politics and the Origins of Welfare States.* New York: Routledge.

Krahe, B., and C. Altwasser. 2006. "Changing Negative Attitudes towards Persons with Physical Disabilities: An Experimental Intervention." *Journal of Community and Applied Social Psychology* 16: 59–69.

Krieger, Nancy, Pamela D. Waterman, Cathy Hartman, Lisa M. Bates, Anne M. Stoddard, Margaret M. Quinn, Glorian Sorensen, and Elizabeth M. Barbeau. 2006. "Social Hazards on the Job: Workplace Abuse, Sexual Harassment, and Racial Discrimination—a Study of Black, Latino, and White Low-Income Women and Men Workers in the United States." *International Journal of Health Services* 36: 51–85.

Kuhn, Thomas S. 1996. *The Structure of Scientific Revolutions.* Chicago: University of Chicago Press.

Kulick, Don. 1998. *Travesti: Sex, Gender, and Culture among Brazilian Transgendered Prostitutes.* Chicago: University of Chicago Press.

Kurashige, Scott. 2002. "Detroit and the Legacy of Vincent Chin." *Amerasia Journal* 28: 51–55.

Kuroiwa, Yoko, and Maykel Verkuyten. 2008. "Narratives and the Constitutions of Common Identity: The Karen in Burma." *Identities: Global Studies in Power and Culture* 15: 391–412.

Lamb, H. R. 1998. "Mental Hospitals and Deinstitutionalization." In *Encyclopedia of Mental Health,* edited by H. S. Friedman, 2: 665–676. San Diego: Academic Press.

Landry, Bart. 2007. *Race, Gender, and Class: Theory and Methods of Analysis.* Upper Saddle River, NJ: Pearson.

Lareau, Annette. 2003. *Unequal Childhoods: Class, Race, and Family Life.* Berkeley: University of California Press.

Larson, Heidi. 1999. "Voices of Pacific Youth: Video Research as a Tool for Youth Expression." *Visual Sociology* 14: 163–172.

Laumann, Edward O., John H. Gagnon, Robert T. Michael, and Stuart Michaels. 2000. *The Social Organization of Sexuality: Sexual Practices in the United States.*

Leasher, M. K., C. E. Miller, and M. P. Gooden. 2009. "Rater Effects and Attitudinal Barriers Affecting People with Disabilities in Personnel Selection." *Journal of Applied Social Psychology* 39: 2236–2274.

Leibovitz, Joseph. 2007. "Faultline Citizenship: Ethnonational Politics, Minority Mobilisation, and Governance in the Israeli 'Mixed Cities' of Haifa and Tel Aviv-Jaffa." *Ethnopolitics* 6: 235–263.

Lenin, Vladimir I. 2007. *The State and Revolution.* Synergy International of the Americas.

Lenzer, Gertrud, and Brian K. Gran. 2011. "Rights and the Role of Family Engagement in Child Welfare: An International Treaties Perspective on Family's Rights, Parents' Rights, and Children's Rights." In

"Taking Child and Family Rights Seriously: Family Engagement and Its Evidence in Child Welfare," special issue, *Child Welfare* 90, no. 4: 157–179.

Levels, M., J. Dronkers, and G. Kraaykamp. 2008. "Educational Achievement of Immigrants in Western Countries: Origin, Destination, and Community Effects on Mathematical Performance." *American Sociological Review* 73, no. 5: 835–853.

Levine, J. 2002. *Harmful to Minors: The Perils of Protecting Children from Sex.* Minneapolis: University of Minnesota Press.

Levine, Judith A., Clifton R. Emery, and Harold Pollack. 2007. "The Well-Being of Children Born to Teen Mothers." *Journal of Marriage and Family* 69 (February): 105–122.

Levit, Nancy. 2002. "Theorizing the Connections among Systems of Subordination." *University of Missouri–Kansas City Law Review* 77: 227–249.

Lewis, L. 2009a. "Introduction: Mental Health and Human Rights: Social Policy and Sociological Perspectives." *Social Policy and Society* 8: 211–214.

——. 2009b. "Politics of Recognition: What Can a Human Rights Perspective Contribute to Understanding Users' Experiences of Involvement in Mental Health Services?" *Social Policy and Society* 8: 257–274.

Link, B. G., B. Dohrenwend, and A. Skodol. 1986. "Socioeconomic Status and Schizophrenia: Noisome Occupational Characteristics as a Risk Factor." *American Sociological Review* 51: 242–258.

Link, B. G., E. L. Struening, M. Rahav, J. C. Phelan, and L. Nuttbrock. 1997. "On Stigma and Its Consequences: Evidence from a Longitudinal Study of Men with Dual Diagnosis of Mental Illness and Substance Abuse." *Journal of Health and Social Behavior* 38: 177–190.

Link, Bruce, and Jo Phelan. 2001. "Conceptualizing Stigma." *Annual Review of Sociology* 27: 363–385.

Linzey, Andrew. 2009. *The Link between Animal Abuse and Human Violence.* East Sussex, UK: Sussex Academic Press.

Lockwood, Elizabeth, Daniel Barstow Magraw, Margaret Faith Spring, and S. I. Strong. 1998. *The International Human Rights of Women: Instruments of Change.* Washington, DC: American Bar Association Section of International Law and Practice.

Loe, Meika. 2006. *The Rise of Viagra: How the Little Blue Pill Changed Sex in America.* New York: New York University Press.

Long, A. B. 2008. "Introducing the New and Improved Americans with Disabilities Act: Assessing the ADA Amendments Act of 2008." *Northwestern University Law Review Colloquy* 103: 217–229.

Longmore, P. K. 2003. *Why I Burned My Book and Other Essays on Disability.* Philadelphia: Temple University Press.

López, Ian Haney. 2006. *White by Law: The Legal Construction of Race.* Rev. and updated 10th anniv. ed. New York: New York University Press.

Lopez, Iris. 1993. "Agency and Constraint: Sterilization and Reproductive Freedom among Puerto Rican Women in New York City." *Urban Anthropology* 22: 299–323.

Lorber, Judith. 2002. *Gender and the Construction of Illness.* Lanham, MD: AltaMira Press.

Lorber, Judith, and Lisa Jean Moore. 2007. *Gendered Bodies: Feminist Perspectives.* New York: Oxford.

Ludvig, Alice. 2006. "'Differences between Women' Intersecting Voices in a Female Narrative." *European Journal of Women's Studies* 13: 245–258.

Luker, Kristin. 2006. *When Sex Goes to School: Warring Views on Sex and Sex Education since the Sixties.* New York: W. W. Norton.

Mackelprang, R. W., and R. D. Mackelprang. 2005. "Historical and Contemporary Issues in End-of-Life Decisions: Implications for Social Work." *Social Work* 40: 315–324.

MacKinnon, Catherine. 1993. "On Torture: A Feminist Perspective on Human Rights." In *Human Rights in the Twenty-First Century: A Global Challenge,* edited by Kathleen E. Mahoney and Paul Mahoney. Boston: Springer Publishing.

Maira, Sunaina. 2004. "Youth Culture, Citizenship and Globalization: South Asian Muslim Youth in the United States after September 11th." *Comparative Studies of South Asia, Africa and the Middle East* 24: 219–231.

Mamo, Laura. 2007. *Queering Reproduction: Achieving Pregnancy in the Age of Technoscience.* Durham, NC: Duke University Press.

Margolis, Eric. 1999. "Class Pictures: Representations of Race, Gender and Ability in a Century of School Photography." *Visual Sociology* 14, no. 1: 7–38.

Martin, Karin A. 1996. *Puberty, Sexuality, and the Self: Boys and Girls at Adolescence.* New York: Routledge.

Massey, Douglas, Jorge Durand, and Nolan J. Malone. 2002. *Beyond Smoke and Mirrors: Mexican Immigration in an Era of Economic Integration.* New York: Russell Sage Foundation.

Matthews, N. 2009. "Contesting Representations of Disabled Children in Picture-Books: Visibility, the Body and the Social Model of Disability." *Children's Geographies* 7: 37–49.

Mayer, Karl Ulrich, and W. Müller. 1986. "The State and the Structure of the Life Course." In *Human*

Development and the Life Course: Multidisciplinary Perspectives, edited by A. B. Sorensen, F. E. Weinert, and L. R. Sherrod, 217–245. Hillsdale, NJ: Lawrence Erlbaum Associates.

Mayer, Karl Ulrich. 2009. "New Directions in Life Course Research." *Annual Review of Sociology* 35: 413–433.

McAdam, Doug. 1999. *Political Process and Black Insurgency, 1930–1970*. 2nd ed. Chicago: University of Chicago Press.

McCall, Leslie. 2001. *Complex Inequality: Gender, Class and Race in the New Economy*. New York: Routledge.

———. 2005. "The Complexity of Intersectionality." *Signs* 30: 1771–1800.

McCarthy, John D., and Mayer N. Zald. 1977. "Resource Mobilization and Social Movements: A Partial Theory." *American Sociological Review* 82: 1212–1241.

McIntyre, Alice. 1997. *Making Meaning of Whiteness: Exploring Racial Identity with White Teachers*. Albany: State University of New York Press.

Mead, George Herbert. 1967. *Mind, Self, and Society: From the Standpoint of a Social Behaviorist*. Chicago: University of Chicago Press.

Mead, S., and M. E. Copeland. 2001. "What Recovery Means to Us: Consumers' Perspectives." In *The Tragedy of Great Power Politics*, edited by John J. Mearsheimer. New York: Norton.

Mendez, Jennifer Bickham. 2005. *From the Revolution to the Maquiladoras: Gender, Labor, and Globalization in Nicaragua*. Durham, NC: Duke University Press.

Menjívar, Cecilia, and Leisy Abrego. 2009. "Parents and Children across Borders: Legal Instability and Intergenerational Relations in Guatemalan and Salvadoran Families." In *Across Generations: Immigrant Families in America*, edited by N. Foner, 160–189. New York: New York University Press.

Merry, Sally Engle. 2006. *Human Rights and Gender Violence: Translating International Law into Local Justice*. Chicago: University of Chicago Press.

Mertus, Julie. 2007. "The Rejection of Human Rights Framings: The Case of LGBT Advocacy in the US." *Human Rights Quarterly* 29: 1036–1064.

Messner, Michael A. 1992. *Power at Play: Sports and the Problem of Masculinity*. Boston: Beacon Press.

Midgley, Mary. 1995. *Beast and Man: The Roots of Human Nature*. London: Routledge.

Miech, R. A., A. Caspi, T. E. Moffitt, B. R. E. Wright, and P. A. Silva. 1999. "Low Socioeconomic Status and Mental Disorders: A Longitudinal Study of Selection and Causation during Young Adulthood." *American Journal of Sociology* 104: 1096–1131.

Mills, Charles W. 1997. *The Racial Contract*. Ithaca, NY: Cornell University Press.

Mittelstaedt, Emma. 2008. "Safeguarding the Rights of Sexual Minorities: Incremental and Legal Approaches to Enforcing International Human Rights Obligations." *Chicago Journal of International Law* 9: 353–386.

Modic, Dolores. 2008. "Stigma of Race." *Raziskave and Razprave/Research and Discussion* 1: 153–185.

Mohanty, Chandra Talpade. 2006. *Feminism without Borders: Decolonizing Theory, Practicing Solidarity*. Durham, NC: Duke University Press.

Mohanty, Chandra Talpade, Ann Russo, and Lourdes Torres, eds. 1991. *Third World Women and the Politics of Feminism*. Bloomington: Indiana University Press.

Moore, Wendy Leo. 2008. *Reproducing Racism: White Space, Elite Law Schools, and Racial Inequality*. Lanham, MD: Rowman & Littlefield.

Morales, Maria Cristina. 2009. "Ethnic-Controlled Economy or Segregation? Exploring Inequality in Latina/o Co-Ethnic Jobsites." *Sociological Forum* 24: 589–610.

Morales, Maria Cristina, and Cynthia Bejarano. 2009. "Transnational Sexual and Gendered Violence: An Application of Border Sexual Conquest at a Mexico-U.S. Border." *Global Networks* 9: 420–439.

Moser, Annalise. 2007. *Gender and Indicators: Overview Report*. Brighton, UK: Institute of Development Studies.

Mossakowski, K. N. 2008. "Dissecting the Influence of Race, Ethnicity, and Socioeconomic Status on Mental Health in Young Adulthood." *Research on Aging* 30: 649–671.

Myers, Kristen, and Laura Raymond. 2010. "Elementary School Girls and Heteronormativity: The Girl Project." *Gender & Society* 24: 167–188.

Nagel, Joane. 2003. *Race, Ethnicity, and Sexuality: Intimate Intersections, Forbidden Frontiers*. New York: Oxford University Press.

Naples, Nancy A. 1991, "Socialist Feminist Analysis of the Family Support Act of 1988."*AFFILIA: Journal of Women and Social Work* 6: 23–38.

———. 1998. *Community Activism and Feminist Politics: Organizing across Race, Gender and Class*. New York: Routledge.

———. 2009. "Teaching Intersectionality Intersectionally." *International Feminist Journal of Politics* 11: 566–577.

———. 2011. "Women's Leadership, Social Capital and Social Change." In *Activist Scholar: Selected Works of Marilyn Gittell*, edited by Kathe Newman and Ross Gittell, 263–278. Thousand Oaks, CA: Sage Publications.

Naples, Nancy A., and Manisha Desai. 2002. *Women's Activism and Globalization: Linking Local Struggles and Transnational Politics.* New York: Routledge.

Narayan, Uma. 1997. *Dislocating Cultures: Identities, Traditions, and Third World Feminism.* New York: Routledge.

——. 1998. "Essence of Culture and a Sense of History: A Feminist Critique of Cultural Essentialism." *Hypatia* 13: 86–106.

Nash, J. C. 2008. "Re-thinking Intersectionality." *Feminist Review* 89: 1–15.

National Drug Strategy Network. 1997. "18-Year-Old Texan, Herding Goats, Killed by U.S. Marine Corps Anti-Drug Patrol; Criminal Investigation of Shooting Underway." National Drug Strategy Network News Briefs. July. http://www.ndsn.org/july97/goats.html (accessed March 23, 2011).

Ngai, Mae M. 2004. *Impossible Subjects: Illegal Aliens and the Making of Modern America.* Princeton, NJ: Princeton University Press.

Nibert, David. 2002. *Animal Rights/Human Rights.* Lanham, MD: Rowman & Littlefield.

Nobis, Nathan. 2004. "Carl Cohen's 'Kind' Arguments for Animal Rights and against Human Rights." *Journal of Applied Philosophy* 21: 43–49.

Nordberg, Camilla. 2006. "Claiming Citizenship: Marginalised Voices on Identity and Belonging." *Citizenship Studies* 10: 523–539.

Núñez, Guillermina, and Josiah McC. Heyman. 2007. "Entrapment Processes and Immigrant Communities in a Time of Heightened Border Vigilance." *Human Organization* 66: 354–365.

Okin, Susan Moller. 1989. *Justice, Gender, and the Family.* New York: Basic Books.

Oliver, Kelly. 2009. *Animal Lessons: How They Teach Us to Be Human.* New York: Columbia University Press.

Omi, M., and H. Winant. 1986. *Racial Formation in the United States: From the 1960s to the 1980s.* New York: Routledge.

——. 1994. *Racial Formation in the United States: From the 1960s to the 1980s.* 2nd ed. New York: Routledge.

Onken, S. J., and E. Slaten. 2000. "Disability Identity Formation and Affirmation: The Experiences of Persons with Severe Mental Illness." *Sociological Practice: A Journal of Clinical and Applied Sociology* 2: 99–111.

Ontario Human Rights Commission (OHRC). 2001. An Intersectional Approach to Discrimination, Addressing Multiple Grounds in Human Rights Claims. OHRC. http://www.ohrc.on.ca/sites/default/files/attachments/An_intersectional_approach_to_discrimination%3A_Addressing_multiple_grounds_in_human_rights_claims.pdf (accessed July 18, 2012).

Orellana, Marjorie Faulstich. 1999. "Space and Place in an Urban Landscape: Learning from Children's Views of Their Social Worlds." *Visual Sociology* 14: 73–89.

Ortiz, Victor M. 2001. "The Unbearable Ambiguity of the Border." *Social Justice* 28: 96–112.

Ouellette-Kuntz, H., P. Burge, H. K. Brown, and E. Arsenault. 2010. "Public Attitudes towards Individuals with Intellectual Disabilities as Measured by the Concept of Social Distance." *Journal of Applied Research in Intellectual Disabilities* 23: 132–142.

Park, Robert E. 1914. "Racial Assimilation in Secondary Groups with Particular Reference to the Negro." *American Journal of Sociology* 19: 606–623.

——. 1928a. "Human Migration and the Marginal Man." *American Journal of Sociology* 33: 881–893.

——. 1928b. "The Bases of Race Prejudice." *Annals of the American Academy of Political and Social Science* 140: 11–20.

Parreñas, Rhacel Salazar. 1998. "The Global Servants: (Im)Migrant Filipina Domestic Workers in Rome and Los Angeles." Unpublished PhD diss., Department of Ethnic Studies, University of California, Berkeley.

Pascal, Celine-Marie. 2007. *Making Sense of Race, Class and Gender: Commonsense, Power and Privilege in the United States.* New York: Routledge.

Pascoe, C. J. 2007. *Dude, You're a Fag: Masculinity and Sexuality in High School.* Berkeley: University of California Press.

Patterson, Charles. 2002. *Eternal Treblinka: Our Treatment of Animals and the Holocaust.* New York: Lantern Books.

Paust, Jordan J. 2004. "Post 9/11 Overreaction and Fallacies Regarding War and Defense, Guantanamo, the Status of Persons, Treatment, Judicial Review of Detention, and Due Process in Military Commissions." *Notre Dame Law Review* 79: 1335–1364.

Pearlin, L., and C. Schooler. 1978. "The Structure of Coping." *Journal of Health and Social Behavior* 19: 2–21.

Penna, David R., and Patricia J. Campbell. 1998. "Human Rights and Culture: Beyond Universality and Relativism." *Third World Quarterly* 19: 7–27.

Pettigrew, T. F., and L. R. Tropp. 2006. "A Meta-Analytic Test of Intergroup Contact Theory." *Journal of Personality and Social Psychology* 90: 751–783.

Pfeiffer, D. 1993. "Overview of the Disability Movement: History, Legislative Record, and Political Implications." *Policy Studies Journal* 21: 724–734.

——. 2001. "The Conceptualization of Disability." In *Exploring Theories and Expanding Methodologies: Where*

We Are and Where We Need to Go, edited by S. N. Barnartt and B. M. Altman, 2:29–52. Oxford: Elsevier Science.

Phemister, A. A., and N. M. Crewe. 2004. "Objective Self-Awareness and Stigma: Implications for Persons with Visible Disabilities." *Journal of Rehabilitation* 70: 33–37.

Pilgrim, D., and A. A. Rogers. 1999. *A Sociology of Mental Health and Illness*. 2nd ed. Buckingham, UK: Open University Press.

Playle, J., and P. Keeley. 1998. "Non-Compliance and Professional Power." *Journal of Advanced Nursing* 27: 304–311.

Ponse, Barbara. 1978. *Identities in the Lesbian World: The Social Construction of Self*. Westport, CT: Greenwood Press.

Population Research Bureau (PRB). 2007. "Is Low Birth Weight a Cause of Problems, or a Symptom of Them?" PBR. http://www.prb.org/Journalists/Webcasts/2007/LowBirthWeight.aspx (accessed January 25, 2012).

Preeves, Sharon E. 2003. *Intersex and Identity: The Contested Self*. New Brunswick, NJ: Rutgers University Press.

Preston, Julia. 2011. "Risks Seen for Children of Illegal Immigrants." *New York Times*. September 20.

Prior, L. 1996. *The Social Organization of Mental Illness*. London: Sage Publications.

Pugh, Allison J. 2009. *Longing and Belonging: Parents, Children, and Consumer Culture*. Berkeley: University of California Press.

Purdy, Laura. 1989. "Surrogate Mothering: Exploitation or Empowerment?" *Bioethics* 3: 18–34.

Quadagno, Jill, and Debra Street, eds. 1995. *Aging for the Twenty-First Century*. New York: St. Martin's Press.

Rainwater, Lee, and Timothy M. Smeeding. 2005. *Poor Kids in a Rich Country*. New York: Russell Sage Foundation.

Raskoff, Sally. 2011. "Welcome Back: Adjusting to Life after Military Service." Everday Sociology Blog. www.everydaysociologyblog.com/2011/12/welcome-back-adjusting-to-civilian-life-after-military-service.html (accessed December 17, 2011).

Ray, Raka, and A. C. Korteweg. 1999. "Women's Movements in the Third World: Identity, Mobilization, and Autonomy." *Annual Review of Sociology* 25: 47–71.

Razack, Sherene. 1998. *Looking White People in the Eye: Gender, Race, and Culture in Courtrooms and Classrooms*. Toronto: University of Toronto Press.

Redwood, Loren K. 2008. "Strong-Arming Exploitable Labor: The State and Immigrant Workers in the Post-Katrina Gulf Coast." *Social Justice* 35: 33–50.

Regan, Tom. 2004. *The Case for Animal Rights*. Berkeley: University of California Press.

Regnerus, Mark D. 2007. *Forbidden Fruit: Sex and Religion in the Lives of American Teenagers*. New York: Oxford University Press.

Reilly, Niamh. 2007. "Cosmopolitan Feminism and Human Rights." *Hypatia* 22: 180–198.

———. 2009. *Women's Human Rights: Seeking Gender Justice in a Globalizing Age*. Cambridge, MA: Polity Press.

Rich, Adrienne. 1980. "Compulsory Heterosexuality." In *Powers of Desire: The Politics of Sexuality*, edited by Ann Snitow, Christine Stansell, and Sharon Thompson, 177–205. New York: Monthly Review Press.

Rich, Michael, and Richard Chalfen. 1999. "Showing and Telling Asthma: Children Teaching Physicians with Visual Narratives." *Visual Sociology* 14: 51–71.

Richards, Patricia. 2005. "The Politics of Gender, Human Rights, and Being Indigenous in Chile." *Gender and Society* 19: 199–220.

Ridge, D., C. Emslie, and A. White. 2011. "Understanding How Men Experience, Express and Cope with Mental Distress: Where Next?" *Sociology of Health and Illness* 33: 145–159.

Riley, J. 2004. "Some Reflections on Gender Mainstreaming and Intersectionality." *Development Bulletin* 64: 82–86.

Riley, M. W., M. E. Johnson, and A. Foner. 1972. *Aging and Society*. Vol. 3: *A Sociology of Age Stratification*. New York: Russell Sage Foundation.

Riley, M. W., R. L. Kahn, and A. Foner. 1994. *Age and Structural Lag: Society's Failure to Provide Meaningful Opportunities in Work, Family, and Leisure*. New York: Wiley.

Riley, M. W., and J. W. Riley Jr. 1994. "Age Integration and the Lives of Older People." *Gerontologist* 3–4, no. 1: 110–115.

Rios, Victor M. 2010. "Navigating the Thin Line between Education and Incarceration: An Action Research Case Study on Gang-Associated Latino Youth." *Journal of Education for Students Placed At-Risk* 15, no. 1–2: 200–212.

Rodan, Garry. 2006. "Singapore in 2005: 'Vibrant and Cosmopolitan' without Political Pluralism." *Asian Survey* 46: 180–186.

Rodríguez, Havidán, Rogelio Sáenz, and Cecilia Menjívar, eds. 2008. *Latina/os in the United States: Changing the Face of América*. New York: Springer.

Rodríguez, Nestor. 2008. "Theoretical and Methodological Issues of Latina/o Research." In *Latina/os in the United States: Changing the Face of América*, edited by H. Rodríguez, R. Sáenz, and C. Menjívar, 3–15. New York: Springer.

Roediger, D. R. 1991. *Wages of Whiteness: Race and the Making of the American Working Class*. London: Verso.

Rogers, Leslie. 1998. *Mind of Their Own: Thinking and Awareness in Animals*. Boulder, CO: Westview Press.

Rogoff, Barbara. 2003. *The Cultural Name of Human Development*. Oxford: Oxford University Press.

Rojas, Fabio. 2007. *From Black Power to Black Studies: How a Radical Social Movement Became an Academic Discipline*. Baltimore: Johns Hopkins University Press.

Romero, Mary. 1988. "Sisterhood and Domestic Service: Race, Class and Gender in the Mistress-Maid Relationship." *Humanity and Society* 12: 318–346.

———. 2006. "Racial Profiling and Immigration Law Enforcement: Rounding Up of Usual Suspects in the Latino Community." *Critical Sociology* 32: 449–475.

Rosenfield, S. 1999. "Gender and Mental Health: Do Women Have More Psychopathology, Men More, or Both the Same (and Why)?" In *Handbook for the Study of Mental Health*, edited by A. Horwitz and T. Scheid, 348–361. Cambridge, UK: Cambridge University Press.

Rosenhan, D. L. 1991. "On Being Sane in Insane Places." In *Down to Earth Sociology*, edited by J. M. Henslin, 294–307. New York: The Free Press.

Ross, Lauren. 2009. "Contradictions of Power, Sexuality, and Consent: An Institutional Ethnography of the Practice of Male Neonatal Circumcision." PhD diss., University of Connecticut, Storrs.

Rossi, Alice S. 1983. "Beyond the Gender Gap: Women's Bid for Political Power." *Social Science Quarterly* 64: 718–733.

Rossi, Federico M. 2009. "Youth Political Participation: Is This the End of Generational Cleavage?" *International Sociology* 24, no. 4: 467–497.

Rowe, John, Lisa Berkman, Robert Binstock, Axel Boersch-Supan, John Cacioppo, Laura Carstensen, Linda Fried, Dana Goldman, James Jackson, Matin Kohli, Jay Olshansky, and John Rother. 2010. "Policies and Politics for an Aging America." *Contexts* 9, no. 1: 22–27.

Rubin, Gayle. 1984. "Thinking Sex: Notes for a Radical Theory of the Politics of Sexuality." In *Pleasure and Danger: Exploring Female Sexuality*, edited by Carol Vance, 267–319. London: Pandora Press.

Rupp, Leila J. 2009. *Sapphistries: A Global History of Love between Women*. New York: New York University Press.

Rutherford, Markella B. 2011. *Adult Supervision Required*. Piscataway, NJ: Rutgers University Press.

Sáenz, Rogelio. 2010a. "Latinos in the United States 2010." Population Reference Bureau. http://www.prb.org/pdf10/latinos-update2010.pdf (accessed July 19, 2012).

———. 2010b. "Latinos, Whites, and the Shifting Demography of Arizona." Population Reference Bureau. http://www.prb.org/Articles/2010/usarizonalatinos.aspx (accessed March 24, 2011).

Sáenz, Rogelio, Cynthia M. Cready, and Maria Cristina Morales. 2007. "Adios Aztlan: Mexican American Outmigration from the Southwest." In *The Sociology of Spatial Inequality*, edited by L. Lobao, G. Hooks, and A. Tickamyer, 189–214. Albany: State University of New York Press.

Sáenz, Rogelio, Maria Cristina Morales, and Maria Isabel Ayala. 2004. "United States: Immigration to the Melting Pot of the Americas." In *Migration and Immigration: A Global View*, edited by M. I. Toro-Morn and M. Alicea, 211–232. Westport, CT: Greenwood Press.

Sáenz, Rogelio, and Lorena Murga. 2011. *Latino Issues: A Reference Handbook*. Santa Barbara, CA: ABC-CLIO.

Safran, S. P. 2001. "Movie Images of Disability and War: Framing History and Political Ideology." *Remedial and Special Education* 22: 223–232.

Said, Edward W. 1979. *Orientalism*. 1st ed. Vintage.

Saito, Leland T. 1998. *Race and Politics: Asian Americans, Latinos, and Whites in a Los Angeles Suburb*. Chicago: University of Illinois Press.

Salzinger, Leslie. 2005. *Genders in Production: Making Workers in Mexico's Global Factories*. Berkeley: University of California Press.

Sampson, Robert J., Patrick Sharkey, and Stephen W. Raudenbush. 2008. "Durable Effects of Concentrated Disadvantage on Verbal Ability among African-American Children." *Proceedings of the National Academy of Sciences of the United States of America* 105, no. 3: 845–852.

San Miguel, Guadalupe. 2005. *Brown, Not White: School Integration and the Chicano Movement in Houston*. College Station: Texas A&M University Press.

Sanbonmatsu, John, ed. 2011. *Critical Theory and Animal Liberation*. Lanham, MD: Rowman & Littlefield.

Sanford, Victoria. 2003. *Buried Secrets: Truth and Human Rights in Guatemala*. New York: Palgrave Macmillan.

Sarbin, T. R., and E. Keen. 1998. "Classifying Mental Disorders: Nontraditional Approaches." In *Encyclopedia of Mental Health*, edited by H. S. Friedman, 2:461–473. San Diego: Academic Press.

Sassen, Saskia. 1999. *Globalization and Its Discontents: Essays on the New Mobility of People and Money*. New York: The New Press.

——. 2006a. *Cities in a World Economy*. 3rd ed. Boulder, CO: Pine Forge Press.

——, ed. 2007. *Deciphering the Global: Its Spaces, Scales and Subjects*. New York: Routledge.

Satterthwaite, Margaret L. 2005. "Crossing Borders, Claiming Rights: Using Human Rights Law to Empower Women Migrant Workers." *Yale Human Rights and Development Law Journal* 8: 1–66.

Scheff, Thomas J. 1999. *Being Mentally Ill: A Sociological Theory*. 3rd ed. New York: Aldine De Gruyter.

Scheid, T. L. 2005. "Stigma as a Barrier to Employment: Mental Disability and the Americans with Disabilities Act." *International Journal of Law and Psychiatry* 28: 670–690.

Schulze, B., and M. C. Angermeyer. 2003. "Subjective Experiences of Stigma: Schizophrenic Patients, Their Relatives and Mental Health Professionals." *Social Science and Medicine* 56: 299–312.

Schwartz, Pepper, and Virginia Rutter. 1998. *The Gender of Sexuality*. Lanham, MD: AltaMira Press.

Scruton, Roger. 2000. *Animal Rights and Wrongs*. London: Claridge Press.

Scull, A. T. 1984. *Decarceration: Community Treatment and the Deviant–a Radical View*. Cambridge, UK: Polity Press.

Segura, Denise. 1989. "Chicana and Mexican Immigrant Women at Work: The Impact of Class, Race, and Gender on Occupational Mobility." *Gender and Society* 3: 37–52.

Sen, Amartya. 1999a. "Democracy as a Universal Value." *Journal of Democracy* 10: 3–17.

——. 1999b. *Development as Freedom*. New York: Random House.

Settersten, R. A., Jr. 2005. "Linking the Two Ends of Life: What Gerontology Can Learn from Childhood Studies." *Journals of Gerontology, Series B: Psychological Sciences* 60B, no. 4: 173–180.

Settersten, R. A., Jr., and J. L. Angel, eds. 2011. *Handbook of Sociology of Aging*. New York: Springer.

Settersten, R. A., Jr., and G. Hagestad. 1996a. "What's the Latest? Cultural Age Deadlines for Family Transitions." *Gerontologist* 36, no. 2: 178–188.

——. 1996b. "What's the Latest II: Cultural Age Deadlines for Educational and Work Transitions." *Gerontologist* 36, no. 5: 602–613.

Settersten, Richard, and Barbara E. Ray. 2010. *Not Quite Adults: Why 20-Somethings Are Choosing a Slower Path to Adulthood, and Why It's Good for Everyone*. New York: Bantam.

Shah, Natubhai. 1998. *Jainism: The World of Conquerors*. Sussex, UK: Sussex Academic Press.

Shakespeare, T., and N. Watson. 2001. "The Social Model of Disability: An Outdated Ideology?" In *Exploring Theories and Expanding Methodologies: Where We Are and Where We Need to Go*, edited by S. N. Barnartt and B. M. Altman, 2:9–28. Oxford, UK: Elsevier Science.

Shakespeare, Tom. 2006. *Disability Rights and Wrongs*. New York: Routledge.

Shergill, S. S., D. Barker, and M. Greenberg. 1998. "Communication of Psychiatric Diagnosis." *Social Psychiatry and Psychiatric Epidemiology* 33: 32–38.

Shevelow, Kathryn. 2008. *For the Love of Animals: The Rise of the Animal Protection Movement*. New York: Henry Holt and Co.

Shin, Y., and S. Raudenbush. 2011. "The Causal Effect of Class Size on Academic Achievement: Multivariate Instrumental Variable Estimators with Data Missing at Random." *Journal of Educational and Behavioral Statistics* 34, no. 2: 154–185.

Shorter, Edward. 1977. *The Making of the Modern Family*. New York: Basic Books.

Shukin, Sharon. 2009. *Animal Capital: Rendering Life in Biopolitical Times*. Minneapolis: University of Minnesota Press.

Shura, Robin, Rebecca A. Siders, and Dale Dannefer. 2010. "Culture Change in Long-Term Care: Participatory Action Research and the Role of the Resident." *Gerontologist* 51, no. 2: 212–225.

SIECUS. 2010. "Fact Sheet: State by State Decisions: The Personal Responsibility Education Program and Title V Abstinence-Only Program." http://www.siecus.org/index.cfm?fuseaction=Page.ViewPage&PageID=1272 (accessed September 5, 2012).

Silvers, A. 1998a. "Formal Justice." In *Disability, Difference, Discrimination: Perspectives on Justice in Bioethics and Public Policy*, edited by A. Silvers, D. Wasserman, and M. B. Mahowald, 13–145. Lanham, MD: Rowman & Littlefield.

——. 1998b. "Introduction." In *Disability, Difference, Discrimination: Perspectives on Justice in Bioethics and Public Policy*, edited by A. Silvers, D. Wasserman, and M. B. Mahowald, 1–12. Lanham, MD: Rowman & Littlefield.

Singer, Peter. 1993. *Practical Ethics*. 2nd ed. Cambridge, UK: Cambridge University Press.

——. 2005. *Animal Liberation*. New York: Harper Perennial.

Sjoberg, Gideon, Elizabeth A. Gill, and Norma Williams. 2001. "A Sociology of Human Rights." *Social Problems* 48, no. 1: 11–47.

Skrentny, John D. 2002. *The Minority Rights Revolution*. Cambridge, MA: Harvard University Press.

Smith, Dorothy E. 1987. *The Everyday World as Problematic: A Feminist Sociology*. Toronto: University of Toronto Press.

——. 1990. *Texts, Facts, and Femininity: Exploring the Relations of Ruling*. New York: Routledge.

Smith, Robert. 2005. *Mexican New York: Transnational Lives of New Immigrants.* Berkeley: University of California Press.

Snipp, C. Matthew. 2003. "Racial Measurement in the American Census: Past Practices and Implications for the Future." *Annual Review of Sociology* 29: 563–588.

Sorenson, John. 2011. "Constructing Extremists, Rejecting Compassion: Ideological Attacks on Animal Advocacy from Right and Left." In *Critical Theory and Animal Liberation,* edited by John Sanbonmatsu, 219–238. Lanham, MD: Rowman & Littlefield.

Soysal, Yasemin. 1994. *Limits of Citizenship: Migrants and Postnational Membership in Europe.* Chicago: University of Chicago Press.

Spirer, Herbert F. 1990. "Violations of Human Rights: How Many? The Statistical Problems of Measuring Such Infractions Are Tough, but Statistical Science Is Equal to It." *American Journal of Economics and Sociology* 49: 199–210.

Stacey, Judith. 1991. "Can There Be a Feminist Ethnography?" In *Women's Words,* edited by Sherna B. Gluck and Daphne Patai, 111–119. New York: Routledge.

Stamp Dawkins, Marian. 2006. "The Scientific Basis for Assessing Suffering of Animals." In *In Defense of Animals: The Second Wave,* edited by Peter Singer. Cambridge, MA: Blackwell Publishers.

Staudt, Kathleen. 1997. "Gender Politics in Bureaucracy: Theoretical Issues in Comparative Perspective." In *Women, International Development, and Politics,* edited by Kathleen Staudt, 3–36. Philadelphia: Temple University Press.

Stein, Dorothy. 1988. "Burning Widows, Burning Brides: The Perils of Daughterhood in India." *Pacific Affairs* 61: 465–485.

Steiner, Gary. 2010. 1987. *Anthropocentrism and Its Discontents: The Moral Status of Animals in the History of Western Philosophy.* Pittsburgh, PA: University of Pittsburgh Press.

Stuart, Tristram. 2006. *The Bloodless Revolution: A Cultural History of Vegetarianism from 1600 to Modern Times.* New York: W. W. Norton and Co.

Sunder, Madhavi. 2003. "Piercing the Veil." *Yale Law Journal* 112: 1401–1472.

Sutter, Molly Hazel. 2006. "Mixed-Status Families and Broken Homes: The Clash between the U.S. Hardship Standard in Cancellation of Removal Proceedings and International Law." *Transnational Law and Contemporary Problems* 783: 1–28.

Switzer, J. V. 2003. *Disabled Rights: American Disability Policy and the Fight for Equality.* Washington, DC: Georgetown University Press.

Symington, Alison. 2004. "Intersectionality: A Tool for Gender and Economic Justice." Association for Women's Rights in Development. http://www.awid.org/content/download/48805/537521/file/intersectionality_en.pdf (accessed September 17, 2012).

Takagi, Dana. 1994. "Maiden Voyage: Excursion into Sexuality and Identity Politics in Asian America." *Amerasia Journal* 20, no. 1: 1–17.

Tarrow, Sidney G. 1998. *Power in Movement: Social Movements and Contentious Politics.* New York and Cambridge, UK: Cambridge University Press.

Tatum, Beverly Daniel. 2003. *"Why Are All the Black Kids Sitting Together in the Cafeteria?" and Other Conversations about Race.* New York: Basic Books.

Terl, Allan H. 2000. "An Essay on the History of Lesbian and Gay Rights in Florida." *Nova Law Review* 24 (spring): 793–853.

Thayer, Carlyle A. 2004. "Laos in 2003: Counterrevolution Fails to Ignite." *Asian Survey* 44, no. 1: 110–114.

Thomas, George. 2004. "Constructing World Civil Society through Contentions over Religious Rights." *Journal of Human Rights* 3: 239–251.

Thomas, James. 2010. "The Racial Formation of Medieval Jews: A Challenge to the Field." *Ethnic and Racial Studies* 33: 1737–1755.

Thomas, James, and David Brunsma. 2008. "Bringing Down the House: Reparations, Universal Morality, and Social Justice." In *Globalization and America: Race, Human Rights, and Inequality,* edited by Angela Hattery, David G. Embrick, and Earl Smith, 65–81. Lanham, MD: Rowman & Littlefield.

Thomas, Nigel, Brian K. Gran, and Karl Hansen. 2011. "An Independent Voice for Children's Rights in Europe? The Role of Independent Children's Rights Institutions in the EU." *International Journal of Children's Rights* 19, no. 3: 429–449.

Thorne, B. 1993. *Gender Play: Boys and Girls in School.* Piscataway, NJ: Rutgers University Press.

Thorne, S., B. Paterson, S. Acorn, C. Canam, G. Joachim, and C. Jillings. 2002. "Chronic Illness Experience: Insights from a Metastudy." *Qualitative Health Research* 12, no. 4: 437–452.

Tiefer, Lenore. 2004. *Sex Is Not a Natural Act and Other Essays.* Boulder, CO: Westview Press.

Timmermans, S. 2001. "Social Death as Self-Fulfilling Prophecy." In *Sociology of Health and Illness: Critical Perspectives,* edited by P. Conrad, 305–321. New York: Worth.

Tinkler, Penny. 1995. *Constructing Girlhood.* Oxfordshire, UK: Taylor and Francis.

Tisdall, E. K. M. 2008. "Is the Honeymoon Over? Children and Young People's Participation in Public Decision-Making." *International Journal of Children's Rights* 16, no. 3: 343–354.

Tolman, Deborah L. 1994. "Doing Desire: Adolescent Girls' Struggles for/with Sexuality." *Gender and Society* 8, no. 3: 324–342.

Tomasevski, Katerina. 1995. *Women and Human Rights*. London: Zed Books.

Torres, Bob. 2007. *Making a Killing: The Political Economy of Animal Rights*. Oakland, CA: AK Press.

Townsend, Peter. 2006. "Policies for the Aged in the 21st Century: More 'Structured Dependency' or the Realisation of Human Rights?" *Aging and Society* 26: 161–179.

Tripp, Aili, and Myra Marx Ferree, eds. 2006. *Global Feminism: Transnational Women's Activism, Organizing, and Human Rights*. New York: New York University Press.

Trucios-Haynes, Inid. 2001. "Why 'Race Matters': LatCrit Theory and Latina/o Racial Identity." *La Raza Law Journal* 12, no. 1: 1–42.

Tuan, Mia. 1999. *Forever Foreigners or Honorary Whites? The Asian Ethnic Experience Today*. New Brunswick, NJ: Rutgers University Press.

Turmel, André. 2008. *A Historical Sociology of Childhood*. New York: Cambridge University Press.

Turner, Bryan S. 1993. "Outline of the Theory of Human Rights." In *Citizenship and Social Theory*, edited by Bryan S. Turner, 162–190. London: Sage.

———. 2006. "Global Sociology and the Nature of Rights." *Societies without Borders* 1: 41–52.

Turner, R. J., B. Wheaton, and D. A. Lloyd. 1995. "The Epidemiology of Social Stress." *American Sociological Review* 60: 104–125.

Uhlenberg, Peter. 2009a. "Children in an Aging Society." *Journals of Gerontology, Series B: Psychological Sciences* 64B: 489–496.

———, ed. 2009b. *International Handbook of Population Aging*. Dordrecht, The Netherlands: Springer.

Uhlenberg, Peter, and Michelle Cheuk. 2010. "The Significance of Grandparents to Grandchildren: An International Perspective." In *Sage Handbook of Social Gerontology*, edited by D. Dannefer and C. Phillipson, 447–458. London: Sage.

Uhlenberg, Peter, and Jenny de Jong Gierveld. 2004. "Age-Segregation in Later Life: An Examination of Personal Networks." *Ageing and Society* 24: 5–28.

Underhill, Kristen, Paul Montgomery, and Don Operario. 2007. "Systematic Review of Abstinence-Only Programmes Aiming to Prevent HIV Infection in High-Income Countries." *British Medical Journal* 335: 248.

United Nations. 1948. "The Universal Declaration of Human Rights." United Nations. www.un.org/en /documents/udhr/index.shtml (accessed December 10, 2010).

———. 1991. "The Protection of Persons with Mental Illness and the Improvement of Mental Health Care." United Nations. http://www.un.org/documents/ga/res/46/a46r119.htm (accessed November 10, 2010).

———. 1995. *UN Report of the Fourth World Conference on Women*. New York: United Nations.

———. 2000. "Gender and Racial Discrimination Report of the Expert Group Meeting." United Nations. http://www.un.org/womenwatch/daw/csw/genrac/report.htm (accessed January 11, 2012).

———. 2001. "Background Briefing on Intersectionality, Working Group on Women and Human Rights, 45th Session of the UN CSW." Center for Women's Global Leadership. http://www.cwgl.rutgers.edu/csw01 /background.htm (accessed March 31, 2011).

———. 2009. *15 Years of the United Nations Special Rapporteur on Violence against Women, Its Causes and Consequences*. Office of the High Commissioner for Human Rights. http://www2.ohchr.org/english/issues/women /rapporteur/docs/15YearReviewofVAWMandate.pdf (accessed January 11, 2012).

United Nations Food and Agriculture Organization (UNFAO). 2006. "Livestock's Long Shadow: Environmental Issues and Options." UNFAO. http://www.fao.org/docrep/010/a0701e/a0701e00.htm (accessed July 20, 2012).

———. 2010. *Gender Dimensions of Agricultural and Rural Employment: Differential Pathways out of Poverty*. Rome: UNFAO, International Fund for Agricultural Development, and International Labour Office.

United States Census Bureau. 2008. "U.S. Population Projections." US Census Bureau. http://www.census .gov/population/www/projections/summarytables.html (accessed January 29, 2012).

United States Department of Health and Human Services. 2010. "Fact Sheet: Sex Trafficking." Administration for Children and Families. http://www.acf.hhs.gov/trafficking/about/fact_sex.html (accessed December 21, 2010).

Valentine, David. 2007. *Imagining Transgender: An Ethnography of a Category*. Durham, NC: Duke University Press.

Van der Kroef, Justus M. 1976. "Indonesia's Political Prisoners." *Pacific Affairs* 49, no. 4: 625–647.

Van Krieken, Robert. 1999. "The 'Stolen Generations': On the Removal of Australian Indigenous Children from Their Families and Its Implications for the Sociology of Childhood." *Childhood* 6, no. 3: 297–311.

Vanwesenbeeck, I. 1997. "The Context of Women's Power(lessness) in Heterosexual Interactions." In *New Sexual Agendas*, edited by L. Segal. New York: New York University Press.

Vegans of Color. 2011. "Liberation Veganism." Vegans of Color. http://vegansofcolor.wordpress.com/tag/animal-rights (accessed March 28, 2011).

Velez, Veronica, Lindsay Perez Huber, Corina Benavides López, Ariana de la Luz, and Daniel G. Solorzano. 2008. "Battling for Human Rights and Social Justice: A Latina/o Critical Race Media Analysis of Latina/o Student Youth Activism in the Wake of 2006 Anti-Immigrant Sentiment." *Social Justice* 35, no. 1: 7–27.

Vermeersch, Peter. 2003. "Ethnic Minority Identity and Movement Politics: The Case of the Roma in the Czech Republic and Slovakia." *Ethnic and Racial Studies* 26: 879–901.

Vialles, Noelie. 1994. *Animal to Edible.* Translated by J. A. Underwood. Cambridge, UK: Cambridge University Press.

Vinck, Patrick, Phuong N. Pham, Laurel E. Fletcher, and Eric Stover. 2009. "Inequalities and Prospects: Ethnicity and Legal Status in the Construction Labor Force after Hurricane Katrina." *Organization and Environment* 22, no. 4: 470–478.

Wagner, Jon. 1999a. "Beyond the Body in a Box: Visualizing Contexts of Children's Action." *Visual Sociology* 14: 143–160.

———. 1999b. "Visual Sociology and Seeing Kids' Worlds." *Visual Sociology* 14.

Waites, Matthew. 2009. "Critique of 'Sexual Orientation' and 'Gender Identity' in Human Rights Discourse: Global Queer Politics beyond the Yogyakarta Principles." *Contemporary Politics* 15, no. 1: 137–156.

Walters, Kerry S., and Lisa Portness, eds. 1999. *Ethical Vegetarianism: From Pythagoras to Peter Singer.* Albany: State University of New York Press.

Walters, Suzanna Danuta. 2001. "Take My Domestic Partner, Please: Gays and Marriage in the Era of the Visible." In *Queer Families, Queer Politics: Challenging Culture and the State,* edited by Mary Bernstein and Renate Reimann, 338–357. New York: Columbia University Press.

Wang, Guang-zhen, and Vijayan K. Pillai. 2001. "Women's Reproductive Health: A Gender-Sensitive Human Rights Approach." *Acta Sociologica* 44, no. 3: 231–242.

Warner, R. 1994. *Recovery from Schizophrenia.* Routledge: London.

Warner, Michael. 2000. *The Trouble with Normal: Sex, Politics and the Ethics of Queer Life.* Cambridge, MA: Harvard University Press.

Warner-Smith, Penny, Lois Bryson, and Julie Ellen Byles. 2004. "The Big Picture: The Health and Well-Being of Women in Three Generations in Rural and Remote Areas of Australia." *Health Sociology Review* 13, no. 1: 15–26.

Weglyn, Michi Nishiura. 1976. *Years of Infamy: The Untold Story of America's Concentration Camps.* Seattle: University of Washington Press.

Weissbrodt, David S., and Clay Collins. 2006. "The Human Rights of Stateless Persons." *Human Rights Quarterly* 28, no. 1: 245–276.

Weitzer, Ronald, ed. 2000. *Sex for Sale: Prostitution, Pornography, and the Sex Industry.* New York: Routledge.

West, Nathaniel. 1841. "A Coppie of the Liberties of the Massachusetts Colonie in New England." In *American History Leaflets 25,* edited by Albert Bushnell Hart and Edward Channing. New York: A. Lovell and Co., 1896. http://www.lonang.com/exlibris/organic/1641-mbl.htm (accessed September 4, 2012).

Whitbeck, Les B. 2009. *Mental Health and Emerging Adulthood among Homeless Young People.* New York: Psychology Press.

Wilkinson, Lindsey, and Jennifer Pearson. 2009. "School Culture and the Well-Being of Same-Sex-Attracted Youth." *Gender and Society* 23, no. 4: 542–568.

Williams, B. 1994. "Patient Satisfaction—a Valid Concept?" *Social Science and Medicine* 38, no. 4: 509–516.

Williams, D. R., Y. Yu, J. S. Jackson, and N. B. Anderson. 1997. "Racial Differences in Physical and Mental Health: Socio-Economic Status, Stress and Discrimination." *Journal of Health Psychology* 2, no. 3: 335–351.

Winter, Bronwyn. 2006. "Religion, Culture, and Women's Human Rights: Some General and Theoretical Considerations." *Women's Studies International Forum* 29, no. 4: 381–394.

Wise, Steven. 2005. *Rattling the Cage: Toward Legal Rights for Animals.* New York: Perseus Press.

Witz, Ann. 2000. "Whose Body Matters? Feminist Sociology and the Corporeal Turn in Sociology and Feminism." *Body and Society* 6, no. 2: 1–24.

Wolf, Diane L., ed. 1996. *Feminist Dilemmas in Fieldwork.* Boulder, CO: Westview.

Women's Refugee Commission. 2011. *The Living Ain't Easy: Urban Refugees in Kampala.* New York: Women's Refugee Commission.

Wood, Charles. 1999. "Losing Control of America's Future: The Census, Birthright Citizenship, and Illegal Aliens." *Harvard Journal of Law and Public Policy* 22, no. 2: 465–522.

World Conference against Racism. 2001. "World Conference against Racism, Racial Discrimination, Xenophobia and Related Intolerance: Declaration." United Nations. http://www.un.org/durbanreview2009/pdf/DDPA_full_text.pdf (accessed July 20, 2012).

World Health Organization (WHO). 2000. *Maternal Mortality in 2000: Estimates Developed by WHO, UNICEF, and UNFPA.* Relief Web. http://www.reliefweb.int/library/documents/2003/who-saf-22oct.pdf (accessed January 20, 2012).

——. 2007. "Community Mental Health Services Will Lessen Social Exclusion, Says WHO." WHO. http://www.who.int/mediacentre/news/notes/2007/np25/en/index.html (accessed January 20, 2012).

——. 2010. *Global Strategies for Women's and Children's Health.* New York: Partnership for Maternal, Newborn, and Child Health.

Wotipka, Christine Min, and Kiyoteru Tsutsui. 2008. "Global Human Rights and State Sovereignty: State Ratification of International Human Rights Treaties 1965–2001." *Sociological Forum* 23, no. 4: 724–754.

Wrench, John. 2011. "Data on Discrimination in EU Countries: Statistics, Research and the Drive for Comparability." *Ethnic and Racial Studies* 34: 1715–1730.

Yang, Alan S. 1998. *From Wrongs to Rights: Public Opinion on Gay and Lesbian American's Moves toward Equality.* Washington, DC: National Gay and Lesbian Task Force Policy Institute.

Yeung, W. J., and D. Conley. 2008. "Black-White Achievement Gap and Family Wealth." *Child Development* 79: 303–324.

Young, Iris. 1990. *Justice and Politics of Difference.* Princeton, NJ: Princeton University Press.

Yuker, H. E. 1994. "Variables that Influence Attitudes toward People with Disabilities: Conclusions from the Data." *Journal of Social Behavior and Personality* 9, no. 5: 3–22.

Yuval-Davis, N. 2006a. "Intersectionality and Feminist Politics." *European Journal of Women's Studies* 13, no. 3: 193–209.

——. 2006b. "Women, Citizenship and Difference." *Feminist Review* 57: 4–27.

Zakaria, Fareed, and Kuan Yew Lee. 1994. "Culture Is Destiny: A Conversation with Lee Kuan Yew." *Foreign Affairs* 73, no. 2: 109–126.

Zheng, Tiantian. 2010. *Sex Trafficking, Human Rights, and Social Justice.* New York: Routledge.

Zitzelsberger, Hilde. 2005. "(In)visibility: Accounts of Embodiment of Women in Physical Disabilities and Differences." *Disability and Society* 20, no. 4: 389–403.

Žižek, Slavoj. 2005. "Against Human Rights." *New Left Review* 34 (May–June): 115–131.

Zuberi, Tukufu, and Eduardo Bonilla-Silva. 2008. *White Logic, White Methods: Racism and Methodology.* Lanham, MD: Rowman & Littlefield.

About the Editors

David L. Brunsma is Professor of Sociology at Virginia Tech. His areas of research are sociologies of human rights and human rights sociologies, racial identity and racism, cognitive sociology and epistemologies, and multiraciality and whiteness, and he is currently working on a major textbook project on the social construction of difference. He is founding co-editor of *Sociology of Race and Ethnicity*, co-editor of *Societies without Borders: Human Rights and the Social Sciences*, and section editor of the Race and Ethnicity Section of *Sociology Compass*. He lives and loves with his family in Blacksburg, Virginia.

Keri E. Iyall Smith's research explores the intersections among human rights doctrine, the state, and indigenous peoples in the context of a globalizing society. She has published articles on hybridity and world society, human rights, indigenous peoples, and teaching sociology. She is the author of *The State and Indigenous Movements* (Routledge), editor of *Sociology of Globalization* (Westview Press), co-editor with Judith R. Blau of *Public Sociologies Reader* (Rowman and Littlefield), and co-editor with Patricia Leavy of *Hybrid Identities: Theoretical and Empirical Examinations* (Brill and Haymarket). She is an associate professor of Sociology at Suffolk University in Boston, Massachusetts, where she teaches courses on globalization, sociological theory, Native Americans, and introductory sociology. She is a former vice president of Sociologists Without Borders.

Brian K. Gran is an associate professor of Sociology and Law on the faculty of Case Western Reserve University. A former lawyer, Gran's sociological research focuses on human rights and institutions that support and hinder their enforcement, with a particular interest in whether law can intervene in private spheres. With David Brunsma and Keri Iyall Smith, he edited *The Handbook of Sociology and Human Rights*. A co-founder of the ASA Human Rights section, Gran serves on the Steering Committee and Council of the Science and Human Rights Project of the American Association for the Advancement of Science. For his research on independent children's rights institutions, Gran has enjoyed support as a Visiting Fellow of the Swiss National Science Foundation and as a Fulbright Scholar to Iceland. He recently had the pleasure of participating in a colloquium on human rights indicators and business held at Cumberland Lodge. Gran is President of the thematic group on Global Justice and Human Rights of the International Sociological Association.

Made in the USA
Las Vegas, NV
08 February 2022

43456403R00083